Attachment in Sport, Exercise, and Wellness

Attachment theory is a concept well known to 'mainstream' psych. informing the literature in areas as diverse as psychodynamics, devels, mental psychology, social psychology, and counselling. This important new book is the first to demonstrate the relevance of attachment theory to the psychology of sport, exercise, and wellness, opening up important new avenues for research and professional practice.

In this book, Sam Carr explains that attachment theory can help us to better understand well-established themes and processes in sport and exercise, including motivation, social relationships, cognitive models of coping, and group processes. By introducing the core elements of attachment theory, and mapping out those areas in which it can inform the knowledge and practice of psychologists working in sport, exercise, and wellness, this book represents an innovative and important contribution to the psychological literature.

Sam Carr is a lecturer in the Department of Education at the University of Bath. His research interests are linked to social relationships in sport-related contexts. He has published a number of articles relating to attachment in the sport and exercise psychology literature.

Routledge Research in Sport and Exercise Science

The *Routledge Research in Sport and Exercise Science* series is a showcase for cutting-edge research from across the sport and exercise sciences, including physiology, psychology, biomechanics, motor control, physical activity, and health, and every core sub-discipline. Featuring the work of established and emerging scientists and practitioners from around the world, and covering the theoretical, investigative, and applied dimensions of sport and exercise, this series is an important channel for new and groundbreaking research in the human movement sciences.

Also available in this series:

Attachment in Sport, Exercise, and Wellness

Sam Carr

Routledge
Taylor & Francis Group

LONDON AND NEW YORK

First published 2012
by Routledge
2 Park Square, Milton Park, Abingdon, Oxon OX14 4RN

Simultaneously published in the USA and Canada
by Routledge
711 Third Avenue, New York, NY 10017

Routledge is an imprint of the Taylor & Francis Group, an informa business

First issued in paperback 2013

British Library Cataloguing in Publication Data
A catalogue record for this book is available from the British Library

Library of Congress Cataloging in Publication Data
Attachment in sport, exercise and wellness / edited by Sam Carr.
p. cm.
1. Sports--Psychological aspects. 2. Attachment behavior. I. Carr, Sam.
GV706.4.A83 2012
796.01--dc23
2011019893

ISBN: 978-0-415-57858-5 (hbk)
ISBN: 978-0-415-85817-5 (pbk)
ISBN: 978-0-203-85203-3 (ebk)

Typeset in Goudy
by Taylor & Francis Books

Contents

Acknowledgements

I am indebted to a number of individuals and organisations for their provision of support during the process of writing this book. I would specifically like to thank (a) Simon Whitmore and Joshua Wells at Routledge for their help and support throughout the process, (b) Colby Pearce and Jessica Kingsley Publishers for kindly agreeing to allow me to reproduce Colby's work in the introductory section of the book, (c) Taylor & Francis and Elsevier publishers for permitting me to include sections of my earlier works in some chapters of this book, and (d) the numerous graduate and undergraduate students who have discussed the various ideas and concepts with me – from our discussions in and out of class I have learned an enormous amount that has undoubtedly helped shape the course of this book.

Perhaps most importantly, in the process of writing this book I have gained significant insight into the concept of attachment within human relationships. Much of this insight has been gained from the opportunity to reflect upon my own close relationships in light of the ideas and concepts I have been lucky enough to engage with during the writing process. I am indebted to the significant attachment figures of my childhood (Mum, Dad, Grandma, and Grandpa) in ways that I could not appreciate prior to writing this book. However, most of all I would like to thank my wife (Ira) and my son (Alex). Without the special attachment we share I would never have mustered the strength, inspiration, or motivation to write this book and you have each taught me more about attachment than I could possibly have learned from my efforts on this book.

Introduction

Some months ago a graduate student came to my office visibly excited after reading the prologue section in Colby Pearce's (2009) text *A Short Introduction to Attachment and Attachment Disorder*. The student felt that although he had been studying attachment theory for a number of years he was so intensely focused upon its numerous intricacies and nuances that he had failed to recognise the striking simplicity that underpins this complexity. With Pearce's permission, I make no apologies for paraphrasing his excellent example below. I agree with my graduate student's initial interpretation.

Pearce (2009) recites a story about three mice. The first mouse resided in a comfortable house that was furnished and supplied with modern conveniences. Inside the house was a button and a hole in the wall and the mouse was able to press the button to receive tasty food through the hole. The mechanism worked well and the mouse appreciated that when he was hungry he would be able to press the button and consistently receive his food. It was comforting to have this knowledge and the mouse liked the predictable nature of his button, only tending to press it when he really needed food.

In contrast, the second mouse (who lived in an identical house) had the misfortune of dealing with a faulty button mechanism. That is, pressing his button only resulted in food being delivered some of the time. There was no predictability to the button mechanism and on some occasions he would receive food immediately on pressing the button whereas on others he would be required to press it 10 or 20 times. At other times it seemed that no matter how often he pressed it nothing was ever going to happen. His distrust of the button led him to be preoccupied with pressing it, even when he was not actually hungry. He would press it many, many times in order to ensure he would have food when he did grow hungry. When the button was fixed he found it hard to trust that it was now in good working order and spent much time storing up food for a rainy day.

Finally, the third mouse lived in a house with a button that consistently failed to work. In short, he never received any food from his button. He quickly came to the understanding that access to food would require him to employ other means and had no belief in the utility of the button. Even when he moved home and found a house with an effectively functioning button his lack of faith in buttons persisted and he continued to find food the way he always had.

The above story highlights how attachment theory can be seen to be grounded in simple assumptions that retain remarkable logical sense even when talk of mice and food is substituted for young children, emotional care, and security. Pearce (2009) has cleverly recognised this in his prologue. However, although there are some simple logical principles at the core of attachment theory, the fact that Bowlby (1969/1982, 1973, 1980) required close to 1000 pages to articulate his ideas suggests that there are complexities, assumptions, and arguments that cannot be overlooked if one is to begin to develop a fuller understanding of Bowlby's position. Furthermore, given that attachment theory has been intuitively appealing to researchers whose ideas are allied to contrasting paradigmatic approaches (e.g. Pearce's example seems couched in behaviourist principles – but attachment theory also reflects ideas that resemble other schools of thought) and from various disciplines it is unsurprising that further methodological and conceptual intricacies have arisen as the ideas have been nurtured and developed according to the assumptions of differing schools of thought.

My intention with this book is to facilitate discussion, debate, and the formulation of ideas in relation to the interface between attachment theory and the fields of sport, exercise, and wellness. Researchers (e.g. Carr, 2009a; Jowett & Wylleman, 2006; Poczwardowski *et al.*; Smith, 2003; Wylleman, 2000) in sport-related fields have already recognised that the understanding of human relationships has a central role to play in the development of our ideas and theoretical frameworks. Accordingly, I believe that attachment theory can serve as a particularly useful lens through which we might examine and better understand the contexts of sport, exercise, and wellness.

Attachment theory offers a particularly useful insight into the interplay between human relationships that are experienced outside of the sport-related context and those that are formulated within it. To this end, previous sport-related research has explored the role of parental relationships from the perspective of a role modelling hypothesis (e.g. Gustafson & Rhodes, 2006), parental belief systems (e.g. Bois *et al.*, 2005), and the construction of the parental motivational climate (e.g. Carr & Weigand, 2001; Carr *et al.*, 1999, 2000). Ullrich-French and Smith (2009) have recognised the importance of exploring how different social relationships in children's lives are interconnected and how they may interact to regulate broader experiences of sport. Attachment theory offers an interesting and new perspective in relation to the reverberation of parental relationships in the sporting context. However, in addition to this, attachment perspectives also offer a way of understanding the reciprocal influence that sporting relationships themselves have on individuals' attachment-related apparatus. Accordingly, the theory offers a framework by which we are able to develop our understanding of the dynamics involved as individuals experience the world of sport and exercise in the context of their attachment-related beliefs, cognitions, and emotions.

In the chapters that follow I seek to provide a platform for initial discussion about the link between attachment theory and some of the most popular theoretical frameworks relating to motivation, cohesion, stress, and coping, and relationships in sport, exercise, and wellness. In Chapter 7 I offer some thoughts related to the integration of attachment theory in the context of exercise, drawing upon ideas about attachment and health to support my argument.

In Chapter 1 I hope to help readers appreciate the predominant assumptions made by attachment theorists. In this chapter, the conceptual history, intricacies, and complexities I mentioned above are sketched and I have sought to provide readers with a basic understanding of the central assumptions at the core of Bowlby's ideas to help them appreciate the numerous complexities that have arisen as the theory has been adapted and extended by researchers.

In Chapter 2 I seek to outline current debate that has largely come to pass as a consequence of attachment theory being embraced by researchers with differing underpinning paradigmatic assumptions. After reading this chapter, readers will hopefully appreciate that broadly contrasting conceptual and methodological ideas (that often reflect differing interpretations of Bowlby's key themes) have given rise to emerging 'schools of thought' within the literature that adopt particular positions in relation to attachment theory. These positions have subsequently given rise to the emergence of specific traditions in relation to the measurement and methodological treatment of attachment. It is my belief that the content in Chapters 1 and 2 is important groundwork for the later discussion of the interface between attachment theory and the contexts of sport, exercise, and wellness.

In Chapter 3 I am concerned with the integration of attachment theory with popular frameworks for motivation research in sport and exercise psychology. Specifically, I seek to explore links with achievement goal and self-determination approaches to human motivation. There are a number of interesting links to be made in these popular research areas. For example, attachment theory puts forward the attachment system as one of a number of psychological 'systems' that are integral to an organism's survival and procreation. The attachment system is hypothesised to be balanced with a system of exploration. That is, the attachment system serves the predominant function of ensuring proximity to the caregiver when threatened or distressed, securing a sense of safety and protection from harm. This sense of security facilitates a sense of confidence and activation of the exploration system to gradually explore the surrounding environment, enhancing individuals' development and individuation. Given their conceptual links, different attachment histories are likely to correspond to different exploration tendencies (e.g. those who find it difficult to develop a sense of attachment security may be less willing to explore or may explore in a more cautious or inhibited manner). The achievement goal constructs that occupy a central role in sport motivation literature are closely linked to the manner in which individuals engage in exploratory environments and this issue is discussed in depth in this chapter. I also explore how issues such as the motivational climate might impinge upon the activation or development of working models of attachment in the sporting context. Furthermore, the chapter also examines how central aspects of self-determination theory (e.g. the basic needs of competence, autonomy, and relatedness) may be integrally linked to the notion of attachment.

Chapter 4 is concerned with the relationship that attachment might share with cohesion and group processes in the context of sport. In this chapter I address issues such as (a) whether cohesion in the context of groups might be seen as a 'buffer' for the attachment concerns of those with insecure attachment histories (serving to dampen their social concerns about rejection and lack of self-worth), (b) how working models of attachment might be seen as a filter in the construction of perceptions about group cohesiveness, and (c) how different conceptualisations of cohesion may have very different implications for a link with attachment theory.

Attachment is strongly linked to the manner in which individuals respond to potentially threatening or stressful experiences. Individual attachment histories tend to reflect the manner in which they process and experience such threat or distress on a cognitive, emotional, and behavioural level. Accordingly, Chapter 5 explores the interface between attachment, stress, and coping in sport-related contexts. I also use this chapter as a space for a discussion of how ideas from attachment shed light on issues related to coping and stress response in the specific context of athletic injury.

Chapter 6 deals with attachment and the notion of sporting relationships, with a specific focus on sporting friendships and coach–athlete bonds. I focus specifically upon conceptual integration in the areas of sport friendship and coach–athlete bonds because a number of authors in this field have begun to implicate attachment theory in their work. Hence, these areas of research provide particularly interesting platforms for discussion and debate. Areas of discussion relate to (a) how internal working models of attachment underpin characteristics of sport friendships, (b) whether sporting relationships (such as the coach–athlete bond) themselves might be considered as attachment bonds, and (c) whether (if they can be considered attachment bonds) relationships in the context of sport have some sort of 'therapeutic potential' as spaces for reworking attachment characteristics.

Finally, Chapter 7 is concerned with attachment in the broader contexts of exercise and health. Ideas are discussed that recognise the usefulness of attachment theory in relation to a number of important research avenues. For example, researchers have outlined how contrasting attachment histories may predispose individuals to different developmental pathways in relation to neurological and physiological development. These differing pathways may have significant implications for physical and mental health and it will be important to identify environmental and lifestyle factors that might buffer this effect. In this chapter I discuss the role of exercise as one such buffer. Furthermore, I also discuss attachment in relation to issues such as cohesion, role modelling, and client–provider relationship formation in the context of exercise and health.

I again ask readers to keep in mind that my ultimate aim for this book is to facilitate discussion, debate, and the formulation of new ideas and research on the interface between attachment theory and sport, exercise, and wellness. I hope the book satisfies this objective and that attachment theory might be carried forward, helping to further enrich the development of research in sport, exercise, and wellness. Additionally, I also hope that such integration can facilitate a reciprocal relationship between the areas of sport and exercise psychology and attachment research, with ideas and findings from the sport-related literature ultimately helping to extend and develop ideas in attachment.

1 Sketching the origins and assumptions of attachment theory

A brief introduction

One of the central tenets of attachment theory is the notion that early childhood lays the foundations for the development of personality through the lifespan. Bowlby's ideas (e.g. Bowlby, 1969/1982, 1973, 1979/2005, 1980) reflected this assumption and he believed that infants are biologically predisposed to form selective bonds with special and proximate caring figures in their environment, proposing that experiences in relation to such bonds are a critical factor in the development of internal working models of the world, the self, and self-in-relation-to-world. Attachment theory proposes that there is evolutionary advantage (Bowlby, 1969/1982) in the capacity to equate concepts such as unfamiliarity, loneliness, and rapid approach with danger, and to seek proximity to an attachment figure in response to such threat is the hypothesised goal of the attachment system. The attachment system therefore serves to regulate, maintain, or obtain proximity to a caregiver (or caregivers), who is perceived to be a secure base from which to engage in environmental exploration (Ainsworth, 1963; Bowlby, 1973). Based upon their experiences and perception of caregiver availability, ability, responsiveness, and willingness in relation to their attachment needs Bowlby (1973) hypothesised that children construct mental models related to their thoughts, memories, beliefs, expectations, and emotional and behavioural apparatus in relation to the self and others. These internal working models are thought to provide the basis for subsequent psychological and social development. The purpose of this chapter is to lay out some of the fundamental tenets of attachment theory and provide a basic overview of its development. Readers interested in a more thorough description of the ideas, concepts, and arguments that frame attachment theory are referred to Bowlby's complete works (e.g. Bowlby, 1973, 1980, 1969/1982).

Historical development

Psychoanalysis

Van der Horst (2009) has suggested that while 'Bowlby was a psychoanalyst by training, he was really an ethologist at heart' (p. 105) and while he embraced psychoanalytic schools of thought on the one hand, he saw shortcomings in relation to issues such as scientific rigour and a perceived overemphasis on internal distortion of early experiences as an explanation for children's emotional problems and psychopathology. Bretherton (1992) has outlined Bowlby's early grounding in the Kleinian (Klein, 1932) object relations approach to psychoanalysis, highlighting how he saw great value in central tenets of this approach, such as the notion that early childhood lays the foundations for the development of personality or the psychopathology surrounding loss. However, a particular point of departure from Kleinian psychoanalysis related to the credence Bowlby allotted to the value of children's actual early childhood experiences in explaining emotional problems, as opposed to internally distorted fantasy (arising, according to Kleinian thinking, from conflict between aggressive and libidinal drives). Bowlby's work led him to believe that actual family experiences in early childhood occupied a more central role in the development of emotional disturbances than Kleinian thought had permitted. He suggested (Bowlby, 1940, p. 23) that 'like nurserymen, psychoanalysts should study the nature of the organism, the properties of the soil, and their interaction' (cf. Bretherton, 1992, p. 761). However, despite such departure from Kleinian thinking it has also been recognised that Bowlby retained an acute recognition of Kleinian ideas. For example, Bretherton (1992, p. 765) has astutely asserted:

> I detect remnants of Kleinian ideas in Bowlby's discussions of children's violent fantasies on returning to parents after a prolonged separation and 'the intense depression that humans experience as a result of hating the person they most dearly love and need' (Bowlby, 1951, p. 57).

Despite points of departure, the above quote suggests that Bowlby continued to recognise some of the central features of psychodynamic ideas, such as the central role occupied by intra-psychic conflict.

By more closely tying the development of emotional disturbances to actual family experiences, Bowlby paved the way for more scientific, rigorous investigation of his hypotheses. This was another aspect of his psychoanalytic grounding that he seemed uncomfortable with:

> As one who strives to be both a clinician and scientist I have been acutely alive to this conflict. As a clinician, I have found Freud's approach the more rewarding ... his series of concepts invoking a dynamic unconscious has been a practically useful way of ordering the data. Yet as a scientist I have felt uneasy about the unreliable status of many of our observations, the obscurity of many of our hypotheses and, above all, the absence of any tradition which demands the hypotheses to be tested.
>
> (Bowlby, 1979/2005, p. 36)

With a greater emphasis on more clear-cut, actual experiences during childhood (e.g. mother–child separation) he was better able to document and trace the effects of such childhood events on the child and on the parent–child interaction. He viewed early research documenting the ill effects of institutionalisation and hospitalisation on children (e.g. Goldfarb, 1943; Skodak & Skeels, 1949; Spitz, 1946) to be heavily linked to the issue of maternal deprivation.

Ethology

For Bowlby, the behavioural system of attachment occupied as important a role as the systems related to feeding, care giving, exploration, and sexual reproduction in terms of its relationship to survival and evolution. He outlined the evolutionary advantages (e.g. safety and survival) of instinctive behaviours that he believed were designed to tie human infants to a primary caregiver and considered that such attachment behaviour was best explained as instinctive and 'built on the same general pattern as in other mammalian species' (1979/2005, p. 37). He described a fixed set of behavioural patterns, such as crying, smiling, and clinging, which he saw primarily as evolutionary behavioural apparatus designed to facilitate the development of a maternal bond:

> It would be odd were the biological security which comes from fixed patterns to have been wholly abandoned. Crying, sucking, and smiling I suspect are some of our many built-in motor patterns and represent nature's insurance against leaving everything to the hazard of learning.
>
> (Bowlby, 1979/2005, p. 51)

In discussing such behaviours Bowlby introduced ethological concepts (Tinbergen, 1951) such as 'sign stimuli', 'social releasers', and 'social suppressors', recognising and exploring the external and internal stimuli seemingly responsible for the activation and termination of these behavioural responses. For example, he viewed (Bowlby, 1979/2005) experimental findings of Ahrens (1954) and Spitz and Wolf (1946), suggesting that the smiles of babies from two months of age (drawn from cross-cultural and cross-racial samples) were specifically evoked by visual configurations similar to the human face, as evidence for potential visual gestalts that act as a 'sign stimulus' for eliciting the specific attachment behaviour of smiling.

Furthermore, he was also attuned to early ethological work (e.g. Hunt, 1941; Lorenz, 1935; Padilla, 1935; Thorpe, 1956; Weidmann, 1956) exploring the existence of 'sensitive phases of development' (typically occurring early in the life cycle), during which certain characteristics are permanently determined or significantly affected, depending on a creature's experiences during the sensitive phase. He explored how specific behavioural responses, their intensity, the precise form they take, and the specific stimuli involved in their activation and termination could be markedly influenced by experiences during these sensitive stages of development. For example, he (Bowlby, 1979/ 2005) was intrigued by Lorenz's (1935) work on 'imprinting' in young goslings; identifying that whereas a young gosling:

> would at first follow any moving object that is within certain wide limits of size, after a few days he will follow only the kind of objects to which he is accustomed, be it mother goose or man; and he does that irrespective of whether he has received food or comfort from the object.
>
> (Bowlby, 1979/2005, p. 47)

Bowlby viewed such findings as interesting evidence of how an interaction between environmental and internal factors during sensitive stages of early development could play a significant role in the development of atypical behaviour.

Bretherton (1992, p. 769) has outlined that in reaction to his openness to ethological principles 'some psychoanalysts accused Bowlby of behaviorism because he supposedly ignored mental phenomena'. However, it seems that he was alert to the complementary spaces occupied by ethology and psychoanalysis:

> in so far as psychoanalysis is dealing with Man as a symbol-using animal with extraordinary capacities for learning and therefore for delaying, distorting, and disguising the expression of instinctual responses, it is exploring a region adjacent and complementary to ethology. In so far as it is dealing with the responses themselves, it seems probable that the disciplines overlap.
>
> (Bowlby, 1979/2005, p. 54)

In many respects, Bowlby's ideas reflected a complex fusion of psychological, ethological, and evolutionary ideas.

The attachment behavioural system

The culmination of Bowlby's engagement with ideas from ethology was his proposal of an innate 'attachment behavioural system' which is a central tenet of attachment theory. Bretherton (1985) has described the attachment system as a 'psychological organization' that exists within individuals and has the predominant goal of regulating behaviours that are designed to maintain and initiate proximity and contact with a discriminate attachment figure. However, it is important to note (Bischof, 1975; Bretherton, 1985) that the internal goal of the system is not proximity or contact per se, but the sense of felt psychological security that is subsequently elicited. Bowlby (1969/ 1982) proposed that the attachment behavioural system is likely to be most 'active' in situations where individuals are under stress, frightened, fatigued, or ill and the system is toned down when the attachment figure provides needed comfort. Furthermore, Hazan and Shaver (1994a) have outlined that the degree of proximity to attachment figures that will likely be required to satisfy the attachment system (when activated by perceptions of threat) is likely to be dependent upon a range of variables, including the level of emotional and physical response to threat, the nature of the environmental threat, and children's age.

Bowlby (1968, 1977) linked this attachment behavioural system with what he proposed to be an inbuilt phylogenetic bias to approach certain classes of stimuli and avoid others. He proposed a 'familiar–strange parameter' that has significant import with regard to survival, hypothesising that 'environmental familiarity' is often synonymous with safety, whereas 'strangeness' is generally responded to with ambivalence (i.e. it can elicit fear and withdrawal or it can elicit curiosity and investigation). The attachment behavioural system serves a protective function that is closely related to the familiarity–strangeness parameter, ensuring that attachment behaviour towards a discriminate figure is activated in strange, novel, or threatening situations (i.e. situations evoking fear and the need for withdrawal) yet does not obstruct exploratory efforts when the degree of strangeness is not excessive. Bowlby suggested that the issue about which of the antithetic individual responses to strangeness (i.e. fear or exploration) predominated would depend upon factors such as the degree of strangeness, the presence or absence of a companion, the maturity of the individual, or the state of health of the individual.

Thus, the attachment behavioural system is hypothesised to function as part of an interrelated group of behavioural systems that serve the overarching objective of maintaining a sense of homeostasis between individual and environment (Bowlby, 1973). The prominence of the attachment system is hypothesised to function homeostatically with the need for exploration. Cassidy (1999) has outlined how the maintenance of proximity and contact with the caregiver would change in accordance with the balance of the systems of attachment and exploration, with the sudden presence of a stranger or onset of physical harm activating the attachment system and diminishing exploratory impulses accordingly. Bowlby (1973) described these behavioural systems as an 'outer-ring' of life-maintaining homeostatic systems that serve to complement what he termed the 'inner-ring' of physiological systems. If the outer-ring systems of attachment and exploration (for example) are able to keep individuals within a familiar environment and maintain a sense of security it is hypothesised as less stressful for the 'inner-ring' systems.

Formation of attachment

It is suggested that in the first two months of life infants do not focus their attention exclusively on their mothers but simply behave in ways that are designed to facilitate the formation of an attachment relationship with a potential attachment figure from the adult world. Bowlby hypothesised that early behavioural and attention-related apparatus are in place as 'nature's insurance' with regard to forming such an attachment bond. For example, Farroni *et al.* (2005) have suggested, with reference to a body of research (e.g. Johnson *et al.*, 1991; Valenza *et al.*, 1996) supporting the notion that newborns' attention is immediately biased towards patterns that resemble human facial configuration, that 'most researchers agree that in their natural environment human infants preferentially orient towards faces' (p. 17245). As a consequence, by 6 or 7 months of life infants already show selective preference with regard to a particular figure to which they direct their attachment-related behaviour, seek proximity to, and object to separation from (Schaffer & Emerson, 1964). Hazan and Shaver (1994a) have outlined that Bowlby believed that such selective preferences develop as a function of (a) who most frequently responds to the child's signals of distress, and (b) the quality of the responses to these signals. Around this period of development, infant and caregiver seem to develop interactional patterns that allow them to communicate, helping to establish a unique relationship between them (Vasta *et al.*, 1999).

Vasta *et al.* (1999) have identified that the development of a discriminate attachment bond becomes more explicit from around the age of 8 months and continues to develop over the course of the first 2 to 3 years. It is no accident that this critical age is also a window for the onset of key developmental milestones in relation to cognitive, emotional, and physical development. For example, Thompson and Limber (1990) have outlined that in this period of development babies begin to acquire cognitive and memory-related abilities that make them more astute to aspects of the environment that are 'familiar' or 'strange'. An increased awareness of this familiar–strange parameter in relation to the environment gives rise to emotional changes, with powerful sensations of fear and anxiety often experienced in what Bowlby considered to be an adaptive response (in terms of survival) to strange situations. These enhanced cognitive and emotional capacities, together with motor developments which permit greater control over the regulation of distance between infant and caregiver, bring an increased need for an attachment figure who reflects a safe haven that a child can retreat to in order to alleviate emotional sensations of fear and anxiety and restore homeostasis. Bowlby suggested that infants' behaviour towards the attachment figure tends to reflect the key functions of the attachment bond; proximity maintenance (seeking and maintaining proximity and protestation at separation), safe haven (the attachment figure is viewed as a haven for retreat in times of distress), and secure base (the attachment figure serves as a base around which exploratory efforts and individuation can begin to develop) functions. Hence, he appreciated that the formation of such bonds is of critical importance, both for the regulation of negative emotion in response to the strange and unfamiliar and for the facilitation of independent exploratory behaviour.

It is also important to note that the above behavioural characteristics of attachment formation are heavily bound to emotionality. Bowlby (1975) recognised that one of the defining features of an attachment bond is the strength of emotional engagement that it elicits. He viewed the emotion surrounding attachment bonds as evidence of their significant evolutionary importance to individual survival. In the short term, being apart from the attachment figure arouses powerful feelings of separation anxiety and protest, which can also involve crying and searching behaviour, and such emotional distress is typically alleviated when an infant is reunited with the caregiver. In the longer term, Bowlby's observations of young children separated from their caregivers for lengthy periods of time (or even permanently) revealed a powerful and predictable sequence of emotional reactions, involving protestation (crying, searching behaviour, and a reluctance to be comforted by an unfamiliar adult figure), despair (sadness), emotional detachment, and extreme anger in some cases upon being reunited with the caregiver. Bowlby hypothesised these emotional reactions as highly adaptive and of obvious importance in an evolutionary sense. For example, he (Bowlby, 1977) viewed anger towards attachment figures (upon being reunited) as part of the emotional apparatus designed to 'add punch' to the efforts to reproach them, to lessen the likelihood of future abandonment. He also saw value in the development of emotional detachment when there seems to be no further hope of reuniting with the caregiver, hypothesising that indefinite expression of distress would, in evolutionary terms, serve only to attract predators and to exhaust the child of energy (Hazan & Shaver, 1994a). The fact that such emotional experiences invariably linked to attachment bonds prompted Bowlby to claim that 'the psychology and psychopathology of emotion is found to be in large part the psychology and psychopathology of affectional bonds' (1979/2005, p. 155).

In the main, sensitive and responsive parenting has been identified as a major contributor to the formation of attachment security in infancy (Ainsworth et al., 1978; De Wolff & van Ijzendoorn, 1997). However, it is worth briefly noting that the attachment literature does not view the formation of attachment bonds as solely a product of parenting characteristics. Hazan and Shaver (1994b) have outlined that 'anything that influences the quality of the caregiver's response ... can be expected to influence the quality of the attachment' (p. 72). For example, Biederman et al. (2001) have linked attachment characteristics in children to parents suffering from anxiety disorders and major clinical depression, and there has also been significant attention devoted to the role of infant temperament differences (e.g. Jang & Chung, 2009; van den Boom, 1994). With regard to infant temperament, it is hypothesised that babies who are more irritable or possess other difficult characteristics may be more difficult to respond to in a sensitive manner or may respond differently themselves to a given level of sensitivity provided by parents.

Internal working models

Over time, through continual transactions, Bowlby (1969/1982, 1973) hypothesised that children begin to develop an internal working model that reflects a generalised mental representation of the world, significant others, and the self in relation to these significant others. This idea was heavily influenced by the work of Kenneth Craik (1943) who had put forward the notion of internalised mental models as a generalised internal representation of the external world that could be employed to guide cognition, emotion, and behaviour. Craik (1943) hypothesised that such mental models were advantageous in evolutionary terms because they save time and energy by removing the need to undertake repeated individual analyses of situations because the internal model serves to generate expectations and hypotheses that guide behaviour in advance. In the context of the attachment relationship between child and caregiver, Bowlby hypothesised that internal working models would guide the child in formulating expectations and behaviour surrounding caregiver availability and responsiveness. For example, if experience over time leads the child to develop an internal representation of the caregiver as someone who cannot be counted on for support and comfort the child often develops an internalised lack of trust in the caregiver. This type of internalised model of the caregiver is likely to guide attachment-related behaviour, perhaps resulting in a more intense and pervasive monitoring of caregiver whereabouts than would be necessary had the child developed more of an internalised certainty in caregiver availability. In addition to expectations in relation to the attachment figure, Bowlby (1973) also hypothesised that internal working models also related to 'whether or not the self is judged to be the sort of person towards whom anyone, and the attachment figure in particular, is likely to respond in a helpful way' (p. 238). Hence, attachment theory also suggests that elements of self-concept and self-perception are also linked to the internal working models that begin to unfold as a consequence of caregiver responsiveness to expressions of attachment needs. For example, Bowlby (1973) believed that when attachment figures provide comfort and support, children develop an internal working model both of the caregiver as loving and supporting and also of themselves as deserving of such love and support. In contrast, when an attachment figure is consistently rejecting, children develop a representation of the caregiver as unavailable and unloving and of themselves as unworthy of support and unlovable. Sroufe and Fleeson (1986) have implied that in the construction of such working models children are essentially constructing and internalising both sides of the parent–child relationship model, also formulating a template about the parental role that they may later enact when they themselves become parents.

In an insightful discussion about the notion of 'internal working models' Bretherton (1985) has outlined that the concept seems to refer to a psychological organisation that is both 'dynamic' (i.e. it is described as a working model) and 'constructed' (i.e. a model implies something that has been constructed). This is important to note because it takes into account issues such as an increasing complexity with regard to the content and function of internal working models that would parallel increasing cognitive and social

complexities that are a function of child development. Bowlby (1980) suggested that new information would therefore continually be assimilated into
earlier versions of working models, updating them in terms of their complexity and sophistication of content. Bretherton (1985) has outlined that
while the basic subsystems underpinning attachment functioning are unlikely
to change (i.e. (a) the need for a homeostatic balance between basic systems
of attachment and exploration, (b) the importance of regulating the attachment
system in relation to attachment figures), the manner in which they are
internally represented and dealt with psychologically is likely to alter with
increasing developmental sophistication. For example, Bretherton (1985) has
highlighted that expressions of attachment behaviour can become more
subtle or cunning (as a function of more sophisticated perceptions and
expectations of the self–caregiver relationship), children become better able
to make judgements about the motives and actions of caregivers, better
able to cope with their own distress (lessening the frequency of activation of
the attachment system), and more astute with regard to appraising threatening
situations. However, Bretherton (1985) has also outlined that such alterations
in the expression of attachment do not imply that the attachment system is
'waning' (p. 12). Rather, they simply suggest that the individual is developing
an increasing degree of psychological sophistication that undoubtedly impacts
the manner in which the attachment system is experienced and regulated.

Ainsworth's work and individual differences in developing internal working models

The 'pattern' and 'tone' of attachment figures' responses to infants' innate
desire for proximity will undoubtedly vary significantly between families and
this could theoretically result in development of an infinite number of possible
internal working models. As Hazan and Shaver (1994a) have pointed out:

> Theoretically and logically speaking, there is no limit to the amount and
> kind of variability that could exist in models of the caregiving environ-
> ment. In reality, however, infants parse the flow of information about
> caregiver behaviours into a limited number of categories corresponding
> to responses to the following question: 'Can I count on my attachment
> figure to be available and responsive when needed?' There are three
> possible answers to this question: Yes, no, and maybe.
>
> (p. 5)

One of Mary Ainsworth's (Ainsworth *et al.*, 1978) significant contributions
to attachment theory was that she developed a laboratory procedure
designed to reflect infants' developing internal working models of attachment
to a key caregiver based upon observations of behavioural responses. Specifically, Ainsworth's Strange Situation Procedure was designed to activate
infants' attachment system by placing them in an unfamiliar environment

(sometimes in the company of a stranger) and by orchestrating brief separations from the caregiver. Furthermore, by also making available an attractive array of toys for the children to play with she attempted to explore interplay between the exploration and attachment systems. Key factors of interest related to whether the presence of the caregiver in the unfamiliar environment would facilitate children's exploration of the toys, the degree to which children sought proximity to the caregiver, the distress experienced during the caregiver's absence, and the role of the caregiver in alleviating distress following brief separation. It was hypothesised that these behavioural responses would serve as indicators of infants' underlying mental models of attachment in relation to their caregiver.

Categorical differences in response to the Strange Situation Procedure were first noted by Ainsworth in her Baltimore study of 23 12-month-old infants and their mothers. Specifically, the study identified distinctly different patterns of responses to the Strange Situation Procedure that corresponded strikingly to distinct features of the relationship between infant and mother in the home. A secure response pattern was evident in the majority of the infants and was manifested when infants showed visible signs of missing their mother during separation, were comforted by her return, and returned to play when they were aware of her presence again. Observations in the home of such infants tended to reveal that the mother was a secure base for exploration within the home and children exhibited little anxiety, anger, and distress during minor separations at home. Furthermore, mothers of such infants engaged sensitively with infants' emotional signals during the first year of life, holding them tenderly, initiating face-to-face contact, and being tuned to their signalling of distress. Insecure-ambivalent infants, in contrast, were preoccupied with their caregiver during the laboratory procedure to the extent that their level of exploratory play was significantly impeded. They also exhibited significantly greater levels of apparent anxiety and anger throughout the procedure. Observations from the homes of such children revealed that they often appeared anxious at home and although mothers were not necessarily rejecting (Main, 1996), they seemed inept with regard to holding the infant and unpredictable with regard to whether or not they would sense, acknowledge, and respond to signals of distress. Finally, insecure-avoidant infants focused predominantly on the toys during the laboratory procedure, did not appear distressed upon separation from caregivers, and avoided general contact with caregivers. Furthermore, these infants tended to engage with the toys with an apparently lower level of enthusiasm and interest than children in the secure category. At home, these infants exhibited high levels of anger towards their mothers and anxiety concerning her whereabouts. Furthermore, observations suggested that these mothers blatantly rejected infants' attachment behaviours and failed to initiate any physical contact in relation to expressions of emotional distress. In relation to the insecure-avoidant categorisation, Main (1996) astutely observed that what Ainsworth appeared to have identified in relation to this type of response was the early development of a form of behavioural expression akin to a psychological defensive mechanism:

> Avoidance on reunion had previously been noted only after long-term separations, where it was interpreted as repression in the making ... Ainsworth had discovered that behavior bearing a phenotypic resemblance to defensive processes could develop out of daily interaction.
>
> (p. 238)

Van Ijzendoorn *et al.* (1999) have outlined how the secure, insecure-ambivalent, and insecure-avoidant categorisations of attachment outlined by Ainsworth reflect what can be termed 'organised' patterns of attachment. That is, each pattern reflects a developed attachment strategy that can be considered 'adaptive' in the sense that it is an internalised pattern of responses that are designed to maximise proximity to the caregiver based upon developed expectations of her typical responses to expression of distress. In this sense, children have an organised response strategy that is a logical reflection of adaptation to the attachment-related features of their environment. However, researchers (e.g. Main & Solomon, 1986, 1990) have also identified a fourth pattern of attachment which has been labelled disorganised. This pattern tends to reflect the absence of a coherent and organised strategy for dealing with distress and the breakdown or absence of a consistent strategy for emotional regulation. Main and Solomon (1990) identified features such as contradictory behaviour (e.g. the infant shows marked distress when separated from the caregiver but then complete indifference when she returns), misdirected behaviour (e.g. seeking proximity to the stranger and not the parent once the parent has returned), 'freezing' (e.g. apparent difficulty in deciding whether to seek proximity to the parent or to avoid her completely), and apprehension (e.g. displaying an apparent fear of the parent following the separation) as indicators of a disorganised pattern of attachment. This attachment strategy has been suggested to be an indication that infants are experiencing anxiety, fear, and distress that they are unable to resolve in an organised fashion because the caregiver seems to simultaneously represent the source of the fear and the potential safe haven (van Ijzendoorn *et al.*, 1999). A disorganised attachment pattern has been suggested to stem from parenting that is abusive or when parents themselves are dealing with unresolved loss of an attachment figure or with issues such as depression or other mental disturbance (Hazan & Shaver, 1994a; van Ijzendoorn *et al.*, 1999).

Stability and multiplicity of attachment models

There are numerous complexities surrounding the central tenets of attachment theory. Most of these issues remain unresolved in the literature and it is therefore helpful to be aware of some of the intricacies that characterise them. Key questions centre around (a) the degree of stability of initial attachment patterns developed with primary caregivers through the lifespan, (b) if it is accepted that individuals can develop multiple models of attachment in relation to multiple others, what is the degree of 'primacy' that early attachment to 'primary' caregivers would occupy within such a network of attachment models, and (c) if individuals do develop 'secondary' models of attachment, how are such models combined with primary models? Before embarking upon discussion of stability and multiplicity of 'attachment models' it is important, as Ainsworth (1993) has pointed out, to keep in mind what is meant by terms such as 'attachment' or 'attachment model' in this context. In accordance with Ainsworth's (1993) definition, readers should keep in mind that the discussion that ensues is referring to an internalisation on the part of the child with regard to the attachment relationship he or she shares with a given attachment figure(s).

Freud (1940, p. 188) argued that the relationship between a child and a mother is 'unique, without parallel, established unalterably for a whole lifetime as the first and strongest love-object and as the *prototype* [italics added] of all later love relations – for both sexes'. While Freud refers exclusively to maternal bonds and is not referring explicitly to attachment in the above statement, from the perspective of attachment theory the quote raises important issues surrounding whether or not there is something primary about the attachment that an infant forms with his/her primary caregiver. Pincus *et al.* (2007) point out that infancy is likely to play a particularly important role in the lifespan of a human being, outlining how the cornerstones of a psychological 'self' are essentially 'carved out' during this critical period of development:

> The human infant's immaturity at birth and extensive dependency on caregivers cannot be underestimated. Humans create ('find') themselves through others, and this cannot be more clearly seen than in human infancy: For an infant to become a self, he or she is dynamically constituted, to a profound extent, through others. A psychological 'self' is shaped out from an immersion with others.
>
> (Pincus *et al.*, 2007, p. 635)

Psychological characteristics developed through key relationships in infancy are therefore more likely to be 'prototypical' as they are developed at a time when the human mind is more akin to a 'tabula rasa' (i.e. more vulnerable, plastic, and open to influence) than in any stages of later life. Viewing attachment patterns formed with primary caregivers in infancy as prototypical suggests that they are likely to have significant and enduring effects.

Hazan and Shaver (1994b, p. 70) have outlined the following view with regard to the stability of early models of attachment:

> Bowlby (1973) explicitly stated ... that working models of attachment are gradually constructed out of experiences throughout infancy,

childhood, and adolescence. Only then do they become relatively resistant to, but still not impervious to, change. Our view is that they are sufficiently stable to warrant consideration and study.

Implicit in the above quote is a sense that models of attachment seem to reflect both a degree of malleability and a degree of consistency. This is consistent with Bowlby's acknowledgement that working models of attachment can change in accordance with an individual's experiences. Indeed, Bowlby espoused a fundamental principle of therapy whereby the therapist would gradually become an attachment figure for the patient, allowing her to slowly build the trust needed in order for the therapist to be viewed as a secure base (Ainsworth, 1993). The formulation of such a secure base in the therapeutic setting allows patients to explore entrenched working models of attachment and related expectations of others and the self, and to gradually 'rework' and 'revise' such models so that they are more in line with realistic present circumstances (Ainsworth, 1993). Clearly, it is therefore feasible to suggest that attachment researchers view the working model of attachment as amenable to modification based upon experience. However, it should be noted that modification does not imply replacement and here it is possible to suggest that a first, prototypical model of attachment (typically constructed out of experiences with primary caregivers) would maintain particular significance because it provides the initial parameters within which subsequent modifications are likely to take place.

Hazan and Shaver (1994a) have therefore outlined how attachment research has been presented with the dilemma that the study of most cognitive-structures is ultimately faced with; the relative degree of plasticity or solidity of the constructs under study. Thompson (2000) has outlined that studies have provided contrasting results with regard to the stability of attachment models. For example, Belsky *et al.*'s (1996) investigation identified that almost half of the infants classified according to Ainsworth's Strange Situation Procedure changed attachment classification after a period of 6–7 months had elapsed. However, in contrast, other studies have identified a remarkable degree of consistency between Strange Situation classifications in infancy and assessments of attachment styles many years later (e.g. Main & Cassidy, 1988; Wartner *et al.*, 1994). Davila *et al.* (1999) have outlined that longitudinal studies employing self-report assessments of attachment (e.g. Baldwin & Fehr, 1995; Davila *et al.*, 1997; Fuller & Fincham, 1995) tend to suggest that approximately 30 per cent of individuals appear to change their attachment styles over time. While it is important to note that differences in relation to researchers' measurement of attachment models could have a significant impact on reported outcomes in relation to stability (the following chapter will address such measurement issues), it is important to keep in mind, as Davila *et al.* (1999, p. 783) have pointed out:

that there is some evidence that whereas many people retain their attachment style, some people change … this brings us to the more pressing question … why do some people change attachment styles?

Bowlby (1969/1982) proposed that working models 'must be kept up to date' (p. 82) in order to retain a level of functional usefulness. For the most part, he proposed that such modification would occur on a small scale and would not be appreciably noticeable. However, he also recognised that at times individuals would experience significant life events that would, perhaps unsurprisingly, result in significant modification of internal working models of attachment. The idea that models of attachment undertake modification in response to contextual changes reflects a contextual model (Davila *et al.*, 1999) of attachment change. In support of this, a number of studies (e.g. Teti *et al.*, 1996; Vaughn *et al.*, 1979) have identified that changes in family stress, living conditions, or factors such as the arrival of new siblings lessen the likelihood that early attachment classifications will be predictive of later classifications. For example, Teti *et al.* (1996) identified that the attachment classifications of first born preschoolers following the birth of a new sibling became significantly less secure and that the decrease in security was significantly related to mothers' experiences of depression and anxiety following the birth of the sibling. Such findings suggest that factors likely to negatively influence the quality of caregivers' reactions to expressions of attachment need may prompt modifications to internal working models.

Furthermore, Crowell *et al.* (2002) identified that changes toward an increasingly secure working model of attachment were evident in a small percentage of adult participants (although it should be noted that this study identified that for the most part models of attachment were remarkably stable) over the first 18 months of marriage. The researchers attributed these changes in working models to a number of factors that characterised the onset of the marriages concerned: (a) an increase in distance from parents, (b) an exposure to new ideas and new people, and (c) new 'ways of being' in relationships. It was hypothesised that these factors facilitated a gradual reconfiguration of working models of attachment formulated in childhood and supported the assumption that under certain circumstances these models are open to modification. It is also interesting to note that there was little reported awareness from participants with regard to changes in models of attachment, suggesting that the process of change may be gradual and not explicitly discernible (Crowell *et al.*, 2002).

Aside from context-related changes as modifiers of working models of attachment, researchers in social psychology have also explored social-cognitive and individual difference models of change. The social-cognitive model (e.g. Baldwin, 1995; Baldwin & Fehr, 1995) suggests that individuals are likely to have internalised multiple models of attachment or 'relational schemata' that could each be activated should the current context provide relevant cues. From this perspective, a 'chronically accessible' relational schema would reflect one's most consistently employed working model of attachment, yet individuals are thought to have numerous accessible working models that can also be activated (and hence influence current thoughts, feelings, and behaviour). In contrast, the individual difference model (e.g. Davila *et al.*, 1997) hypothesises attachment changes to be a function of differences in 'proneness to attachment change'. From this perspective, some people are more prone to attachment changes not simply because of contextual changes but because they have a stable internal vulnerability to fluctuation. In a two-year longitudinal study of young women making the transition into adulthood Davila *et al.* (1997) supported this proposition and identified that women with a history of personal and family dysfunction (psychological illness, parental divorce) were significantly more prone to attachment style fluctuations. The authors provided evidence that such fluctuation in attachment models in these individuals was more a function of a 'personal tendency to fluctuate' than a simple response to contextual changes. They noted that such individuals' tendency to experience changes in attachment models was more likely a reflection that they themselves had a specific form of insecurity that made them vulnerable to oscillations in models of attachment.

Multiple attachment figures and models of attachment

Bowlby (1969/1982) recognised a tendency for infants to have a selective preference for one particular caregiver. He labelled this monotropy and argued that there was a clear evolutionary advantage in having a primary attachment figure to turn to in times of distress to avoid potential confusion or threats to safety. Hazan and Shaver (1994b) have argued that most attachment researchers would agree that the majority of human infants do become attached to a primary caregiver (although it is generally accepted that this is not necessarily always the mother) but this does not preclude the possibility that infants and children might form multiple secondary attachment bonds with significant others and there is no doubt that they do. For Hazan and Shaver (1994b), when a bond with a significant other satisfies the criteria put forward for being an attachment (e.g. it includes proximity maintenance, secure base, and safe haven behaviours) it is likely to form one of multiple attachment bonds that constitute an attachment 'hierarchy' or 'network' of individuals that are each perceived to serve attachment functions (although it is likely that they do not all have the same relative degree of importance with regard to such functions). Important points of debate in relation to multiple attachment relationships (i.e. relationships in which individuals perceive that they can meet attachment needs) relate to whether or not an individual having multiple attachment figures implies that all of these relationships will necessarily contribute to an individual's internal working model of attachment. Furthermore, as Kobak (2009) has discussed, individuals who have multiple figures whom they indicate serve attachment functions could also be a simple reflection of an individual with a particular working model of attachment, comfortable with relying on 'any port in a storm'.

Bretherton (1985) outlines how, in its most technical sense, the term 'attachment figure' is referring to the use of the caregiver for the functions outlined by Hazan and Shaver (1994b) above (secure base, safe haven, proximity maintenance). However, they argue that this does not imply that attachment figures will necessarily occupy other important relational roles (such as play). It is conceivable that a child's predominant attachment figure may not be the figure that they utilise for significant play experiences but, on the other hand, a primary attachment figure might simultaneously operate as the main playmate. It is important to recognise that the relative 'uses' of various significant adults in children's lives may differ with regard to the specific relational functions that they serve. For example, studies from specific cultural groups have identified that relationships between mothers and children are sometimes exclusively biased towards attachment functions. Brazelton (1977) reported that Mexican Indian mothers showed little to no attempt to initiate play or social interaction with their children yet were simultaneously very attentive to children's expressions of distress. Furthermore, studies of Western cultures have shown that the relative importance of mothers has been more significant with regard to an attachment function whereas the relative importance of fathers has been more significant with regard to play (e.g. Lamb, 1976, 1977). However, in contrast, Colin's (1987) data suggested that 24 per cent of children directed stronger attachment-related behaviour toward their fathers, suggesting that in certain circumstances (i.e. the fathers concerned were all observed to play a substantial role in their child's day-to-day care) there is no reason to believe that the primary attachment figure is always the mother. Such relative differences with regard to the attachment functions served by specific significant others are reflected in hierarchical conceptualisations of attachment figures (e.g. Trinke & Bartholomew, 1997).

Even within a single relationship, Bowlby (1980) highlighted the issue of multiplicity with regard to models of attachment. For the most part, it is suggested that minor inconsistencies in day-to-day care giving behaviour on the part of a parent would occur but that a child would nonetheless extract a degree of perceived consistency from his or her experience that would permit the crystallisation of an internal working model. However, Bowlby (1980) did note that at times the degree of inconsistency experienced in a given relationship is so great that it becomes extremely difficult to develop a generalised level of expectation. Ainsworth (1993) highlights the example of a child's actual experiences in relation to his mother's care giving behaviour being significantly distinct from what he is both told to believe and wishes to believe with regard to her thoughts and behaviour. In such instances, Bowlby (1980) argued that a child may form dual working models of the mother, with one model becoming cognitively accessible and the other becoming inaccessible (but perhaps nevertheless exerting an influence subconsciously).

Across the literature, the issue of multiple models of attachment remains debatable, with differences in the conceptualisation of attachment figures and the measurement of attachment making it difficult to draw definitive conclusions. Main (1985) has suggested that individuals tend to form a gen-eralised view of attachment figures that reflects a state of mind with regard to attachment which will serve to guide future interactions that are relevant to the attachment system. However, as Ainsworth (1993) has commented, 'there is no reason to believe that no other working models could be formed' (p. 476) and the literature has conceptualised interesting avenues of research in relation to multiple working models with regard to various indi-vidual attachment figures and also to group-related attachment con-ceptualisations such as the family (Marvin & Stewart, 1990). From the perspective of 'the family as a secure base', researchers (e.g. Byng-Hall, 1995; Marvin & Stewart, 1990) have argued that a family often also 'provides a reliable network of attachment relationships in which all family members of whatever age are able to feel sufficiently secure to explore' (Byng-Hall, 1995, p. 46). Hence, the idea individuals can hold working models that reflect an internal conceptualisation of the family unit as a source of security (as opposed to, or in addition to an aggregated abstraction of multiple models from individual relationships) is a further extension to this issue in attachment research.

Adult attachment

Bowlby (1979/2005) hypothesised attachment to be an integral part of human existence through the lifespan. Attachment theory's proposal of relatively enduring cognitive representations constructed initially out of early attach-ment experiences has implications for adulthood in the sense that such working models will influence the manner in which aspects of adult life are psychologically experienced. Of particular significance is Bowlby's conten-tion that early relationship experiences provide a model for how subsequent relationships are played out. In this sense, the expectations of the self and others that constitute central elements of internal working models of attachment will undoubtedly play a central role in constructing new rela-tionships in adulthood. Hence, researchers (e.g. Bartholomew, 1990; Shaver *et al.*, 1996) have suggested that the long-term effects of early attachment experiences are predominantly a function of the persistence of internal working models into adulthood. However, it is also necessary that the sig-nificant attachment bonds that played a central role in initial development of attachment working models in childhood are gradually (but never entirely) relinquished, and that additional affectional bonds are formed with close significant others through adulthood. These new affectional bonds may also serve to modify and rework internal working models over time.

Bartholomew and Shaver (1998, p. 41) have suggested that 'as a person moves along ... increasingly differentiated [life] pathways, it is quite possible for internal working models of relationships with parents to diverge from working models of romantic relationships'. Hence, the complexity surrounding internal working models of attachment is likely to increase significantly with progression into adulthood.

In social psychology Hazan and Shaver (1994a; Shaver & Hazan, 1988; Shaver *et al.*, 1988) have employed attachment theory as a framework for understanding adult romantic relationships and for conceptualising adult romantic love. For example, in a now classic study Hazan and Shaver (1987) translated Ainsworth's categorisations of infant attachment patterns to adult romantic love relations, asking participants to choose descriptors that best reflected their style of adult love relations (i.e. secure, insecure-avoidant, insecure-anxious). Secure individuals (in relation to their romantic love relations) had relationships that tended to be characterised by high levels of trust, happiness, and friendship, whereas insecure-anxious individuals tended to experience a rollercoaster of emotionality in love relations, tending to be jealous, obsessive, and unhealthily preoccupied with their partners. These styles were found to be linked to parenting experiences in childhood, with secure individuals reporting more accepting and sensitive parenting than insecure individuals. The researchers claimed that this was a preliminary indication that working models of attachment from childhood may well exert an active influence on experiences of close relationships in adulthood, highlighting similarities between their findings and Bowlby's initial ideas.

Despite similarities between adult attachment and attachment in early childhood there are also a number of important distinctions that are worth noting. First, attachment relationships in adulthood tend to be reciprocal in nature in the sense that both partners tend to provide and receive care (Hazan & Shaver, 1994a). This is clearly not the case in early childhood relations, when the relationship is unidirectional. This distinction may have important implications that make attachment relations in adulthood increasingly complex and intricate. For example, withholding or failing to provide adequate care in a reciprocal relationship can stimulate anxiety or anger on the part of the receiver (as in parent–child dyads). However, in a reciprocal relationship the partner experiencing anger or anxiety is also a mutual provider of such care and their emotional responses to a perceived lack of received care may influence the likelihood or quality of their provision in return (e.g. 'Why should I be there for you when you were not there for me?'). Second, with maturity individuals are increasingly able to derive a sense of felt security from attachment figures without such a significant need for physical contact and proximity (although Hazan & Shaver, 1994a, contend that the need for physical contact will not diminish completely). Ainsworth (1993) has outlined how representational processes make it possible to maintain the working model of the attachment figure, for example, without the same reliance on factors such as proximity. Bowlby outlined how the goal of the attachment system in adulthood (i.e. a perceived availability of the attachment figure) depends more significantly on cognitive factors such as the belief that lines of communication are open, the perception that physical accessibility exists if need be, and trust that the attachment figure will be available if necessary. Finally, researchers (e.g. Hazan & Shaver, 1994a; Kobak, 2009) have also discussed that, unlike parent–child dyads, adult attachment relationships are often simultaneously also sexual or affiliation-based relationships, meaning that they will involve a more complex fusion of the attachment system, the sexual system, the care giving system, and the affiliation system. This distinction is important when examining attachment in the sense that factors such as proximity seeking or emotional responses to actual and hypothetical loss (which are often indicators of attachment) could be primarily motivated by other behavioural systems (e.g. individuals might display striking emotional reactions to perceived loss of a given other because of a loss of sexual need satisfaction). Furthermore, formation of additional attachments in adulthood may well arise out of initial relationships that are originally motivated by sexual or affiliation needs. Such issues point to the complexities that characterise the field of attachment research in adulthood.

Conclusion

Ainsworth (1993) commented that:

> Bowlby has made it quite clear that his theory is eclectic in its origins. His genius, however, lies in the way he has integrated a collection of concepts together to form a coherent and comprehensive theory that is still open ended and subject to revision/extension through the research for which it has provided a useful guide.
>
> (p. 476)

This chapter has attempted to sketch out some of the predominant assumptions of the theory, highlighting (a) the array of concepts that Bowlby integrated into a coherent set of assumptions, and (b) how these specific assumptions within the framework are nonetheless open to revision and extension as research unfolds. Hazan and Shaver (1994b) have noted that Bowlby required the best part of 1000 pages in order to articulate his theory fully. It should therefore be noted that the intention of this chapter has been merely to help readers familiarise themselves with some of the fundamental tenets of the framework.

Notable by its absence in this chapter is the devotion of attention to what has been referred to as the emergence of 'two traditions' in attachment research (e.g. Bartholomew & Shaver, 1998; Jacobvitz *et al.*, 2002). In short, the 'open ended' nature of attachment theory and the fact that it is 'open to revision' (highlighted from Ainsworth's above quote) have given rise to the development of distinct lines of research related to attachment. On the one hand are researchers who 'tend to think psychodynamically, be interested in clinical problems, prefer interview measures and behavioral observations over questionnaires, study relatively small groups of subjects, and focus their attention on parent–child relationships' (Bartholomew & Shaver, 1998, p. 27). On the other hand are personality and social psychologists 'who tend to think in terms of personality traits and social interactions, be interested in normal subject populations, prefer simple questionnaire measures, study relatively large samples, and focus on adult social relationships, including friendship, dating relationships, and marriages' (Bartholomew & Shaver, 1998, p. 27). Not surprisingly, these different lines of research give rise to significant distinctions in terms of how attachment research is conceptually underpinned, how attachment is measured, and how results are interpreted. Hence, sensitivity to this distinction is recommended. In the following chapter, measurement issues with regard to attachment are discussed and it is hoped that the chapter will go some way towards articulating the differences between these two traditions in attachment research.

2 Contrasting perspectives and measurement in adult attachment research

Introduction

Bowlby claimed that attachment has significant implications for human beings 'from the cradle to the grave'. The notion that the effects of attachment might endure beyond childhood and throughout the lifespan has fuelled significant lines of research relating to attachment in *adulthood*. Specifically, the influence of persistent (although the theory does not preclude the idea that such models can be subject to reformulation and increasing complexity over the lifespan) internal working models of the self and the self in relation to others proposed by attachment theory is hypothesised to extend into experiences of cognition, affect, and behaviour in close relationships that are encountered in adulthood. Consequently, researchers have been concerned with constructing studies that permit robust examination of such important hypotheses. In the concluding section of the previous chapter it was noted that the research on adult attachment has diverged into two distinct lines of research. These lines of research are both derived from the theoretical assumptions at the heart of Bowlby's theory (Jacobvitz *et al.*, 2002), yet have evolved according to underlying assumptions and measurement techniques of contrasting sub-cultures (Bartholomew & Shaver, 1998). Many of the distinctions between these two lines of enquiry are reflected in the manner in which researchers allied to each have approached the measurement of attachment in adulthood and it is the purpose of this chapter to outline these measurement techniques within each school of thought. It is intended that such an outline will assist readers in developing an appreciation both of the different measurement techniques that exist with regard to attachment and also of the subtle conceptual distinctions that differences between them reflect. Such an appreciation is important (a) so that sport researchers will be able to make informed and conceptually sensible decisions when adopting an attachment perspective, and (b) so that research conducted in sport is developed in accordance with the evolution of lines of enquiry in the broader field of attachment.

The Adult Attachment Interview: a clinical/developmental conceptualisation

In the previous chapter it was noted that some researchers in the field of adult attachment 'tend to think psychodynamically, be interested in clinical problems, prefer interview measures and behavioral observations over questionnaires, study relatively small groups of subjects, and focus their attention on parent–child relationships' (Bartholomew & Shaver, 1998, p. 27). Many of the underpinning assumptions made by researchers allied to this tradition of attachment research are reflected in the Adult Attachment Interview (AAI; George *et al.*, 1985). Building upon the work of Mary Ainsworth and her colleagues in developmental psychology (e.g. Ainsworth *et al.*, 1978), Mary Main and colleagues from developmental and clinical psychology (e.g. George *et al.*, Kaplan, & Main, 1985, 1996; Main & Goldwyn, 1998; Main *et al.*, 1985) explored the idea that adult 'states of mind' with respect to attachment relationships with their parents in childhood are related to the parenting behaviour that they themselves exhibit toward their offspring and subsequently to the attachment styles that unfold in their offspring in early childhood. This line of enquiry seems particularly important in helping to substantiate a hypothesised degree of persistence with regard to working models of attachment through the lifespan. The AAI was developed as part of this research programme, in order to tap into adults' states of mind regarding attachment from their childhood.

The AAI examines adults' current representations of their childhood relationships with parents (Bartholomew & Shaver, 1998). Hesse (1999) has outlined that the interview takes between 60–90 minutes to complete. Participants are required to think of five adjectives that they feel describe their childhood relationship with their mother, five adjectives to describe their childhood relationship with their father, to provide anecdotal evidence in support of their adjective choices, to speculate with regard to the reasons underpinning their parents' behaviour, and to recall any perceived changes in the quality of their relationship with parents through childhood. Furthermore, individuals are also required to discuss their attachment-related experiences with parents during childhood, such as what typically happened when they were upset, ill, hurt, or separated from attachment figures (Jacobvitz *et al.*, 2002). The AAI coding system assesses adults' discussions and recollections of their childhood relationships with parents based upon investigator coding of *how* participants describe their experiences, and not on the content of their recollections (Jacobvitz *et al.*, 2002). The assumption here is that the coding procedure taps into 'adults' unconscious processes for regulating emotion' (Jacobvitz *et al.*, 2002, p. 208), predominantly through the analysis of defensive processes and characteristics of discourse (such as anger, coherence, and viability of content). Trained coders of the AAI conceptualise attachment patterns that are primarily derived from Ainsworth's traditional classification system (Ainsworth *et al.*, 1978).

Specifically, the interview is coded according (a) to 5 rating scales that reflect the 'probable quality' (Shaver & Mikulincer, 2002, p. 136) of childhood experiences, with quality of relations (loving, abusive, neglecting etc.) with mother and father analysed separately, and (b) 12 scales which are designed to reflect individuals' current state of mind with regard to these experiences (e.g. evidence of anger, coherence of discourse, idealisation).

Attachment classification is derived from a composite judgement of these rating scales and they are hypothesised to reflect specific forms of affect-regulation in relation to discussion of attachment experiences (Shaver & Mikulincer, 2002; Hesse, 1999). According to Shaver and Mikulincer (2002), individuals are classified as *secure* if they describe 'positive relationships in a clear, convincing, and coherent manner or if negative relationships are described coherently with an appropriate degree of perspective' (p. 136). Mary Main has described a coherent interview accordingly:

> a coherent interview is both believable and true to the listener; in a coherent interview, the events and affects intrinsic to early relationships are conveyed without distortion, contradiction or derailment of discourse. The subject collaborates with the interviewer, clarifying his or her meaning, and working to make sure he or she is understood. Such a subject is thinking as the interview proceeds, and is aware of thinking with and communicating to another; thus coherence and collaboration are inherently intertwined and interrelated.
>
> (Slade, 1999, p. 580)

Sonkin (2005) has outlined that factors such as the coherence of discourse described above are likely to reflect something about the attachment status of individuals. This is because recounting one's life story is likely to evoke both subtle and powerful emotional responses that will partially influence the manner in which one's story is relayed. Powerful emotions evoked by the narrative may result in a variety of responses that could serve to derail the content of what is relayed, to distort such content, or for individuals to become so absorbed in the discourse that they lose awareness of the interview procedure. AAI researchers view such features of discourse as highly informative with regard to attachment states of mind. For example, individuals are coded as *insecure-dismissing* if their narrative seems to dismiss the importance of their early attachment relationships, idealises them without any substantial evidence in support of such idealisation, or is particularly brief and uninformative. A classification of *insecure-preoccupied* is assigned when coders judge narrative recollection to be disrupted by anger, anxiety, or preoccupation when the relationships are discussed (Shaver & Mikulincer, 2002). For such individuals, the past seems to 'significantly intrude' on their coherent discussions of attachment in the present and narratives can appear lengthy, entangled, and hard to follow (Sonkin, 2005).

Hence, the AAI purports to tap into probable internal working models of attachment that individuals have internalised based upon their own childhood parental relationships. The researchers (George *et al.*, 1985) initially sought to verify the predictive validity of their classification system by exploring how AAI classifications related to individuals' own parenting behaviour and to the Strange Situation classification that their children were assigned according to independent ratings of Ainsworth's protocol. In support of their hypothesis, George *et al.*'s (1985) initial predictive study confirmed that infants classified as *insecure-avoidant* in the Strange Situation Procedure had parents who were themselves classified as *insecure-dismissing* on the AAI. Furthermore, infants who were classified as *insecure-anxious* in the Strange Situation had parents who were classified as *insecure-preoccupied* in relation to their AAI narratives, whereas *securely* attached infants had parents who were classified as *secure* (Bartholomew & Shaver, 1998). This pattern of predictive findings has been replicated many times in the literature (see van Ijzendoorn, 1995) and provides compelling evidence in favour of an enduring internalised attachment representation linked to childhood experiences that manifests itself in individuals' relational behaviour in adulthood.

Following in the tradition of narrative representational methodologies in attachment research, it is worth noting that recent developments in this tradition have seen the introduction of the Adult Attachment Projective (AAP; George & West, 2001, 2003). The AAP follows in the footsteps of researchers that have attempted to utilise *projective* methodology in the context of attachment research with children (e.g. Kaplan, 1987; Jacobsen *et al.*, 1994; McCarthy, 1998; Slough & Greenberg, 1990; Shouldice & Stevenson-Hinde, 1992). Specifically, the AAP hypothesises that 'the shifting balance of adaptive and defensive processes, guided by mental representations of attachment, can be evidenced in adults' story responses to pictures of hypothetical attachment situations' (George & West, 2001, p. 31). Adults are presented with a series of eight line drawings (one neutral and seven attachment-related) depicting events that have been hypothesised to activate attachment (e.g. illness, isolation, separation). The line drawings (e.g. 'Bench' – a youth sitting alone on a bench, 'Bed' – a child and woman sit facing each other at opposite ends of a child's bed) are constructed in such a way that only the event is identifiable and potentially biasing features such as facial expressions are unidentifiable. As with the AAI, participants' projected responses in terms of what they believe is happening in the drawings are analysed by trained coders and features such as coherence, content of discourse, and defensive processes are rated to determine overall attachment classification. In general, individuals classified as *secure* on the AAP portray characters as drawing upon internal resources, see attachment figures as a means of addressing attachment stress, and identify a general belief in the importance of relationships in their stories by expressing the desire to be connected to others and giving descriptions of balanced, reciprocal interactions (George & West, 2001). In contrast, *dismissing* (conceptually akin to insecure-dismissing classification on the AAI) individuals tend to construct stories that avoid or ignore direct expressions of attachment and portray close relationships as unnecessary and ineffective. Similar to dismissing individuals, *preoccupied* (again akin to AAI insecure-preoccupied classification) individuals also fail to portray narratives that view attachment as a viable mechanism for resolving stress. However, the authors note that preoccupied individuals are especially interesting because they 'are able to identify what needs to be done to re-establish attachment equilibrium; they just do not take steps to accomplish it ... this suggests that these individuals often seem preoccupied with the processes that contribute to resolution but not the productive outcome' (George & West, 2001, p. 52).

Social psychological conceptualisations and self-report

In the previous chapter, Hazan and Shaver's (1987) classic study of attachment in the context of romantic relationships was briefly outlined. This study reflected the beginnings of a second independent line of research within adult attachment research, pursued by psychologists 'who tend to think in terms of personality traits and social interactions, be interested in normal subject populations, prefer simple questionnaire measures, study relatively large samples, and focus on adult social relationships, including friendship, dating relationships, and marriages' (Bartholomew & Shaver, 1998, p. 27). Hazan and Shaver's (1987) study employed Bowlby's ideas on attachment to reason that chronic loneliness in adulthood was likely to be associated with an insecure attachment style and that individuals' orientations towards romantic relationships could be an offshoot of previous attachment experiences. They translated Ainsworth's classifications of attachment (i.e. secure, insecure-avoidant, insecure-anxious) from the Strange Situation Procedure into a self-report descriptor (Hazan–Shaver Attachment Self-Report; Hazan & Shaver, 1987). Participants were required to reflect upon their romantic relationships and to select the statement (which reflected either a secure, avoidant, or anxious style of attaching to romantic partners) that they felt was most self-descriptive. These self-selected 'styles' were found to be linked to parenting experiences in childhood, with 'secure' individuals in romantic relationships reporting more accepting and sensitive parenting than insecure individuals. Such findings were viewed as an indication that early attachment experiences may link to the manner in which adult romantic relations are negotiated in the context of attachment theory. A significant amount of research has subsequently been conducted using various adaptations of this self-report measure and has generally suggested that such self-selected adult attachment styles are related to cognitive, affective, and behavioural outcomes linked to close relations, as well as to retrospective reports of experiences with parents during childhood (see Shaver & Hazan, 1993; Shaver & Clark, 1994).

Both the AAI (George et al., 1996) and the Hazan–Shaver Attachment Self-Report (Hazan & Shaver, 1987) are based around a typology of attachment styles or states of mind that can ultimately be traced back to

Ainsworth's earlier conceptualisations of attachment in infancy. However, other researchers in the developing self-report tradition have adopted different approaches to tapping attachment security. Sperling *et al.* (1996) have suggested that the current available self-report measures of attachment have proceeded from slightly different conceptual angles and have also referred to differing relationship contexts (e.g. romantic relations versus parental relations). As such, researchers should exercise caution with regard to selecting an instrument that is best suited to their research questions and conceptual assumptions. For example, measures such as the Reciprocal Attachment Questionnaire (RAQ; West *et al.*, 1987) and the Adolescent Attachment Questionnaire (AAQ; West *et al.*, 1998) have paid specific attention to the *degree* to which individuals might be considered securely or insecurely attached, providing a continuous assessment (i.e. more/less security) of a number of conceptual indicators of attachment security put forward by Bowlby (1969/1982, 1973, 1980). The AAQ, for example, assesses *adolescents'* perceptions of their relationship with an *adult attachment figure* on three subscales that are each in line with one of Bowlby's specific conceptual ideas that surround an attachment relationship. For example, the first subscale, 'availability', is based upon Bowlby's (1973) contention that an attachment figure must be available and responsive to the adolescent's attachment-related distress and anxiety. This subscale (e.g. 'I'm confident that my Mum/Dad will try to understand my feelings') therefore taps into perceptions of the attachment figure as reliably responsive and available to the adolescent's attachment needs. The second subscale, 'angry distress' (e.g. 'I get annoyed at my Mum/Dad because it seems I have to demand his/her care or support'), is conceptually linked to Bowlby's (1973) contention that anger is likely to be directed towards attachment figures when attachment needs and desires are frustrated, and the final subscale, 'goal-corrected partnership' (e.g. 'I feel for this person when he/she is upset'), reflects Bowlby's (1969/1982) suggestion that attachment bonds are characterised by an increasing sense of empathy towards the attachment figure and the attachment figure is respected as a separate individual with needs and feelings. Hence, the AAQ claims to provide an assessment of the quality of attachment relationships grounded in the central tenets of Bowlby's work. In contrast, measures such as the Hazan–Shaver Attachment Self-Report are based more heavily upon specific 'classifications' or 'types' of attachment.

Accordingly, developments in the self-report tradition have questioned whether or not categorical assessment of attachment styles captures individual differences as effectively as continuous assessment methods, particularly where statistical power is concerned (Roisman, 2009). From this perspective, researchers have identified that attachment patterns are more likely to be continuously distributed and that such distribution is most adequately reflected according to a two-dimensional model of individual differences (e.g. Bartholomew & Horowitz, 1991; Brennan *et al.*, 1998; Feeney *et al.*, 1994b; Fraley & Waller, 1998). The predominant premise from this perspective is that systematic variation in adult attachment differences tends to centre around two major *dimensions* of attachment which have been labelled *attachment-related anxiety* (concern about the availability and responsiveness of partners in close relationships) and *attachment-related avoidance* (discomfort with reliance upon others for attachment-related purposes) by Brennan *et al.* (1998). These dimensions have been described by Shaver and Mikulincer (2002, p. 135) as 'best conceptualised as regions in a two-dimensional space that is conceptually parallel to the space defined ... in Ainsworth *et al.*'s (1978) summary of research on infant-mother attachment'. Specifically, *low* levels of *both* attachment-related anxiety and avoidance correspond to a 'secure' classification according to Ainsworth's system. *High* levels of attachment-related anxiety and *low* levels of avoidance are conceptually consistent with an insecure-anxious classification according to Ainsworth's taxonomy. The region of space where attachment-related anxiety is low and avoidance is high is conceptually parallel to Ainsworth's insecure-avoidance. However, with regard to this 'avoidant' area of the conceptualisation researchers (e.g. Bartholomew & Horowitz, 1991; Bifulco *et al.*, 2002a, 20002b) have identified that in adult research there appears to be a conceptual distinction between *dismissive* avoidance (low levels of attachment-related anxiety and high levels of avoidance) and *fearful*-avoidant (high levels of both anxiety and avoidance) styles of attachment. Variation in the two dimensions of attachment has been captured by self-report measures such as the Experiences in Close Relationships Questionnaire (e.g. ECR-R; Fraley *et al.*, 2000), including 18 items that assess attachment-related avoidance (e.g. 'I prefer not to be too close to romantic partners', 'I find it easy to depend on romantic partners') and 18 items that assess attachment-related anxiety (e.g. 'I often worry that my partner doesn't really love me', 'I often worry that my partner's feelings for me are not as strong as my feelings for him/her') on a continuous Likert scale.

As the above section indicates, assessment of attachment within the social psychological tradition has generally been conducted through self-report (Stein *et al.*, 1998). However, recent developments in social psychiatry (e.g. Bifulco *et al.*, 2002a, 2002b) have witnessed the development of an interview tool that is hypothesised to gauge individuals' current working models with regard to attachment. The Attachment Style Interview (ASI; Bifulco *et al.*, 2002a, 2002b) provides an interview assessment of adults' attitudes to close relationships in general and of their attachment-related behaviour in current close relationships in order to gauge patterns of thinking in relation to attachment. The interview provides the platform for assessment of an array of constructs that are hypothesised to be closely linked to internal models of attachment (i.e. levels of mistrust, constraints on closeness, degree of proximity seeking, desire for company, self-reliance, comfort with separation, and anger) and, in conjunction with behavioural information about current close relationships, enables attachment classification in accordance with attachment 'styles' (i.e. insecure attachment styles of enmeshed, fearful, dismissive, and withdrawn-avoidant, in addition to a secure style) and relative 'strength' of these styles (e.g. mild, moderate, or marked). It is proposed that the more detailed and descriptive content (ASI classifications are based predominantly upon content of discourse and not on coherence or evidence of distortion) of attachment-related characteristics portrayed in an interview allows for more in-depth assessment of attachment styles. The interview has been employed in the social psychological and clinical literature and has been shown to be a reliable and valid method of assessing attachment styles (e.g. Bifulco *et al.*, 2002a, 2002b; Figueirido *et al.*, 2006).

It is also worth mentioning that there has also been significant development within an experimental paradigm that has served to further our understanding of certain aspects of attachment theory. Much of this work has emanated from researchers who tend to work within the social psychological tradition of research. For example, Mikulincer *et al.* (2002) focused upon subliminal activation of the attachment system in adult subjects to examine how symbolic threat activated attachment-related thoughts that would subsequently influence performance during a series of cognitive tasks (i.e. lexical decision tasks and a Stroop colour-naming task). In one of their studies participants were subliminally primed (i.e. words were presented for 20 ms – which was below the threshold for conscious awareness) with words that reflected either threat (e.g. failure, separation) or neutral primes (e.g. hat) and primes were quickly followed by the presentation of a name or nonsense word string (either the name of an attachment figure, a close figure who served no attachment function, a known figure, an unknown figure, or a nonsense word string). Participants were required to respond by deciding whether what had been presented was a legible 'word' (e.g. a name) or a 'non-word' (e.g. a nonsense letter string). Results indicated that when participants had been primed with a threat word they were significantly faster to react to the names of the figures they had earlier indicated as attachment figures. Hence, the subliminal priming of threat words enhanced participants' sensitivity towards *attachment figures* and *not* to any other named figures. The researchers suggested that such findings are support for the idea that the attachment system may be subconsciously aroused by detection of threat, and that such arousal of the attachment system has the capacity to influence cognitive processes, potentially shaping state of mind and behavioural responses. In later discussions of their findings (Shaver & Mikulincer, 2005) the authors have also suggested that such experimental work provides useful support for important psychodynamic assumptions such as the idea that subconscious factors can play a significant role in driving attachment-related mental processes.

Other conceptualisations of attachment have viewed working models of attachment not only in terms of stable personality dimensions but also as 'dynamic systems' that, under certain environmental circumstances, are malleable in accordance with environmental changes (Fraley & Brumbaugh 2004; Mikulincer & Shaver, 2007). For example, Feeney and Noller (1992) tracked attachment patterns of young adults over a ten-week period and identified that the formation of a steady relationship was associated with increases in self-reported attachment security and decreases in insecurity. Furthermore, the work of Gillath and colleagues (e.g. Gillath & Shaver, 2007; Gillath et al., 2006) has provided evidence that attachment states of mind can be 'primed' (e.g. by imagining one's partner as either responsive and sensitive or unresponsive and insensitive) and that such primed states of mind have meaningful influences on how participants think and feel in relationship-related scenarios that can persist for a reasonable time period. Gillath et al. (2009) have concluded that:

> it seems clear that at least life events (especially those pertaining to close relationships), and experimental activation of close relationship schemas, temporarily affect people's attachment style or levels of security and insecurity. Moreover, these temporarily fluctuations are not simply 'noise' but result in meaningful behaviour ... attachment style fluctuates across moments in time and situations, albeit within a range constrained in part by a person's stable dispositions.
>
> (p. 363)

This has resulted in the development of the SAAM (State Adult Attachment Measure; Gillath et al., 2009), a self-report instrument designed to capture short-term fluctuations in attachment states of mind. Such developments may have particularly interesting applications within the field of sport as researchers begin to examine how the attachment states of mind of athletes and performers might be linked to important cognitive and affective functions that have implications for performance and well-being.

Similarities and differences between traditions

The two above-mentioned research traditions and the measurement techniques allied to each can be viewed as similar from certain angles. For example, both lines of research are ultimately grounded in the conceptual assumptions of attachment theory put forward by Bowlby and Ainsworth, and each has stimulated interesting studies that can be argued to provide support for the fundamental tenets of the theory (Bartholomew & Shaver, 1998). Furthermore, there have been measurement techniques from each tradition (e.g. the AAI and the Hazan–Shaver Attachment Self-Report) that have *categorised* individuals' attachment status in a manner that has broadly approximated the traditional categories identified in Ainsworth et al.'s (1978) studies with infants. Given this apparent overlap it is perhaps unsurprising that researchers have looked to examine the degree to which measurement techniques from within the two subcultures appear to converge.

Examination of convergence between the two traditions has produced equivocal results. On the one hand, Shaver et al.'s (2000) investigation has identified that Collins and Read's (1990) self-report dimensions (which are conceptually similar to the dimensions of attachment-related anxiety and avoidance forwarded by Brennan and colleagues) were statistically predicted by AAI coding scales in a sample of married women. Results identified that the two self-report scales assessing attachment-related avoidance could be predicted with multiple Rs of .48 and .52 and the scale assessing attachment-related anxiety could be predicted with a multiple R of .30. Furthermore, when the regressions were reversed all but one of the AAI coding scales could be predicted by self-report items and the researchers reported conceptually meaningful links between self-report items and the AAI constructs predicted. Shaver and Mikulincer (2002, p. 137) have suggested that such correlation does not necessarily imply 'that scores on the two kinds of measures are identical in meaning, which they most certainly are not, but shows that both are related in sensible ways to shared central concepts of attachment theory'. Other studies have also identified significant correlation between the AAI and self-report measures. In their development of the AAQ (discussed above), West *et al.* (1998) examined the correspondence between AAI classification and *adolescents'* scores on the AAQ self-report subscales *in relation to a nominated key caregiver*. Data suggested that securely classified individuals on the AAI reported significantly higher perceptions of *availability* of their key caregiver on the AAQ, preoccupied individuals on the AAI reported significantly higher levels of *angry distress* toward caregivers, and those classified as dismissing on the AAI reported lower scores on the *goal-corrected partnership* scale. The authors therefore suggested that their self-report measure relates 'in a meaningful way' (p. 670) to the AAI classification system. Despite such reports of association between AAI classifications and various measures of self-reported attachment, there are also studies (e.g. Borman & Cole, 1993; Holtzworth *et al.*, 1997) that have failed to identify a correlation between measures from the two traditions. For example, Holtzworth-Munroe *et al.* (1997) found no association between the AAI and self-report measures of attachment, prompting the researchers to suggest 'there was a lack of convergence between the AAI and questionnaire measures of attachment, suggesting that the AAI does not measure the same construct the questionnaires do' (p. 327). Roisman *et al.* (2007) have suggested that it is 'disconcerting' (p. 679) that researchers have interpreted these equivocal findings with regard to convergence between the two measurement traditions in radically different ways. They outline how Shaver *et al.*'s (2000) data concerning measurement convergence (discussed above) has been labelled as 'robust' evidence for similarity between the two traditions by some social psychologists (Bartholomew & Moretti, 2002), yet 'small' (Bernier & Dozier, 2002) or 'modest' (Jacobvitz *et al.*, 2002) by developmental researchers. It is clear that while there may be broad conceptual similarities between the traditions, there are also distinct differences between them.

One of the key differences between the measurement traditions has been the perception that the AAI taps into attachment-related *unconscious* processes, whereas self-report measures are thought to assess adults' *conscious* appraisals of themselves in the context of a specific relationship (e.g. romantic others or a key caregiver, depending upon the specific self-report questionnaire). This important difference has been highlighted as a concern by Jacobvitz *et al.* (2002) in an interesting commentary on the measurement of adult attachment. For example, they outline how identification of an avoidant attachment style (or insecure-dismissing according to AAI terminology) via self-report is dependent upon participants *openly disclosing* that they have difficulties trusting or depending upon others. In contrast, on the AAI it is often the case that an openness, awareness, and comfort with discussing and revealing such issues in relationships would serve to indicate a *secure* classification. Insecure-dismissing individuals on the AAI are classified via dismissing discussions of relationships with parents, utilising strategies such as false idealisation of parental figures or an insistence on lack of memory. There may also be evidence of conflicting statements from adults who are insecure-dismissing on the AAI which provide evidence of idealisation and a subconscious unwillingness to recognise one's true childhood experiences. Jacobvitz *et al.* (2002) have outlined an interesting example from their work of how such issues bring into question comparisons between self-report and AAI measures of attachment.

> one father in our sample claimed his parents were wonderful and very loving but failed to provide evidence that this was so. He claimed to have little memory of his childhood, but one of the few experiences he recalled entailed an incident in which his father beat him uncontrollably for running a tractor into a tree. The issue, then, is whether dismissing adults, such as this father in our study, would openly acknowledge their own relationship difficulties on a self-report measure. His initial claims that his parents were very loving lead us to suspect he would classify himself as secure on a self-report measure.
>
> (p. 208)

Additionally, Jacobvitz *et al.* (2002) have identified other distinctions between the two procedures with regard to identifying insecure-preoccupied (often labelled as insecure-anxious in self-report) individuals. They have outlined how such individuals openly report (on self-report) feeling uncomfortable without close relationships, worry about being unloved, or scare others away with their fierce desire for closeness. However, in the AAI procedure such individuals exhibit an emotional preoccupation with parental relationships, often rambling at length, failing to find the right words to describe their ideas, and finding it difficult to provide a coherent and meaningful discourse. Jacobvitz *et al.* (2002) have questioned whether such individuals would be capable of such a logical, calculated evaluation of themselves as is required in self-reported attachment measures. Furthermore, Jacobvitz *et al.* (2002) discuss how the AAI also allows for differentiation of individuals within the secure categorisation. Specifically, given that the AAI attends to both *how* individuals discuss their experiences and to the *content* of those experiences, it has been possible for AAI researchers to identify some individuals who are securely attached in terms of the manner in which they *recount* experiences, yet portray experiences that are *negative* in *content* (e.g. of abusive or neglecting parents). Such individuals have been labelled as 'earned secure' by AAI researchers on the grounds that they appear to have 'earned' or 'worked for' their secure attachment state of mind *in spite of* early experiences. This is in contrast to 'continuous secure' adults, who appear to be securely attached in terms of both *how* they recount their experiences *and* the content of experiences that they recount. Such subtle distinctions between AAI classified secure individuals has been demonstrated as potentially meaningful in the literature. For example, Paley *et al.* (1999) identified that 'earned secure' husbands showed less positive affect and more ambivalence towards their wives during a problem-solving task than 'continuous secure' husbands. Hence, measures that do not detect such subtle differentiation (within what has generally been identified by self-report measures as a single 'secure' category) may well overlook important information.

Conceptually, then, there are arguments questioning the convergent validity of adult attachment measures emerging from the predominant research traditions that have each made significant contributions to the field. As can be noted from the above discussion, a significant element of these arguments centres around whether or not it is possible for individuals to consciously and accurately perceive their general style of relating to others, or whether individuals habitually utilise psychological defences such as distortion and bias that would serve to mask detection of attachment states of mind via self-report. Identification of correlation between measures from the two schools of thought in some ways provides little clarification with regard to this debate. On the one hand, moderate correlation between the AAI and self-report *could* suggest that both measures are tapping into related constructs, both closely linked to the tenets of attachment theory. On the other hand, moderate association between the two measures could also suggest that stronger, more perfect correlation between them is *dampened* by the fact that individuals have a tendency to misreport (e.g. bias, defence, distortion) experiences of close relations on self-report, dampening overall association with the AAI (which is ostensibly more sensitive to such factors).

Jacobvitz *et al.* (2002) have reviewed data exploring the relationship between attachment classifications using AAI versus self-reported and individuals' self-reported levels of functioning in relation to various aspects of their romantic relationships. In accordance with the tenets of attachment theory, they suggested that one might expect that attachment classifications (whether assessed via AAI or self-report) would relate to the quality of various aspects of romantic relations. Hence, even if attachment classifications are assessed using the AAI, one would still expect such an assessment of working models of attachment to demonstrate some predictive validity in relation to self-reported aspects of relationship functioning. Interestingly, Jacobvitz *et al.*'s (2002) review highlights that a small handful of research has refuted the idea that AAI classifications are related to self-reported levels of relationship functioning, identifying no relationship between AAI classifications and variables such as self-reported levels of trust (Holtzworth-Munroe *et al.*, 1997) and perceptions of intimacy and love in a marriage (Paley *et al.*, 1999). In contrast, they report a number of studies from the self-report tradition that have identified significant links between self-reported attachment classification and self-reported levels of trust (Mikulincer, 1998b; Simpson, 1990) and an array of other relationship-related outcome variables such as commitment, relationship satisfaction, sexual attitudes, sexual behaviour, and interpersonal communication patterns (see Feeney, 1999 for a review). While some caution is required when interpreting such findings (e.g. the larger number of studies exploring such hypotheses within the self-report tradition make a body of support for such links more likely), Jacobvitz *et al.* (2002) view such differences as potential evidence for obvious discrepancies between the measurement traditions. They highlight how the requirement to consciously appraise relationships when they are mentioned in various self-report outcome measures is likely simply to arouse the psychological defences of insecure-preoccupied or insecure-dismissing (according to AAI) individuals, compromising the validity of their self-reported outcome variables. For this reason, it is believed that self-reported assessments of trust, intimacy, or other meaningful relationship outcomes will be meaningfully associated with AAI classifications because preoccupied and dismissing individuals' self-reports of their relationships are not 'true' reflections of their perceptions and will therefore not be meaningfully associated with AAI classification (which has purportedly 'factored out' such interference). Contrastingly, in self-report studies both attachment style classifications *and* relationship function variables have been assessed via self-report. Hence, systematic distortions and defences will likely influence *both* variables, rendering significant association more likely.

One way of getting around such difficulties is to focus upon research that has examined the link between attachment classifications (generated from the AAI and self-report) and actual *behaviour* in relationship contexts. While self-reports of relationship functioning could be potentially distorted by psychological biases and defences, actual behaviour in relationship contexts could be a truer expression of attachment-related functions as it is more likely to reflect true feelings. Accordingly, bodies of research have also attempted to explore how the AAI and self-report methods of classifying attachment status link to relationship behaviour. With regard to the AAI, research (discussed earlier, see van Ijzendoorn, 1995) has identified a remarkable association between individuals' AAI classification status and parenting behaviour towards their own infants. Specifically, secure individuals have been observed to demonstrate significantly more sensitivity to the distress signals of their infants. Furthermore, in the context of romantic relationships studies have also identified that secure classifications on the AAI are associated with significantly less withdrawal behaviour from partners (compared to dismissing individuals) and more positive affect during problem-solving discussions (Paley *et al.*, 1999), significantly lower levels of controlling and distancing behaviour (compared to dismissing partners) (Babcock *et al.*, 2000), and significantly more positive behaviour (in women) and less negative behaviour (in men) during relationship conflict (Creasey, 2002). Hence, when measures of behaviour are employed as indicators of relationship functioning (as opposed to self-report) AAI classifications have shown improved predictive capacity.

However, self-report measures of attachment have also demonstrated significant association with behavioural functioning in romantic relationships. For example, Simpson *et al.* (1992) observed how partners behaved in a waiting room after they had been told that the female partner would be taking part in an anxiety-provoking task. Results suggested that self-reported insecure-avoidant individuals exhibited greater distancing behaviour toward their partner during stress. Furthermore, Fraley and Shaver (1998) identified an association between an avoidance dimension self-report scale and observations of couples' behaviour on separation. Observations suggested that attachment avoidance was associated with lower levels of the expression of sadness and contact-seeking behaviour, and higher levels of avoidant behaviour. Such data suggest that self-report measures of attachment styles are also able to predict behavioural expressions of relationship functioning in a conceptually meaningful way.

In a recent meta-analysis Roisman *et al.* (2007) examined the bivariate association between AAI and social psychological self-report measures of attachment style in ten published studies ($n = 961$) and identified that the average association between the classification systems from the two measurement traditions was 'trivial to small' ($r = .09$) according to Cohen's (1992) criteria. Furthermore, in the same paper, the authors also reported data in relation to the relative ability of both AAI and self-report measures of attachment style to predict various aspects of relationship functioning (i.e. reported emotional tone, observed collaboration, and emotional appraisals of interaction) in a sample of 50 engaged couples. Results identified that AAI and self-report dimensions of attachment predicted different outcome variables and were in some cases associated differently with the same outcome. For example, self-reported appraisals of attachment style were significantly related to adults' reported levels of the emotional tone that characterised their relationship, whereas AAI dimensions were very trivially associated with such appraisals. On the other hand, AAI scores were significantly associated with couples' observed collaboration, whereas self-reported dimensions of attachment showed no meaningful relationships with this outcome variable. The authors have suggested the following with regard to their findings:

We believe that this report ... emphasizes that Bowlby's theoretical account is in fact a broad framework, capable of inspiring generative research focused on adults' appraisals of attachment-related concerns, as it has done in social psychological research, as well as the ways in which early life experiences are integrated in the discourse of adults ... In our view, both methodological traditions in adult attachment research have proved excellent stewards of Bowlby's theoretical legacy. Nonetheless ... the generally trivial-to-small overlap identified here between the two attachment measurement traditions suggests results from the AAI and self-report literatures should not be cited and discussed in narrative reviews as if the measures were interchangeable.

(p. 694)

Hence, recent research would suggest that while the two traditions are perhaps conceptually united by Bowlby's assumptions, it is difficult to deny that there is also an element of distance between them with regard to empirical convergence.

In their discussion about what current and potential attachment researchers are to make of the complex differences between the two traditions, Bartholomew and Shaver (1998) suggest keeping in mind that Bowlby wrote about 'developmental pathways along which children and adults travel' (p. 41), 'shifting' in attachment security in accordance with important life events such as the formation and quality of new close relationships, the death or loss of attachment figures, and even the therapeutic relationship. They argue that in moving along such developmental pathways it is plausible to suggest that the internal working models of relationships that individuals initially carve out with parents may diverge from the models of newly formed close relationships, gradually evolving into a complex 'tree' with branches that reflect the amendments, additions, and evolutions of earlier internal models of attachment that are a response to the attachment-related developmental experiences mentioned above. Such development in the complexity of internal working models is likely to give rise to increasing complexity with regard to how such working models might function, with particular branches of the 'tree' perhaps more active in terms of influencing cognition, affect, and behaviour in specific relationship contexts (e.g. the 'branch' of the working model that has evolved specifically from experiences in romantic relations would be more likely to feature in experiences of romantic relationships). Hence, Bartholomew and Shaver (1998) suggest that attachment measures should be chosen according to the domain of interest, with those wishing to tap into individuals' most general representation of attachment being advised to combine measurement techniques to form latent attachment variables.

Conclusion

Sport researchers hoping to integrate attachment theory into their research questions will undoubtedly be faced with issues related to the measurement and identification of attachment styles or states of mind. It is therefore critical that such researchers are able to approach their research questions with a sound methodological rationale for their decisions. This chapter has attempted simply to outline how measures of adult attachment differ in a number of ways. Notwithstanding fundamental differences in relation to paradigmatic stance, different measurement approaches also reflect departures in relation to the relationship experiences that they tap (e.g. parental, romantic), the method they employ (e.g. interview, self-report), the features they identify as attachment 'indicators' (e.g. unconscious features of discourse, conscious self-reported appraisals), and the manner in which they organise attachment data (e.g. categories, continuous dimensions). Given such distinct differences, it is perhaps unsurprising that convergence between the various measures of attachment has been difficult to systematically identify. As Bartholomew and Shaver (1998) have suggested, each of the currently used measures of attachment characteristics is associated with a body of empirical findings that lends support to Bowlby's conceptual framework and for the author, Bartholomew and Shaver (1998) aptly identify the key point for researchers to keep in mind:

> When we step back from the details of specific measures and measure-specific findings, the results produced by attachment researchers are all compatible with the possibility that various forms of adult attachment arise from a continuous but branching tree of attachment experiences, beginning in infancy and developing throughout the life course.
>
> (p. 42)

3 Attachment and sport motivation

Regardless of social strata or cultural origin, examples of both children and adults who are apathetic, alienated, and irresponsible are abundant. Such non-optimal human functioning can be observed not only in our psychological clinics but also among the millions who, for hours a day, sit passively before their televisions, stare blankly from the back of their classrooms, or wait listlessly for the weekend as they go about their jobs. The persistent, proactive, and positive tendencies of human nature are clearly not invariantly apparent.

(Ryan & Deci, 2000, p. 68)

Introduction

In the above quote Ryan and Deci (2000) encapsulate the central role occupied by motivation in human life and offer an appreciation as to why the development of understanding in relation to motivation is of critical importance. Furthermore, the phenomena they describe are not peculiar to the context of sport, with apathy, alienation, passivity, and lack of engagement equally common in physical education (PE) classrooms, fitness clubs, and on sports fields across the globe. Sport psychology has recognised the importance of developing understanding of human motivation in the wider contexts of sport, exercise, and PE, and there is a burgeoning body of literature devoted to sport- and exercise-related motivation (see Duda, 2005, 2007; Frederick-Recascino, 2004; Hagger & Chatzisarantis, 2007; Roberts, 2001; Vallerand, 2007; Wang & Biddle, 2007).

Undoubtedly, the term 'sport motivation' incorporates an array of theoretical frameworks and sets of ideas, each with significant implications and important contributions to make. However, this chapter specifically seeks to integrate ideas from attachment theory with two of the most popular motivational frameworks in the sport psychology literature: achievement goal theory (e.g. Dweck & Leggett, 1988; Elliot, 1997; Elliot & McGregor, 2001; Nicholls, 1984) and self-determination theory (e.g. Deci & Ryan, 1985; Ryan & Deci, 2000). Each of these theories has extensive applications in sport and exercise and has significantly enhanced our understanding of motivation-related cognition, affect, and behaviour in sport settings. The sporting research (e.g. Carr, 2009a) is beginning to recognise the important conceptual links that these specific frameworks share with the attachment literature, and has called for developments in sport motivation research that carefully consider conceptual integration with influential frameworks from mainstream psychology. To this end, this chapter explores the important links that attachment theory shares with achievement goal and self-determination models, recognising critical areas for integration and research, and appreciating the practical and theoretical importance of such links. It is hoped that, by better 'organising' the key ideas and thoughts surrounding the integration of attachment theory with the motivational frameworks of achievement goal and self-determination theories, researchers will be able to appreciate the potential that attachment theory has for advancing the sport motivation literature.

Achievement goal models

Achievement goal approaches to the study of motivation afford competence a central role in the understanding of motivation. The psychological importance of competence-related cognition, affect, and behaviour has been well established (e.g. Dweck & Elliot, 1983; Elliot & Dweck, 2005) and competence has been identified as a fundamental human need (e.g. Deci & Ryan, 1990; White, 1959), the satisfaction of which has been theorised to energise much of everyday thought, feeling, and behaviour. Achievement goals have been defined as the purpose, or cognitive-dynamic focus, of competence-related behaviour (Maehr, 1989). As the literature has evolved, different theorists have used slightly different nomenclature and a number of models have been advanced (Ames, 1992; Dweck & Leggett, 1988; Elliot, 1997; Elliot & McGregor, 2001; Harackiewicz *et al.*, 1998; Maehr & Midgley, 1991; Nicholls, 1984; Pintrich, 2000) with different interpretations regarding the precise antecedents, definition, nature, and number of achievement goals. For this reason, Elliot (2005) has suggested that researchers referring to the general overarching conceptual ideas that unite these various achievement goal 'theories' might be advised to point out that they are referring to a general 'achievement goal approach'.

The predominant focus of 'achievement goal approaches' has emanated from the idea that achievement goals reflect how individuals construe competence in a given situation or context (e.g. Ames, 1984; Dweck, 1986; Dweck & Leggett, 1988; Elliot, 1997; Nicholls, 1984, 1989). Endorsing *mastery goals* (often labelled *task-involved goals* in the sport literature, see Duda, 1992), individuals essentially focus themselves on the development and demonstration of competence via personal improvement and learning. Elliott and Dweck (1988) have suggested that such individuals are essentially concerned with the question 'How can I best acquire this skill or master this task?' In contrast, *performance goals* (often referred to as *ego involved goals* in the sport literature) centre around a focus on the demonstration or proving of competence levels (or the avoidance of incompetence) relative to normative or other-referenced standards. When performance goals are salient individuals are essentially concerned about demonstrating success (or avoiding failure) by securing a favourable comparison of their ability with that of others.

It has been suggested that such achievement goals provide the framework within which individuals interpret and react to achievement experiences and they have been implicated in evoking qualitatively different patterns of cognition, affect, and behaviour (Ames & Archer, 1988; Dweck & Leggett, 1988; Elliott & Dweck, 1988; Nicholls, 1989). A large body of research has provided evidence that achievement goals are associated with an array of motivationally significant cognitive, affective, and behavioural outcome variables such as the interpretation of effort, reaction to failure, task choice, and anxiety (for a review see Ames, 1992; Dweck & Leggett, 1988; Duda, 1992; Duda & Hall, 2001; Harwood *et al.*, 2008; Urdan, 1997). In the specific context of sport and physical activity the constructs have also been linked to important outcomes such as intrinsic motivation, affective patterns, and moral belief systems (see Carr, 2006; Duda, 1992, 1993, 1996; Duda & Hall, 2001; Duda & Whitehead, 1998; Harwood *et al.*, 2008).

There is evidence to support the suggestion that adoption of achievement goal frameworks and associated motivational responses are significantly linked to social and cultural milieu (see Ames & Archer, 1988; Biddle, 2001; Kaplan *et al.*, 2002; Treasure, 2001; Urdan & Turner, 2005). It has been suggested that individual differences in personal achievement goals are, to some extent, a function of factors such as situational goals operating in the context of wider socialisation experiences, including home life and parenting (e.g. Ablard & Parker, 1997; Ames & Archer, 1987; Parsons *et al.*, 1982; Stipek & Hoffman, 1980). Ames (1992) has contended that various socialising agents (e.g. parents, peers, coaches, and teachers) can impact achievement goals through the emphasis of an environmental goal structure. That is, through the instructional climate they provoke and personal evaluation systems, social agents may be responsible for invoking *mastery-* or *performance-*oriented motivational climates for children's sport and physical activity. Research has consistently identified that the quality of the motivational climate that children detect from their parents, peers, teachers, and coaches in sport and PE contexts is linked to the development of their achievement goals (e.g. Carr, 2006; Carr & Weigand, 2001; Morris & Kavussanu, 2008; Ntoumanis & Biddle, 1999; Papaioannou *et al.*, 2008) and additional, related motivational outcomes (e.g. Kavussanu & Roberts, 1996; Vazou *et al.*, 2006).

In the sport and PE literature researchers (e.g. Barkoukis *et al.*, 2007; Carr, 2006; Cury *et al.*, 2002; Morris & Kavussanu, 2008) have begun to devote attention to achievement goal frameworks incorporating a distinction between 'approach' and 'avoidance' goals (e.g. Elliot & Church, 1997; Elliott

& Harackiewicz, 1996; Elliot & McGregor, 2001; Middleton & Midgley, 1997). For example, Elliot's (1997) trichotomous achievement goal framework defines mastery goals in a similar manner to traditional dichotomous goal models (e.g. Dweck, 1986; Nicholls, 1984) but segregates performance goals into *performance-approach* and *performance-avoidance* categories. According to this framework, individuals focused on performance-approach goals concern themselves with demonstrating their superior competence levels relative to others, whereas individuals who are focused on performance-avoidance goals attempt to avoid appearing inadequate and demonstrating incompetence relative to others. Elliot and McGregor (2001) have further extended this trichotomous goal model to include an additional bifurcation of mastery goals incorporating a *mastery-approach* and *mastery-avoidance* goal distinction. Within this conceptualisation, mastery-approach goals reflect a focus on striving to achieve improvement, personal progression, and learning. Mastery-avoidance goals are conceptualised to be a focus upon striving to avoid *not* demonstrating mastery. These multiple achievement goals are thought to be manifestations of the underlying dispositional motives of the *need to achieve* and the *need to avoid failure* (e.g. Atkinson, 1957; McClelland, 1951) and the influence of these higher-order motives is hypothesised to be channelled through representational goal conceptualisations that individuals internalise in specific contexts. Achievement goals are therefore viewed 'as "focused needs" ... concretized "servants" of their higher order achievement relevant motives' (Elliot & Church, 1997, p. 219).

Achievement goal models and attachment theory: conceptual links

Attachment theory has interesting conceptual links with the achievement goal models currently popular in the sport and physical activity literature. To demonstrate where achievement goal theorists might locate some of the key links between the theories, Elliot and Reis (2003) have focused upon the 'innate behavioral control systems' that attachment theory (Bowlby, 1969/1982, 1988) proposes as integral to an organism's survival and procreation; the systems of *attachment* and *exploration*. A key assumption of attachment theory is that the *attachment system* serves the predominant function of ensuring proximity to the caregiver, securing safety and protection from harm. However, despite this, it is equally important that infants are compelled by an *exploration system* to gradually explore their surrounding environment, further enhancing their development and likelihood of future survival (Elliot & Reis, 2003).

Aside from influencing the function of the *attachment system*, it is also proposed by attachment theory that individuals' underlying attachment styles are likely to dictate the manner in which their *exploration system* operates (e.g. Bowlby, 1988; Cassidy & Berlin, 1994; Moss & St Laurent, 2001). A *secure attachment style* is more likely to *promote* environmental exploration as infants permit themselves to explore unimpeded, safe in the knowledge that their caregiver is consistently available when they need to retreat to a secure base. An *insecure-ambivalent style* of attachment detracts from the quality of exploration experiences because infants are thought to be consistently preoccupied with whether or not the caregiver will be available and responsive should they feel the need to retreat to safety and an *insecure-avoidant style* is also suggested to hamper exploration because the child is simultaneously attempting to deal with the unavailability of the caregiver, making it difficult to develop the same level of interest in exploratory experiences.

For Elliot and Reis (2003), it is the system of *exploration* outlined above that is particularly important for achievement motivation research. In developing an understanding of the conceptual links between attachment styles and exploratory tendencies, achievement goal theorists can begin to recognise how working models of attachment might also relate to constructs that are central to achievement goal models. Bowlby (1988) and Ainsworth (1990) both hypothesised that the link between attachment and the nature of individuals' exploratory experiences would continue beyond infancy and throughout the lifespan. That is, the attachment styles that children, adolescents, and adults develop have been hypothesised to be linked to the quality of exploration of their surrounding environment. Beyond infancy, researchers have focused upon variables such as cognitive curiosity, interest in leisure-time activities, and intellectual openness (e.g. Green & Campbell, 2000; Mikulincer, 1997) as indicators of exploration systems in adults and have identified (e.g. Green & Campbell, 2000) that insecure dimensions of attachment are linked to lower levels of the desire to explore one's physical, social, and intellectual environment, whereas secure attachment was linked to higher levels of such exploratory impulses.

Related to this, Elliot and Reis (2003) have outlined what they consider to be conceptual similarity between the concept of *effectance motivation* central to competence-based frameworks of achievement (i.e. 'the desire for effective, competent interactions with the environment, and … an innate, organismic propensity that impels the individual to investigate, manipulate, and master the environment', Elliot & Reis, 2003, p. 318) and the *system of exploration* put forward by attachment theory. Such conceptual similarity between effectance motivation and exploratory systems central to attachment theory is thought to be linked to achievement motivation because secure internal working models of attachment are more likely to promote positive, approach-based, mastery-oriented systems of exploration devoid of concerns about failure. Such attachment styles are less likely to promote concerns with the prospect of failure because a secure working model of attachment leads one to believe that attachment figures are readily available, accepting, and supportive, regardless of achievement outcomes. In contrast, an insecure attachment style may well provoke less adaptive systems of competence-based exploration where individuals are overly concerned about the prospect of failure because they do not expect attachment figures to be readily available, accepting, and supportive, and they are oriented towards avoiding situations that might lessen the likelihood of securing such responses (e.g. failure). Hence, it is suggested that 'securely attached persons are able to construe achievement situations as a positive challenge and fully engage in the appetitive pursuit of competence, whereas insecurely attached persons construe achievement situations as a threat and self-protectively avoid incompetence' (Elliot & Reis, 2003, p. 319).

In the context of Elliot and McGregor's 2 × 2 model of achievement goals, Elliot and Reis (2003) provided initial evidence that attachment styles are linked to contextual achievement goals and to the higher-order achievement motives that such goals are hypothesised to serve. Specifically, they identified that secure attachment styles were associated with greater levels of a higher-order need for achievement and mastery-approach goals, and to lower levels of the need to avoid failure, mastery-avoidance goals, and performance-avoidance goals. Insecure attachment styles were linked to higher levels of the need to avoid failure, mastery-avoidance goals, and performance-avoidance goals, and lower levels of the need to achieve and mastery-approach goals. Elliot and Reis (2003) made no conceptual predictions regarding the link between attachment characteristics and performance-approach goal pursuit and they identified null results with regard to this link. However, they suggested that such null results may reflect the fact that the assessment of performance-approach goals often reflects additional underpinning motives, such as self-presentational concerns, and is therefore often *not* simply a reflection of an appetitive pursuit of normative competence. Given the hypothesised approach-based, appetitive nature of performance-approach goals, they have proposed that secure attachment may positively predict performance-approach goal pursuit if researchers can ensure that exclusively competence-based assessment of performance-approach goals is employed. The performance-approach goal construct requires further scrutiny in this area and it will be interesting to further examine the operation of the construct within secure and insecure attachment frameworks.

Given that sport research (e.g. Conroy *et al.*, 2003; Elliot & Conroy, 2005; Morris & Kavussanu, 2008) has begun to embrace the hierarchical model of multiple achievement goals put forward by Elliot and McGregor (2001), the field of sport and physical activity has the potential to contribute to the understanding of how attachment styles fit into this motivational framework. Sport is a context where individuals have the opportunity to explore and develop their cognitive, physical, and social selves, and achievement goals in sport have been shown to influence the quality of such exploration. It is therefore important that researchers establish whether or not the propensity to explore the sporting context in qualitatively different fashions (i.e. contrasting achievement goals) is linked to mental representations of attachment.

A body of achievement goal research in the context of sport and physical activity has identified children's perceptions of the motivational climate as a predictor of a variety of motivational outcome variables (e.g. Carr & Weigand, 2001; Morris & Kavussanu, 2008; Papaioannou et al., 2008; White et al., 1998). Typically, such studies have identified that where they perceive an environmental emphasis on aspects of sport involvement such as demonstration of superior ability, avoidance of mistakes, or success without effort, children are more likely to develop contextual responses characterised by worry, anxiety, and negative affect. Conversely, environmental emphasis on factors such as the embracing of mistakes, learning, and personal development regardless of mistakes and comparative ability have been linked to lower levels of anxiety and more positive motivational characteristics. Bowlby (1969/1982) hypothesised that working models of attachment may be particularly salient during fear- or anxiety-inducing situations, where arousal of the attachment system is likely set into play individuals' 'working models' of attachment, which subsequently are thought to guide the manner in which individuals resolve, think about, and respond to the condition that elicits their fear (Madigan et al., 2006). Given the potential threat to self-esteem and competence perceptions, and the anxiety-provoking conditions that seem to be associated with highly performance-oriented motivational climates in sport, it is feasible to suggest that such environments may well be rife with the sorts of situations that are more likely to set into play individuals' working models of attachment. In such situations researchers (Madigan et al., 2006; Weimer et al., 2004) have suggested that individuals with less secure working models of attachment ultimately have a history of being faced with the frightening realisation that, when in need of protection, the caregiver is unlikely to provide a haven of safety. Accordingly, there is a large body of literature in support of the idea that attachment styles are related to distress regulation, with secure individuals more likely to appraise such situations as benign, to rely on social and emotional support, to view themselves as better able to cope with the situation without defensively distorting their perceptions of self and others (e.g. Collins & Read, 1990; Mikulincer & Florian, 1995; Mikulincer et al., 1993; Mikulincer, 1998a). In contrast, avoidant and anxious individuals have a tendency to appraise such situations as threatening, to doubt their ability to cope, to rely on defensive perceptions of self and others in order to cope, and to utilise different methods of coping such as hyperactivation of distress-related cues, inhibition of proximity seeking (avoidant individuals), and an increased sense of self-reliance (e.g. see Collins & Read, 1994; Mikulincer & Florian, 1998). Given that a reliance on social and emotional support and an inability to maintain a level of self-belief, task-relevant concentration, and trust in others are likely to be adaptive responses to anxiety-inducing performance-oriented motivational climates, individuals who possess working model of attachment where such responses are readily activated in stressful situations may be at a psychological disadvantage. It may therefore be important for sport researchers to investigate the manner in which attachment styles are related to individuals' responses to the motivational climate.

Researchers should also consider issues related to the 'priming' or 'activation' of specific models of attachment. To this end, attachment literature (e.g. Rowe & Carnelley, 2003; Shaver *et al.*, 1996; Sibley & Overall, 2007, 2008) has suggested that individuals may hold multiple models of attachment and that the activation of these models may be governed by cognitive factors such as 'schema accessibility' (i.e. the ease with which specific models of attachment 'spring to mind' in response to environmental cues). It may be, for example, that children's attachment models of relationships with parents are particularly likely to be 'active' (and, as a consequence, *influence* or *moderate* subsequent responses) in interactions that 'cue' the parent–child attachment schema. This idea is linked to the psychodynamic concept of transference first proposed by Freud (1912/1963) and more recently experimentally supported by Andersen and her colleagues (e.g. Andersen & Berk, 1998; Andersen & Glassman, 1996), where working models of the self and the self in relation to a specific other can be 'triggered' by factors that 'cue' their accessibility. From this perspective, it may be particularly interesting to examine whether, for example, parent–child attachment models appear to have a more prominent role in moderating responses to motivational climates involving interactions likely to be similar to parent–child dyads (i.e. the coach/teacher motivational climate) compared to interactions that might be considered less similar to parent–child relations (i.e. the peer motivational climate). Abercrombie (1984) has suggested that the conventional model of teaching–learning situations has enormous similarities with the parent–child relationship and, as a consequence, is more likely to activate schemata (such as working models of attachment) that are based upon such a relationship model. Hence, in the context of relationship models such as PE teacher–pupil and coach–athlete dyads there may be reason to expect a level of 'activation' of underlying models of attachment. Consequently, models of attachment may be *more likely* to moderate responses to the motivational climate emphasised by these social agents.

Despite a high level of support for its stability, a number of authors have also provided evidence for temporary fluctuations in attachment styles in response to major life events and contextual factors (e.g. Baldwin & Fehr, 1995; Feeney & Noller, 1992; Gillath & Shaver, 2007; Gillath *et al.*, 2009; Hammond & Fletcher, 1991). For example, Feeney and Noller (1992) tracked young adults over a ten-week period and identified increases in reports of attachment security and decreases in reports of attachment insecurity in response to the formation of a stable romantic relationship. Additionally, priming studies have identified changes in attachment security over very short time periods. For example, Gillath and colleagues (e.g. Gillath & Shaver, 2007; Gillath *et al.*, 2009) have demonstrated that priming individuals by asking them to imagine their partner as either responsive and sensitive or unresponsive and insensitive resulted in meaningful changes in momentary attachment-related responses and thoughts about relationships. Hence, as Gillath *et al.* (2009, p. 363) have suggested 'these temporary fluctuations are not simply "noise" but result in meaningful behavior ... in other words, attachment style fluctuates across moments in time and situations, albeit within a range constrained in part by a person's stable dispositions'. Viewing attachment styles as more malleable constructs offers interesting possibilities of investigation for sport researchers interested in examining the sport-related constructs such as achievement goals that have been hypothesised to be linked to attachment styles. For example, it would be interesting to explore whether temporary alterations in levels of attachment security in response to life events such as relationship break-ups experienced by athletes are linked to temporary alterations in the achievement goals that are conceptually tied to such attachment states. Experimental priming studies would also provide an interesting insight into whether manipulated changes in attachment states in the laboratory also correspond with changes in the manner in which individuals subsequently approach achievement tasks with regard to achievement goals. However, it should be noted that such experiments would currently throw up additional challenges for sport researchers, such as the difficulty that is currently evident in assessing achievement goals on a momentary level (see Harwood & Hardy, 2001; Harwood *et al.*, 2000; Treasure *et al.*, 2001).

Self-determination theory

It is not intended that this section provide a complete overview of self-determination theory (SDT) in all its complexity (readers are referred to Ryan & Deci, 2004 and Hagger & Chatzisarantis, 2007 for more complete reviews). Rather, in this section an outline of the theory is sketched and areas that are particularly important in making conceptual links with attachment ideas are given attention. SDT (e.g. Deci & Ryan, 1985; Ryan & Deci, 2000) is best described as a macro-theory of human motivation, encapsulating a range of issues from personality development, self-regulation, global psychological needs, and non-conscious processes, to the relations of culture to motivation, and the impact of social environments on motivation, affect, behaviour, and well-being (Deci & Ryan, 2008). The theory is essentially concerned with the degree to which human behaviours can be considered to be determined by the self and is comprised of four sub-theories: *cognitive evaluation theory, organismic integration theory, causality orientations theory*, and *basic needs theory*.

A central assumption of SDT revolves around the idea that individuals possess a primary predilection toward the development of a unified sense of self (Ryan & Deci, 2004), striving to integrate, within themselves and with others, new ideas and experiences that are encountered. However, SDT proposes that a *predilection* towards growth and actualisation by no means guarantees that individuals will attain this psychological objective, and there are clear and identifiable social-contextual factors that have the potential to enhance or thwart its accomplishment. Hence, the SDT framework views growth and integration as dependent upon the social-contextual provision of key psychological nutriments necessary to nourish actualisation (Ryan & Deci, 2004). To this end, it is hypothesised that individuals possess basic psychological needs; the needs for *competence*, *autonomy*, and *relatedness*. In *basic needs theory* Ryan and Deci (2000) have adopted a working definition of these psychological needs that is closely aligned with the physiological understanding of the term. That is, the needs are specifiable requirements necessary for organisms to survive and thrive and 'withholding such an element will lead reliably to deterioration of growth and integrity, whereas making it available will lead to maintenance and enhancement' (Ryan & Deci, 2004, p. 7). The needs of competence, autonomy, and relatedness provide a framework for examining how social-contextual factors can enhance or inhibit psychological growth and actualisation by supporting or thwarting such needs. The need for *competence*, which has also been recognised as a central element of human motivation in achievement goal frameworks, reflects the innate propensity to experience a sense of efficacy and confidence in one's interactions with the surrounding environment (e.g. White, 1959), stimulating individuals to seek out challenges and to enhance and develop their capacities. The need for *relatedness* is closely tied to ideas (e.g. Bowlby, 1979/2005; Harlow, 1958) suggesting that humans have an inbuilt propensity to feel a psychological sense of connectedness and belonging to other human beings. This need reflects a deep-rooted desire to justify one's existence by feeling that one is integral and accepted by others. Finally, as Ryan and Deci (2004, p. 8) have articulated, *autonomy* is the need for individuals to 'experience their behaviour as an expression of the self, such that, even when actions are influenced by outside sources, the actors concur with those influences, feeling both initiative and value with regard to them'.

The extent to which the above basic needs are satisfied by given social contexts is hypothesised to be linked to the direction and persistence with which individuals engage in goal-directed behaviour (Hagger & Chatzisarantis, 2007) and the needs are a central element of each of the SDT sub-theories. *Cognitive evaluation theory* has specifically concerned itself with the idea of *intrinsic motivation* as the epitome of self-determined motivation. Intrinsic motivation has been defined as the doing of an activity for its inherent satisfactions rather than for some separable consequences (Ryan & Deci, 2000) and cognitive evaluation theory has linked its maintenance and development with environment-related satisfaction of the basic psychological needs (Deci *et al.*, 1999; Ryan & Deci, 2007). Indeed, it is proposed (e.g. Deci & Ryan, 1980) that basic needs are 'necessary conditions for the maintenance and enhancement of intrinsic motivation' (Ryan & Deci, 2007, p. 3).

Beyond intrinsic motivation, there are other types of behavioural regulation that have been suggested to underpin individuals' motivation in various contexts. *Organismic integration theory* (Deci & Ryan, 1985) proposes a motivational regulation *continuum* that conceptualises motivations as ranging from highly autonomous (e.g. 'pure' intrinsic motivation) to highly controlling regulations (i.e. 'pure' extrinsic motivation), recognising that certain extrinsically motivated actions can sometimes become 'internally motivated' in the sense that they begin to serve internal rather than external goals (Ryan & Deci, 2007). This framework has focused on 'types' of motivation that vary in the degree to which they are self-determined (i.e. external regulation, introjected regulation, identified regulation, intrinsic motivation and amotivation). *External regulation* is the least self-determined form of motivation and reflects a behaviour that is undertaken for external reasons, such as a specific reward or because of pressures from external authorities. *Introjected regulation* reflects a slightly more autonomous action in the sense that behaviours are carried out based upon *self-imposed* feelings of guilt or pressure, reflecting an internalised belief that individuals 'ought' to undertake a specific behaviour, not that they 'want' to (Wang *et al.*, 2002). This motivational regulation moves beyond external regulation in the sense that it is an *internalisation* of external pressures. *Identified regulation* is a more self-determined form of motivation and reflects behaviours that are undertaken because individuals have adopted them as part of a personal value and choice system. Hence, the behaviour is adopted out of 'want,' and not guilt or pressure. In addition, amotivation essentially reflects an absence of motivation, where individuals appear to no longer recognise a perceived purpose for engaging in the activity (Vallerand, 2001) and cannot identify a link between actions and worthwhile outcomes. It is predicted within organismic integration theory that more self-determined forms of motivation would be associated with more positive outcomes and dependent upon psychological need satisfaction, and there has been a wealth of research to support these contentions (see Ryan & Deci, 2000, 2004, 2007).

Causality orientation theory examines individual differences in the tendency to engage in and seek self-determined behaviours. For example, a specific situation can be interpreted as informational by one person and controlling or amotivational by another. There are hypothesised to be personality-based orientations that predispose individuals to such differences and press them to seek out an informational, controlling, or impersonal aspect within each situation in order to regulate their behaviour (Deci & Ryan, 1985b; Rose *et al.*, 2005). It is suggested that this interpretation will interact with social-contextual factors and characteristics of a given situation, resulting in a final interpretation that is a blend of personal and environmental characteristics. It is feasible that one might exhibit more self-determined motivation types towards a particular activity yet exhibit more controlled motivation towards another activity. However, causality orientation theory proposes the existence of a more global motivational orientation that would to some degree transcend contextual differences and be experienced across domains. Deci and Ryan (1985b) have identified three causality orientations: autonomy, control, and impersonal. The autonomy orientation is based around the concept of choice and individuals strive to be self-determining, seeking out opportunities to achieve this. The control orientation reflects a predilection to search for control and pressure, either imposed by others, within the self (e.g. guilt), or by the environment (reward contingencies). According to Rose *et al.* (2005), individuals 'search out' controlling aspects (internal and/or external) in order to regulate their behaviour and often 'find themselves doing things because "they are told to", "they should", "they have to" or "they must"' (p. 401). The impersonal orientation is based on individuals' feeling that they are not able to regulate their behaviour in order to achieve desired outcomes and there is an amotivated aspect to the orientation.

As a framework that recognises the role of specific social-contextual and individual difference factors in satisfying basic psychological needs and stimulating subsequent motivational regulation (and associated cognitive, affective, and behavioural responses), SDT has been particularly popular in bodies of applied literature such as health, education, and sport, where human motivation is a particularly salient issue. Indeed, the sport and exercise motivation literature houses a burgeoning body of SDT-related research that demonstrates the theory's utility in sport-, PE-, and exercise-related contexts (see Hagger & Chatzisarantis, 2007 for a complete review). In support of the assumptions of cognitive evaluation theory, there has been a strong body of research promoting the relationship between intrinsic motivation and self-determination, identifying that intrinsic motivation is more likely when sport-related environments facilitate basic need satisfaction, promoting a sense of competence and autonomy (see Blanchard & Vallerand, 1996; Cadorette *et al.*, 1996; Frederick & Ryan, 1995; Vallerand *et al.*, 1987; Vallerand & Reid, 1984). The motivational regulations put forward by organismic integration theory have also been identified as significant predictors of important psychological variables related to sport, PE, and exercise involvement (see Chatzisarantis *et al.*, 2003; Goudas *et al.*, 1994; Mullan & Markland, 1997; Pelletier *et al.*, 1995), and there has been evidence that basic need satisfaction and social-contextual support of basic needs is again likely to underpin the development of these specific motivational regulations and their cognitive, affective, and behavioural concomitants (see Edmunds *et al.*, 2008; Reinboth & Duda, 2006; Reinboth *et al.*, 2004; Sarrazin *et al.*, 2002; Wilson & Rodgers, 2004). Furthermore, causality orientation theory has also been implicated in sport-, PE-, and exercise-related contexts. For example, in the PE literature Taylor *et al.* (2008) identified PE teachers' personal autonomy causality orientations to be significantly involved in the prediction of teacher psychological need satisfaction and self-determined motivation, which subsequently predicted teachers' use of motivational teaching strategies presented to pupils. Rose *et al.* (2005) have also provided evidence that individuals' causality orientations may relate to the stability of their involvement in exercise.

SDT and attachment theory: conceptual links

There are a number of areas that offer interesting avenues of research for sport and exercise psychologists interested in implicating attachment frameworks in self-determination research. An interesting study by La Guardia *et al.* (2000) has demonstrated the potential for exploring formation of secure attachment in adult relationships using *basic needs theory* as a primary point of reference. Proceeding from the assumption that attachment security to primary caregivers *in childhood* has been hypothesised by attachment theorists (e.g. Bowlby, 1969/1982; Sroufe, 1990) to result from caregiver *sensitivity, responsiveness,* and *availability,* La Guardia *et al.* (2000) suggested that *beyond childhood* the formation of secure attachment relationships with additional *adult attachment figures* is also likely to result from the basic qualities of sensitivity, responsiveness, and availability on the part of the relationship partner. Accordingly, they elected to focus upon *within-person variation* in attachment security both within and across different relationships in individuals' lives (e.g. Shaver *et al.*, 1996; Sibley & Overall, 2007, 2008) and hypothesised that within-person variation in attachment security across adult attachment figures would relate to variation in the degree to which each attachment referent was able to offer a relationship characterised by *sensitivity, responsiveness,* and *availability.* Furthermore, they conceptualised attachment figures' provision of sensitivity, responsiveness, and availability in accordance with the basic psychological needs proposed by SDT, hypothesising that 'sensitive,' 'responsive', and 'available' relationship partners are ones who promote individuals' experiences of the basic psychological needs proposed in SDT. From this perspective, a conceptual argument exists to suggest that relationship partners who support the needs for competence, autonomy, and relatedness would be more likely to fit the definition of a 'sensitive' caregiver or attachment figure in the attachment literature (e.g. Bretherton, 1987; Sroufe & Waters, 1977) and would subsequently be more likely to facilitate a secure attachment relationship.

To test their hypothesis La Guardia *et al.* (2000) assessed individuals' reported attachment security in relation to four key attachment relationships in their lives (i.e. mother, father, romantic partner, and friend), in addition to reported levels of the degree to which each relationship was felt to satisfy competence, autonomy, and relatedness needs. Results provided evidence for both *within-* and *between-person* variability in attachment security. Specifically, attachment security varied *between individuals,* therefore supporting the existence of stable individual difference factors such as the 'internal working models' of attachment proposed by Bowlby. However, attachment security also varied across the relationships *within individuals' lives* and this variation was related to the specific characteristics of each relationship. Of particular interest was the finding that the *within-person* variability in attachment security across relationships was significantly accounted for by the degree to which the relationships in question satisfied the basic psychological needs for competence, autonomy, and relatedness. Specifically, greater need satisfaction was related to higher levels of attachment security and, although the need for relatedness seemed to be the strongest predictor, all of the basic needs contributed to the prediction. The authors concluded that 'attachment security seems to go hand in hand with psychological need fulfilment' (La Guardia *et al.*, 2000, p. 380).

The idea that the basic needs component of SDT may offer insight into systematic variation in felt attachment security has interesting implications for sporting research. The findings of La Guardia *et al.* (2000) suggest that the formation of new, secure adult attachment relationships may be partially dependent upon the degree to which such relationships are able to facilitate the satisfaction of individuals' basic psychological needs. Researchers have recently begun to appreciate the significance of 'close' social relationships within sport and have explicitly recognised the benefits of sharing high-quality friendships (e.g. Smith, 2003; Weiss & Smith, 2002) and coach–athlete bonds (Jowett & Wylleman, 2006; Poczwardowski *et al.*, 2006; Wylleman, 2000). Indeed, recent suggestions (e.g. Carr, 2009a; Jowett & Wylleman, 2006) have put forward attachment theory as a potentially fruitful lens for examining sporting relationships and there is the potential that sporting figures, such as coaches, themselves have the potential to be considered 'attachment figures'. Although it is currently not known whether the close relationships that develop between athletes, coaches, and peers within sport can be considered as 'attachment relationships' akin to those shared with romantic partners and close adult friends (more detailed attention is devoted to this issue in Chapter 6), there are arguments as to why such relationships might evolve into attachment relationships. Hazan and Shaver (1994a) have argued that, on a fundamental level, 'for an attachment to form there must be a strong force promoting closeness' (p. 11), which ultimately leads to the relationship figure serving as a safe haven in times of distress and offering a secure base from which strong emotional ties can be formed (see Hazan & Shaver, 1994a; Trinke & Bartholomew, 1997). Accordingly, future investigation of the formation of attachment relationships within the context of sport will likely and necessarily concern itself with examining the fundamental existence and formation of attachment bonds within sport. To this end, the basic needs component of SDT may prove to be a useful lens in helping to understand the specific factors involved in the initial development of attachment relationships between athletes and their peers or coaches. La Guardia *et al.*'s (2000) findings suggest that the satisfaction of the basic human needs in a given relationship may well be a precursor to the development of secure attachment bonds and it will be interesting to explore the development of attachment bonds in sporting relationships while paying careful attention to the manner in which the relationship satisfies feelings of competence, autonomy, and relatedness. It could be hypothesised, for example, that where athletes and coaches share a bond, conceptually close enough to be considered an attachment relationship, the relationship may be more likely to blossom into a *secure* attachment for the athlete when basic needs of competence, autonomy, and relatedness are perceived to be satisfied.

There may also be scope for examining the links between different elements of SDT and individuals' attachment *styles* (i.e. more stable representations of self and others). A fundamental assumption of SDT (e.g. Deci & Ryan, 1985; Ryan & Deci, 2000) that has been well supported in the sporting literature (see Chatzisarantis & Hagger, 2007; Frederick-Recascino, 2004) is the notion that intrinsic motivation for an identified activity is more likely to be elicited and sustained in conditions that foster the needs for competence, autonomy, and relatedness. Consequently, factors that impact these psychological needs have the potential to limit the degree of intrinsic motivation experienced in a given activity or context. Individuals' attachment styles have the potential to limit their experiences of competence, autonomy, and relatedness in the context of sport and initial evidence suggests that attachment styles are significantly related to constructs that would limit the experience of these important psychological needs.

For example, Schwartz et al. (2007) have recently presented evidence to suggest that attachment styles are linked to individuals' underlying motivation related to affiliation in social contexts. Specifically, more *securely* attached individuals were more likely to seek affiliation with others for emotional support than for social comparison or attention. Those who experienced an inclination towards *avoidance* (discomfort with closeness and dependency) in their attachment styles were significantly *less* motivated to affiliate with others for emotional support and those who experienced an inclination towards attachment *anxiety* (about loneliness and abandonment) in their attachment styles were more likely to seek affiliation with others for attention and social comparison than for emotional support. Furthermore, in the context of youth sport, Carr (2009b) has recently provided evidence that the models of attachment which adolescents develop with their parents are related to the quality of friendships subsequently experienced in the sporting context. Specifically, adolescents who held more secure models of attachment with their parents were more likely to experience sporting friendships characterised by esteem enhancement, support, loyalty and intimacy, and an ability to resolve conflict. Such findings are in line with conceptual predictions of attachment theory and suggest that attachment styles may be influential in more *general* social interactions outside of intimate relationships (with parents and romantic partners). The manner in which individuals relate to peers in the context of sport may have a significant impact on the extent to which they are able to develop feelings of competence, autonomy, and relatedness (Jago et al., 2009). For example, sporting friendships characterised by a high level of self-esteem enhancement and support are more likely to bolster and protect individuals' sense of competence in response to the sporting environment. Furthermore, those who actively seek out emotional support and closeness are more likely to experience the sense of relatedness and belongingness that come from such support. Consequently, there are conceptual reasons to suggest that insecure attachment styles may render individuals more likely to experience thwarted levels of the basic psychological needs proposed in SDT, subsequently decreasing the likelihood of intrinsic motivation.

The earlier conceptual links identified between attachment styles and achievement goal orientations (i.e. Elliot & Reis, 2003) provide additional reasons to suggest that basic psychological needs might be thwarted when individuals hold insecure attachment styles. Elliot and Reis (2003) identified that insecure attachment styles were linked to *greater endorsement of performance-avoidance goals* and to lower levels of mastery-approach goals. In the context of the approach-avoidance model of achievement goals, endorsement of performance-avoidance goals has been suggested as particularly likely to undermine intrinsic motivation. Elliot and Harackiewicz (1996, p. 463) have outlined that 'the performance-avoidance goal ... is focused on avoiding incompetence, and this avoidance orientation is viewed as evoking processes that are antithetical to the very nature of the intrinsic motivation construct'. Indeed, an achievement focus that orients individuals towards the self-protective withdrawal of resources and disrupts concentration and task involvement is likely to limit the potential for experiences of competence. It is for this reason that an attachment style associated with an increased reliance on performance-avoidance goals would be considered a threat to the development of feelings of competence and subsequent intrinsic motivation. Studies incorporating hierarchical modelling techniques would be able to shed light on the manner in which attachment styles are related to basic psychological need satisfaction and subsequent motivational regulation in sport. Such studies would enable examination of whether contextual variables such as friendship quality, affiliation motives, and achievement goals in sport are 'mid-level' constructs via which attachment styles exert an indirect influence on contextual levels of motivation.

Conclusion

The integration of attachment theory offers numerous avenues of research that will ultimately serve to enhance the development of the achievement goal and self-determination literature in sport. There appears to be conceptual evidence to suggest that in attachment styles sport researchers may identify an important personality-related variable that has a central role to play in the contextual regulation of key motivational constructs such as achievement goals, responses to the motivational climate, and levels of intrinsic motivation. Furthermore, the implications of linking attachment styles to the quality of sporting involvement will help to identify how critical relationships from individuals' past can have widespread consequences for the manner in which they negotiate the different domains of their lives, reinforcing the notion that early parent–child relations are a critical factor in 'setting up' the quality of future sport involvement. Additionally, sport researchers also have the potential to help further recent developments (e.g. Gillath *et al.*, 2009) in the attachment literature related to the exploration of attachment models as a fluctuating construct. To this end, exploring how experimentally induced and natural fluctuations in attachment security are tied to changes in sport motivation would offer important insight into the manner in which the everyday experiences encountered in most individuals' lives have an impact on the manner in which they approach their sporting involvement. It is hoped that this chapter will serve as a catalyst for future research in the integration of attachment and sport motivation.

4 Attachment and group cohesion in sport

The earliest records of cohesion are written descriptions of military battles in ancient Greece. Specifically, the battle in 480 BC between the Spartan warriors and the Persian army has been used to depict the powerfulness of group cohesion. The outnumbered Spartans managed to hold their ground for several days against the powerful Persians ... they stood 'shoulder to shoulder, shield to shield, in the narrow pass to prevent the Persians from invading ... a symbol of unity and cohesion' (Siebold, 1999, p. 8).

(Carron et al., 2007, p. 117)

Introduction

Carron et al. (2007) recognise in the quote above the significance of the construct of group cohesion for humankind. Siebold (1999) has suggested that cohesion has undoubtedly been important since a time when prehistoric hunters used 'teamwork, coordination, mutual aid, and small group actions to bring down large game and obtain meat and raw materials for their clans' (p. 7). Furthermore, the notion of group cohesion is also of critical importance in evolutionary terms and research in environmental biology has suggested that animal species are equipped with behavioural apparatus specifically designed to maintain group cohesion (e.g. Janik & Slater, 1998; Lusseau & Newman, 2004). Indeed, an understanding of group cohesion is likely to be significant across a range of academic domains, including military, evolutionary, organisational, and educational psychology.

The field of sport too is undoubtedly a site of critical importance for the investigation of issues related to group cohesion. Sport teams are naturally occurring groups that can provide a useful insight into the nature of group cohesion. Indeed, examples abound of scenarios where seemingly 'less talented' sport teams have overcome overwhelming odds and succeeded, attributing their successes to factors such as a 'team bond', 'teamwork', or 'group chemistry' (Carron et al., 2007, p. 117). Carron et al. (2007) also astutely point out that there are equally abundant examples of situations where exceptionally talented teams of individuals have failed to succeed in sport due to an apparent absence of the ability to work together as a team, to respect each other, and to form a coherent unit. As an example, Carron *et al.* (2007) refer to the 2004 US Olympic men's basketball team (the Dream Team), who, despite possessing by far the most talented group of individuals, were defeated in the opening round of the competition by Puerto Rico, with the lack of success attributed to an absence of group chemistry in the US team. Furthermore, beyond anecdotal examples there has also been a body of research in sport that has served to highlight the link between cohesion and an array of positive outcome variables, such as decreased state anxiety (Eys *et al.*, 2003), enhanced performance (Carron *et al.*, 2002), increased satisfaction (Widmeyer & Williams, 1991), increased work output (Prapavessis & Carron, 1997), and reduced perceptions of social loafing (Naylor & Brawley, 1992).

In this chapter I attempt to integrate the sport-related literature on group cohesion with attachment theory. Specifically, the chapter seeks to provide a brief review of the literature on cohesion (briefly addressing definition, conceptualisation, and research findings) before exploring the avenues of research that might be explored when these ideas are integrated with concepts and assumptions from bodies of attachment literature.

Cohesion in sport: a brief review

In the sport psychology literature the most significant contribution to the development of understanding around the concept of cohesion in sports teams has resulted from the ideas of Albert Carron and his colleagues (e.g. Carron, 1982, 1988; Carron *et al.*, 1998; Carron *et al.*, 2007; Widmeyer *et al.*, 1985). Carron *et al.* (1998) have defined cohesion as a 'dynamic process reflected in the tendency for a group to stick together and remain united in the pursuit of its instrumental objectives and/or for the satisfaction of member needs' (p. 213). They further note that this definition reflects some of the fundamental properties of cohesion: (a) that it is multidimensional (i.e. there are multiple reasons for groups to 'stick together' and for one group this may be unity for the sake of task accomplishment, whereas for another it may be unity from a social point of view), (b) that it is dynamic (the dimensions of cohesion can change over time), (c) that it is instrumental (group cohesion is a reflection of the purpose of the group and as such can be said to exist as a function of the instrumental objective), and (d) that it contains an affective dimension (social relationships are either developed or initially present in groups). Carron *et al.* (1998) have suggested that their working definition of cohesion has 'won general acceptance from group dynamics theoreticians' (p. 213) and can therefore be considered as a conceptually sound starting point for research.

In their early research on the dynamics of cohesion in sport teams Carron and Chelladurai (1981) utilised self-report measures to assess high school athletes' perceptions of five identified aspects of cohesion within their sporting groups: (1) the value attached to group membership, (2) the sense of belonging individuals felt toward the group, (3) the level of enjoyment individuals gained as a function of group membership, (4) the level of teamwork perceived to exist within the group, and (5) the degree of closeness within the group. Based upon their analyses, they reduced their data to two overriding factors that seemed most aptly to explain the variance in athletes' perceptions of elements of cohesion: (1) individual-to-group cohesion (which consisted of the value attached to group membership, enjoyment as a function of membership, and a sense of belonging), and (2) group-as-a-unit (consisting of teamwork and member closeness dimensions). Subsequent work led to important conceptual developments in the way that the construct was conceptualised.

Carron and his colleagues (e.g. Carron *et al.*, 1998; Widmeyer *et al.*, 1985) have since recognised that important 'organising properties' and assumptions require consideration when attempting to address research questions related to cohesion. First, it has been assumed in much of their work that cohesion (which is essentially a characteristic of a *group*) can be tapped by gauging *individual* perceptions of the construct. Carron and Spink (1995) have even suggested of cohesion that it is 'cognition about the group that exists in the minds of individual group members' (p. 91; cf. Hogg, 1992). Carron and his colleagues have defended this assumption by suggesting (a) that the assessment of *group* characteristics via *individual* perceptions of group features is supported by a history of research from the wider field of social psychology (e.g. Bandura, 1986; Kenny & Lavoie, 1985), and (b) that groups possess observable properties that are both *experienced* and *personally integrated* by group members. Consequently, the perceptions members have of the group are thought to permit a reasonably accurate approximation of group characteristics.

Second, it has also been suggested that researchers should recognise that the perceptions individuals hold of the group can be tapped in relation to (a) their perception of the group as a whole (e.g. does the member perceive the *group* to exhibit various properties of cohesion?), and (b) their personal relationship or attraction to the group (e.g. does the member perceive *themselves* to be attracted to the group?). Carron *et al.* (1998) have defined these further organising structures as *group integration* (i.e. the individual perceptions of group features as a whole) and *individual attractions to group* (i.e. the perception of personal attraction to the group).

Finally, a distinction between 'social cohesion' (i.e. a 'unity in socialising together,' Hardy *et al.*, 2005, p. 167) and 'task cohesion' (i.e. a 'unity around group objectives and goals,' Hardy *et al.*, 2005, p. 167) has also been made. This critical distinction between two important dimensions of cohesion has been recognised in the wider literature on group dynamics (e.g. Fiedler, 1967; Hersey & Blanchard, 1969) and is also reflected in the main definition of cohesion provided by Carron *et al.* (1998) above. In his earlier work (e.g. Carron, 1982) Carron was critical of a bias in cohesion research toward the construct of social cohesion and he suggested that in sport groups such a bias was 'indefensible' (p. 128). The arguments that he made highlighted issues such as (a) the fact that many sport-related groups were highly cohesive yet exhibited low levels of social cohesion (suggesting other factors can bring about a cohesive group), (b) social cohesion does not fully reflect cohesion as a construct, and (c) that social cohesion is not always a necessary or sufficient condition for group formation (Siebold, 1999).

The development of the Group Environment Questionnaire (GEQ; Widmeyer et al., 1985) was based upon the conceptual thinking outlined above and the inventory seeks to measure member perceptions of group cohesion according to these assumptions. The GEQ is an 18-item self-report measure that assesses individual perceptions of cohesion with regard to four dimensions: (1) Group integration-task (individuals' perceptions of closeness and bonding in the *group as a whole* in relation to *task cohesion* – 'Our team is united in trying to reach its goals for performance'), (2) Group integration-social (individuals' perceptions of closeness and bonding in the *group as a whole* in relation to *social cohesion* – 'Members of our team do not stick together outside of practices and games'), (3) Individual attractions to the group-task (individuals' perceptions of *personal involvement with and attraction to* the group in relation to *task cohesion* – 'I do not like the style of play on this team'), and (4) Individual attractions to the group-social (individuals' perceptions of *personal involvement with and attraction to* the group in relation to *social cohesion* – 'Some of my best friends are on this team'). Readers are referred to Carron et al. (1998) for a thorough review of this measure.

There has been a large body of research on cohesion in sport. The majority of this research has been guided by the assumptions outlined above and there is a strong suggestion that there are a number of personal benefits for those involved in cohesive sporting groups. It is beyond the scope of this chapter to provide a through review of this literature but readers are refer-red to Carron et al. (1998, 2007) and Widmeyer et al. (1993) for comprehensive outlines. For example, cohesion has been linked to lower levels of state anxiety (e.g. Eys et al., 2003), to increased satisfaction (e.g. Widmeyer & Williams, 1991), to increased group norm conformity (e.g. Prapavessis & Carron, 1997), to greater sacrifices for the sake of the team (e.g. Prapavessis & Carron, 1997), to enhanced work output (e.g. Prapavessis & Carron, 1997), to self-esteem (Julian et al., 1966), to likelihood of sharing the responsibility for team failure (e.g. Brawley et al., 1987), and to lower perceptions of social loafing by team mates (Naylor & Brawley, 1992). It is also worth noting that the role of cohesion is becoming increasingly important in exercise settings too, with exercise, dieting, and other health-based initiatives being increasingly conducted in the context of groups (Carron et al., 2007). Studies have made important discoveries in support of the idea that increased cohesion in the context of exercise groups is associated with important variables such as adherence (Carron & Spink, 1993; Fraser & Spink, 2002; Spink & Carron, 1993).

Groups and attachment theory: conceptual links in the literature

Byng-Hall (1995) has suggested that individuals are invariably exposed from the outset not only to dyadic relationships but also to groups, with the most significant of these groups being the immediate family unit. Smith *et al.* (1999) have argued that, from an evolutionary perspective, 'closeness and dependence on groups is arguably as fundamental as closeness to an individual caregiver ... our humanoid ancestors could not have survived outside the group any more than an infant can survive without parental care' (p. 96). Accordingly, Smith *et al.* (1999) have suggested that because closeness and dependence are fundamental needs then they are not only likely to colour experiences of dyadic relationships but also the manner in which people relate to groups.

Smith *et al.*'s (1999) influential paper sought to outline a conceptual case for integrating attachment theory with group processes. While they recognised that there are fundamental differences between the close dyadic relationships typically investigated in attachment research and group interactions (e.g. most group relations are likely to be less central or 'close' than romantic or parental relations), Smith *et al.* (1999) also outlined that there are reasons to believe that an attachment perspective may also be useful in conceptualising group functioning. They proposed that attachment theorists (e.g. Baldwin *et al.*, 1996; Collins & Read, 1994) have provided evidence that individuals can hold multiple models of attachment (varying in terms of chronic accessibility) based upon their relational experiences with previous and current relationship partners (e.g. mother, father, friend, romantic partners). Hence, the notion of an 'attachment style' (i.e. construction of a specific mental model of the self and the 'other' to which the self relates) may be a fundamental psychological 'template' which individuals employ to conceptualise many relationships they experience in their lives. Accordingly, Smith *et al.* (1999) reasoned that if attachment reflects a fundamental mechanism by which relationships are experienced then it is plausible to suggest that 'people also have models of themselves as group members and models of groups that in combination affect their thoughts, emotions, and behaviours regarding group memberships' (p. 96). Byng-Hall (1995) has suggested that similar to building up individual models of attachment with key caregivers in early life, children are also developing *collective* mental models of the *family* as a reliable and *collective* base from which they might be able to explore the world in safety. From this perspective, it is possible to depict the attachment system as an 'organising force' that serves to provide a template for how models of various critical 'relationships' in individuals' lives are experienced, judged, and constructed; some of these relationships may be experienced with group entities.

Accordingly, Smith *et al.* (1999) have conceptualised attachment to groups in a manner similar to Brennan *et al.*'s (1998) continuous two-dimensional approach in the adult attachment literature; the dimensions of *group attachment anxiety* and *group attachment avoidance* were proposed. Specifically, it was suggested that high levels of group attachment anxiety would reflect a lack of belief in one's worth as a group member and anxiety about being accepted as a member of personally valued groups (with behavioural features such as 'trying to please' or to 'fit in' being logical consequences). Conversely, low levels of group attachment anxiety would lead to an implicit belief in one's value to the group and a lack of concern with group acceptance. High levels of group attachment avoidance were reflected in a lack of desire for and belief in the utility of closeness and dependence in groups (behavioural consequences might be isolation and distancing), whereas a low level of the construct reflected acceptance and comfort with these group features (Smith *et al.* 1999). It was tentatively suggested that such general attachment-related orientations toward groups might be a consequence of earlier experiences in familial or peer group settings. However, this issue has received little attention in the attachment literature.

Smith *et al.* (1999) developed self-report assessments for their hypothesised dimensions of group attachment and, in a series of studies, they examined their factor structure and utility in predicting a number of variables related to group functioning. Results provided support for the hypothesised factor structure and also suggested (a) that group attachment anxiety (e.g. 'I often worry my group will not always want me as a member') was negatively associated with general feelings of warmth towards the group, aspects of collective self-esteem (e.g. 'I am a worthy member of the group I belong to'), frequency and duration of time spent in groups, and solving conflict with group members in a cooperative manner, and positively associated with the desire to avoid conflict and disagreement for fear of upsetting the group, and (b) that group attachment avoidance (e.g. 'Often my group wants me to be more open with my thoughts and feelings than I feel comfortable being') was negatively associated with all of the above-mentioned constructs with the exception of frequency and duration of time spent in groups (no significant correlation). Furthermore, the researchers also examined how measures of group attachment anxiety and avoidance completed with reference both to *groups in general* and a *specific group* (i.e. with reference to a particular group only) related to measures of anxiety and avoidance in romantic relationships. Results revealed that the anxiety dimension in romantic relationships was strongly positively correlated with the anxiety dimension for groups in general and moderately positively correlated with anxiety for a specific group. Avoidance in romantic relationships was moderately positively correlated with avoidance for groups in general and weakly correlated with avoidance for a specific group. Additionally, there was no relationship between dimensions of *romantic* attachment and the various group functioning variables (e.g. feelings of warmth towards the group, collective self-esteem, frequency of time spent in groups, and attitude to group conflict), whereas these variables were significantly related to measures of both general and specific group attachment. This led the researchers to conclude that *group* attachment constructs are related but not identical to *relationship* measures of attachment and that they also possess predictive power in relation to various group constructs that distinguishes them from relationship attachment.

However, Rom and Mikulincer's (2003) research has suggested that romantic attachment *is* also highly likely to exert an influence on group interactions on the premise that romantic attachment should provide an indication of key aspects of individuals' internal conceptualisations of the self in relation to others. Conceptually, they have suggested that the working models of self and others that are thought to characterise attachment styles in romantic relationships consist of structural features that one might expect to exert an influence on existence in groups: (a) representations of the self and others (e.g. attachment anxiety is linked to negative perceptions of the self and doubts about worth in the eyes of others, which may lead to a general negative expectation of others in groups and appraisal of group interactions as potentially distressing/rejecting; avoidant individuals are more likely to dismiss the benefits of interactions with others and relationships with group members may be perceived as less valuable), (b) episodic memories (e.g. attachment anxiety biases memory towards the recall of painful relational episodes and ensures they are accessible on a chronic level; avoidance is linked to a more defensive and repressive memory system, where negative memories are less accessible), (c) interaction goals (e.g. anxious individuals are likely to formulate interaction goals around gaining approval, love, warmth, and support from group members to accommodate previous relational shortcomings and meet attachment needs; avoidant individuals are more heavily inclined toward self-reliance and distancing in an emotional sense), and (d) regulatory strategy (e.g. anxious individuals are more prone to hyperactive attachment-related thoughts and behaviours and may be more likely to use group contexts for socio-emotional purposes, drawing them away from task-related functions; avoidant individuals have a tendency to dismiss and avoid emotional goals and may be less likely to focus on socio-emotional aspects of group involvement).

In a series of studies, Rom and Mikulincer (2003) supported their assumptions and found that dimensions of attachment anxiety and avoidance in relation to romantic relationships were linked to important features of group interaction. First, attachment anxiety negatively predicted appraisals of self-efficacy in task-oriented group contexts and positively predicted appraisals of the group situation as a threat, heightening negative emotions such as fear and anxiety. Attachment avoidance negatively predicted positive emotional responses (e.g. pleasure, pride) and was also linked to heightened negative emotions. Second, participants were asked to recall and describe three task-oriented group interactions from group-based activities. Attachment anxiety was linked to recalling events characterised by a negative hedonic tone and by negative perceptions of the self in the context of the group. Avoidance was also linked to recalling experiences characterised by a negative hedonic tone but to a negative perception of *other* group members as opposed to the *self*. Third, attachment anxiety was positively associated with the objectives of acquiring security and love from the group, whereas avoidance was linked to objectives of maintaining distance and self-reliance. Finally, attachment anxiety was associated with a decrease in self-reported *instrumental* functioning in the context of the group (i.e. contribution to *instrumental* group goals and tasks) and avoidance was linked to a decreased *socio-emotional* functioning (i.e. the extent to which the person contributed to morale and group atmosphere) during group missions. The researchers argued that these findings are conceptually coherent with attachment theory as a predictive framework. In a further extension they also corroborated Smith *et al.*'s (1999) findings identifying that measures of romantic attachment were associated with measures of attachment to groups in conceptually expected directions but also that attachment to group measures accounted for variance in group functioning variables over and above relationship attachment measures.

Attachment and cohesion

Carron and his colleagues (e.g. Carron *et al.*, 1998) have suggested that cohesion can be conceptualised and measured according to different units of analysis. That is, on an *individual level* it is the individual group member who reflects the unit of analysis (and each *individual's* perception of cohesion is typically related to other *individual* variables of interest such as a person's adherence or commitment), whereas on a *group level* it is aggregated group statistics (e.g. the *group* mean of *all members'* perceptions of cohesion) that form cells of analysis. It is worth noting that each of these conceptualisations has been criticised in the wider literature on cohesion. For example, Mudrack (1989) has suggested that it does not seem fitting that 'researchers are forced to examine *individuals* in order to gain a glimpse of *the group*' (p. 38, original emphasis) and Evans and Jarvis (1980) suggested that:

> cohesion is uniformly recognized as a group phenomenon, yet its measurement generally involves measuring the levels of attraction of individual members and averaging them. This technique assumes, with little justification, that the whole is no greater than the sum of its parts.
> (p. 359)

Hogg (1993) further outlines the problems that this causes on the grounds that psychology is by definition the study of the mental processes that occur *inside* the human brain. Discussing group processes, he argues:

> we are making summary statements about human aggregates … non-psychological entities because psychology cannot occur either outside the human mind or among separate psychological entities. Group and individual levels of analysis are thus independent, and yet

group cohesiveness researchers try to describe the former in terms of the latter.

(Hogg, 1993, p. 90)

Such measurement distinctions raise interesting possibilities in relation to attachment theory. *Individual* units of analysis are perhaps most obviously suited to an exploration of the link between attachment characteristics and perceptions of group cohesion. In relation to the above arguments, Carron *et al.* (1998) have suggested that *individual* perceptions of team cohesion are beliefs that 'are a product of the member's selective processing and personal integration of group-related information' (p. 217). It seems logical to assume that on an individual level such 'selective processing' and 'personal integration of group-related information' would be subject to a degree of influence from *relevant internal psychological apparatus* that the individual possesses. Such characteristics could be assumed to influence the construction of individuals' selective processing, perceptions, and integrations in relation to a given group or team and models of attachment may be important in this respect. For example, individuals with high levels of attachment avoidance or anxiety (whether this is thought of in terms of attachment to the *group* or to interpersonal relations in general) may possess mental models that serve to reduce the likelihood that they will be attracted to the group and perceive it to be cohesive and unified. If individuals' appraisals of the self in the context of the group, appraisals of the group's expectations of the self, the hedonic tone of memories of group experiences, personal objectives surrounding group involvement, and socio-emotional and instrumental functioning in groups have been linked to dimensions of attachment (e.g. Rom & Mikulincer, 2003; Smith *et al.*, 1999) it seems reasonable to suggest that individual appraisals of aspects of team cohesion (as conceptualised in the GEQ) would also demonstrate associations. For example, it might be hypothesised that GEQ dimensions such as *individual attraction to the group-social* (ATG-S, e.g. 'I'm not going to miss the members of this team when the season ends') would be negatively linked to attachment avoidance (e.g. due to an internal working model that tends to devalue the emotional and social utility of others, emphasising group goals of self-reliance and distance, and de-emphasising socio-emotional goals) and positively linked to attachment anxiety (e.g. due to an internal working model that tends to heighten awareness and concern with the emotional and social utility of others, emphasising group socio-emotional goals). Exploration of the associative patterns between perceptions of cohesion in sport and dimensions of attachment will likely provide interesting insight for sport cohesion researchers and attachment theorists alike, and may help to establish the extent to which individual perceptions of group cohesion are a function of internal psychological characteristics that bias or filter how the group is perceived and experienced.

It is also important to explore issues such as the perceptions of group members as a function of the attachment styles of *other* members. Such investigations could begin to shed light on how members' assessments of cohesion are not only influenced by their *own* attachment characteristics but also those of *other* team members (which would suggest that individuals' attachment styles translate into behavioural and emotional characteristics which are perceived by and of consequence to other group members). Bonito (2002) has suggested that this type of investigation would require researchers to embrace the concept of interdependence, 'the consequence and effect of one's behaviours and thinking on what other members do and think' (p. 416). Studies seeking to explore these types of questions would benefit from employing sophisticated analytical approaches that are designed to investigate such issues in social groups. For example, Kenny and his colleagues have provided detailed explanations of frameworks such as the Actor-Partner Interdependence Model (APIM; Cook & Kenny, 2005; Kashy & Kenny, 2000; Kenny & Cook, 1999) which enables researchers to distinguish between issues such as *partner effects* (i.e. the extent to which specified characteristics of the *self* are a function of specified characteristics of *other members*) and *actor effects* (i.e. the extent to which specified characteristics of the *self* are a function of other specified elements of the *self*). In the context of attachment it would be interesting to examine how individuals' perceptions of aspects of group cohesion are related to *their own* attachment characteristics (actor effects) and to the attachment characteristics of *other group members* (partner effects).

In research with dating couples, Campbell *et al.* (2001) examined the predictive role of both actor and partner attachment styles (tapped using two continuous self-report measures of anxiety and avoidance) on couples' observed behavioural interactions while the female partner was waiting to engage in an anxiety-provoking task. Results identified an actor effect whereby individuals with higher levels of attachment avoidance exhibited higher levels of criticism, irritation, distancing, and negative emotion toward their partners. Additionally, a partner effect was also identified, demonstrating that when individuals' *partners* had higher attachment avoidance then the individuals themselves were more likely to demonstrate negative emotion, irritation, and criticism toward their partner. The researchers explained the *partner* effect by reasoning that when one's *partner* has high attachment avoidance then one's experiences with that person are likely to lead one to *expect* that partner either to withdraw from offers of emotional support when he or she is distressed or to fail to provide adequate care giving responses when one is distressed oneself. Hence, such expectations of *the other* may well lead to negative responses in situations of distress due to frustration, anger, and feelings of helplessness. Extending such ideas into the context of small groups in sport may prove interesting. Close-knit sports teams will undoubtedly face situations that are distressing for the team as a whole or for individual members, and the manner in which individuals behave toward each other in such moments could (a) have a bearing on the development of group cohesion and (b) be a reflection of working models of attachment. It would be interesting to explore how individuals' behavioural responses in the context of sports teams are a function of their own attachment styles and of the attachment styles of other members in the group. Such questions would be complicated by factors such as group size, level of group interaction, nature of group, and stage of group development. That is, it might be suggested that expectations about the level of support one can expect from other members when distressed, or the responses of others to one's own offers of emotional support could only be constructed when one has forged close enough relationships to generate such expectations. In the context of many sports teams (close-knit groups that spend months in each other's company under stressful and changing conditions) there is reason to believe that athletes get to know each other on a level that is sufficient for such construction to occur.

Beyond a linear link between attachment and cohesion

Researchers might also look beyond a linear hypothesis relating to whether various models of attachment (in relation to the group or to other relationship referents) are linked to group cohesion or to factors that might influence its development. Siebold (1999) has advocated that cohesion researchers recognise the complex, non-linear, and shifting nature of the correlations that cohesion shares with various important outcome variables. In sport research there has been an appreciation of cohesion with respect to its circular relationship with various outcome variables (e.g. Carron, 1982; Carron & Ball, 1978; Slater & Sewell, 1994) and in the attachment literature there has also been a suggestion that attachment may not be a simple linear predictor of cohesion but that cohesion may be a moderator of the relationship between attachment characteristics and various group outcome variables. For example, Rom and Mikulincer (2003) outlined that the negative relationship they identified between self-reported attachment anxiety and levels of self-reported in-group instrumental functioning (contribution to instrumental tasks and goals) was moderated by group level measures of cohesion (i.e. aggregated scores of perceptions of cohesion across all group members). The researchers suggested that 'high levels of group cohesion seemed to act as a psychological buffer against the negative effects of attachment anxiety on instrumental functioning' (p. 1228). In further discussing their findings they put forward the hypotheses (a) that high levels of group cohesion may well activate a sense of attachment security that serves to dampen the hyperactivating strategies of individuals with attachment anxiety, facilitating the use of psychological resources for group-task purposes, and (b) that high group cohesion may signify that the predominant goals of anxious individuals (support, closeness, availability of others) have been satisfied in the context of the group, deactivating their attachment-related concerns and allowing them to allocate resources elsewhere. Such hypotheses also raise interesting issues for sport researchers and suggest that there may be reasons to believe that fostering cohesion within sports teams could have significant implications for offsetting some of the negative aspects of group involvement that individuals with insecure attachment characteristics are prone to experiencing. Given that the sporting literature has indicated that the perceived behavioural characteristics of coaches and sport leaders are linked to perceptions of group cohesion (e.g. Turman, 2003; Westre & Weiss, 1991) this may provide another significant justification for coaches to pay particular attention to facilitating its development.

Cohesion as more than interpersonal attraction

As a final word on the integration of attachment theory with group cohesion research in sport it is worth noting that the developments in attachment research that have formed the basis of this chapter have in many ways benefited from the fact that the researchers have conceptualised cohesion in the context of *interpersonal attraction* (i.e. members' reports of attraction to the group). In an insightful and critical discussion of group cohesion research, Hogg (1993) has suggested that when one thinks of cohesion solely in terms of interpersonal attraction then one might go so far as to suggest that one has 'no theory of *group* cohesiveness – just theories of interpersonal attraction among individuals in small interactive aggregates' (p. 91). He goes on to suggest that it seems highly unlikely that cohesion in many groups amounts to *no more* than simple interpersonal attraction among members of that group (although interpersonal attraction is undoubtedly a feature). In discussing other ways to think about cohesion in social groups, Hogg (1993) has recommended that it is important to consider other factors that might underpin cohesiveness, such as depersonalised social attraction; the idea that attraction among members of interpersonal groups may be different from *genuine* interpersonal attraction. He describes depersonalised social attraction as:

> attraction to the group as that group is perceived to be embodied, in terms of its defining attributes, by specific group members. The object of positive attitude and feelings is not actually the unique individual person, but the group prototype that he or she embodies. Targets are relatively interchangeable – they are depersonalized.
>
> (p. 95)

Hence, in this argument cohesion need not always be a consequence of a genuine interpersonal attraction to the group members but of the fact that members and 'the group' embody something of relevance to the social identity of individuals, providing them with a motivation to maintain the group and its function.

Carron's work in the context of sport has also recognised that an over-emphasis on interpersonal attraction as the sole reason for cohesion in sports teams is inadequate. For example, he has suggested that athletes 'may not know each other initially, they may never come to like one another, but they may stay together (cohere) in order to continue to compete in the league' (1982, p. 127, parentheses in original). Furthermore, he goes on to express the opinion that the conceptualisation of cohesion as interpersonal attraction 'as an exclusive or principal manifestation of cohesiveness in sport groups is indefensible' (1982, p. 128). Such comments highlight that sport may be a context where the extent to which cohesiveness is likely to be a function of genuine interpersonal attraction is likely to vary greatly and should not be considered 'a given'. This is reflected in the conceptualisation of the GEQ.

This may have significant implications for the integration of attachment theory with sport cohesion research and researchers should keep this in mind. Conceptually, it is possible to predict that when the *predominant* reasons for cohesiveness within a given group are *depersonalised* (as opposed to genuine member interpersonal attraction) then the significance of attachment characteristics in predicting cohesion *and* the specific *role* of attachment characteristics may differ. For example, in Rom and Mikulincer's (2003) study (discussed earlier) cohesion was found to offset the negative relationship between attachment anxiety and individual instrumental functioning in group tasks. It was suggested that this may be a function of the fact that high group cohesion signified to anxious individuals that the support, closeness, and availability of others was readily accessible in the group, lessening their concern with such issues and enabling a more instrumental focus. However, such a hypothesis is likely to be dependent upon the extent to which cohesion is defined in terms of interpersonal attraction. That is, in a group where cohesion is *genuinely* a function of a high degree of *interpersonal attraction* (closeness, support, emotional bonding) among members it makes sense to suggest that member perception of such cohesion might serve to alleviate some of the anxieties and concerns that group situations typically evoke for anxiously attached individuals. However, if such cohesion is perceived to be a function of *depersonalised attraction* (such as the social identity hypothesis forwarded above by Hogg, 1993) then it may be less likely that such cohesiveness would signify the closeness and support that serves to alleviate attachment-related concerns in group contexts. Hence, researchers will need to be particularly alert to the idea that the various relationships that attachment characteristics share with group cohesion and group-related constructs may in large part be a function of the specific *reasons* for the cohesiveness within the group. Such issues make for potential research questions and it would be interesting to explore whether specific dimensions of cohesion as it is conceptualised in the GEQ are more likely to offset any negative relationships between attachment anxiety, avoidance, and various group outcomes. It might be hypothesised that social dimensions of cohesion are more likely to moderate such negative effects as they are more likely to signify the availability of support and closeness in the group, deactivating attachment concerns of anxious individuals.

Conclusion

This chapter sought to examine the potential for integration of the attachment literature with cohesion as it has been conceptualised in sport research. It should be kept in mind that the attachment literature that has formed its basis has been exclusively conducted according to the social psychological tradition of attachment research. From a measurement perspective the assumption has therefore been that individuals' conscious recollection of their attachment-related beliefs, concerns, and behaviours in relation to groups (i.e. Smith *et al.*, 1999) or to interpersonal relations (i.e. Rom & Mikulincer, 2003) is an accurate indication of internal working models. As discussed in the previous chapter, such assumptions overlook the role of defensive processes and unconscious conceptualisations of working models of attachment. For example, in the tradition of psychodynamic research it is feasible that individuals might exhibit deep-rooted and unconscious emotional, physiological, and behavioural responses to attachment-related recollections of the collective *family unit* in early life that serve as an indicator of an internal model that would influence how they subsequently relate to collective others. This possibility has been put forward by Byng-Hall (1995) but has received no empirical attention that I am aware of.

The social psychological research to date is encouraging with regard to the significance of attachment theory in the context of small group functioning. Research has suggested (a) that individuals may form specific styles of attachment toward groups that can serve to influence the quality of their group-related experiences on a cognitive, affective, and behavioural level, (b) that even general working models of attachment that are unrelated to groups (i.e. romantic relationship attachment) may dictate that individuals possess specific mental structures in relation to interpersonal relationships that are reflected in the manner in which they experience group contexts, and (c) that the research in relation to the above reveals associations that are conceptually coherent with attachment theory. It befits sport researchers to begin to unravel the potential contributions that the theory might make to the development of the sport cohesion literature.

Furthermore, the idea that aspects of group cohesion can serve to moderate the negative features of group involvement associated with endorsement of insecure models of attachment (i.e. with attachment anxiety) is encouraging. If aspects of group cohesion serve to signify closeness, availability, and support in the context of the group and subsequently deactivate attachment-related concerns, then this suggests that cohesion may have a particularly important role to play. Research has suggested that long-term experiences of therapy (e.g. Fonagy *et al.*, 1996; Korfmacher *et al.*, 1997) and significant interpersonal life changes (e.g. Hamilton, 2000) can bring about shifts in individuals' attachment patterns. This is partially attributed to the discovery of a 'site' where individuals are able to feel a reliable sense of acceptance, support, and security that may have been lacking in previous relationships. It is interesting to speculate on whether long-term involvement with close-knit groups has the potential to bring about similar meaningful changes. If perceptions of cohesion can alleviate attachment concerns in the short term, then investigation of longer-term effects may prove insightful. This might implicate aspects of sports team involvement such as cohesion as potentially important in terms of the wider psychological development of members' attachment characteristics.

5 Attachment, reactions to stress, and coping in sport

Introduction

There are numerous stressors that can arise from sport and exercise participation. These may include dealing with experiences of failure, injury, trauma and pain, the psychological demands of competition, a lack of confidence, and coach stress (e.g. Dale, 2000; Gould *et al.*, 1993; Holt & Hogg, 2002; Nicholls & Polman, 2007). Nicholls and Polman (2007) have suggested that if athletes are unable to cope effectively in the face of such stressors then it is likely that (a) certain elements of performance will suffer (Lazarus, 2000), and (b) that levels of satisfaction, motivation, and commitment will be detrimentally affected (e.g. Holt & Dunn, 2004; Klint & Weiss, 1986; Smith, 1986).

In the sport literature coping with stress has been thought about on a number of levels. First, researchers have discussed *trait* and *process* conceptualisations. According to the trait approach, individuals are suggested to possess relatively stable 'styles of coping' that they 'bring with them' into various stressful situations and which remain influential in dictating coping responses across time and conditions (Carver *et al.*, 1989). Alternatively, process models (e.g. Lazarus, 1999; Lazarus & Folkman, 1984) of coping have viewed coping with stress as a dynamic process dependent upon individuals' attempts to manage constantly changing perceptions of situational demands in light of whether or not they are appraised to strain or exceed perceptions of available internal resources (i.e. beliefs about the self's capabilities to deal with a given stressor). Lazarus and Folkman's (1984) model of appraisal has received significant attention in the sport psychology literature.

Lazarus (1999) suggested that *cognitive appraisal* is an important variable associated with coping with stress and has conceptualised both *primary* and *secondary* appraisal processes. Primary appraisal is suggested to involve a cognitive evaluation related to whether current environmental circumstances and stressors are perceived to be of importance in relation to the individual's valued goals, intentions, and thoughts about the self. For example, Lazarus (1999) suggested that if individuals perceive a given situation to be of little consequence with regard to these issues then there is likely to be nothing 'at stake' to provoke a stress response in the first place. However, when appraisal leads to the conclusion that current circumstances *are* of significance to the individual and threaten an aspect of their well-being, Lazarus (1999) outlined a number of possible appraisal outcomes: (a) there is a sense of harm or loss because damage has *already* been incurred, (b) there is a sense of threat about *anticipated* harm, loss, or damage in the future, (c) there is a sense of *challenge* about a looming struggle with the environmental stressor, or (d) there is a *perceived benefit* to the looming encounter. Secondary appraisal is suggested to reflect individuals' evaluations of the *resources* (internal and external) that are available to them in order to cope with the stressors encountered and Nicholls and Polman (2007) outline that this is especially important when primary appraisal has indicated that threat is imminent. The sporting literature has suggested that how athletes *appraise* potentially threatening situations is a significant factor in dictating the manner in which they attempt to cope on a behavioural level (e.g. Anshel & Delany, 2001; Anshel *et al.*, 2001). For example, Anshel and Delany (2001) identified that athletes who made more negative appraisals of stressful sporting events (i.e. they perceived them as harmful and did not believe they had the resources to cope with them effectively) were more likely to rely on negative, avoidance-style coping mechanisms. Positive appraisals were linked to positive, approach-type coping techniques.

Nicholls and Polman (2007) have highlighted that there are various *categories* of coping strategies that have been employed by the sporting literature to help organise the different ways individuals go about coping with stressful situations. Clearly there are numerous mechanisms that individuals might employ in their attempts to cope with stressors encountered in sport. For example, positive coping strategies might include communicating with and seeking support from others, emotional regulation, relaxation, and active problem solving, whereas negative strategies might include anger, blaming others, and mechanisms of avoidance (Ayers *et al.*, 1996; Fanshawe & Burnett, 1991). Nicholls and Polman (2007) have outlined problem- (i.e. strategies intended to change the external situation) and emotion- (i.e. strategies intended to deal with the emotional response the situation provokes in individuals) focused, avoidance (i.e. behavioural [physical self-removal] and cognitive [psychological distancing] efforts to disengage from the situation), and approach (i.e. confronting the stressor head-on and trying to reduce its effects) coping mechanisms as *macro level* descriptions of coping strategies. Beyond this, a micro level categorisation has also emerged, with researchers creating subcategories of coping strategies within macro level categories. For example, problem-focused coping has been subdivided into strategies such as (a) assertive confrontation, (b) planning and goal setting, and (c) information seeking.

Generally, the ability to cope with stressors encountered during sport has been highlighted as an integral part of successful performance (e.g. Hardy *et al.*, 1996). Researchers have implicated coping mechanisms as predictors of (a) objective performance outcomes under experimentally induced stressful conditions (e.g. Anshel & Anderson, 2002; Krohne & Hindel, 1988), (b) self-reports of performance-related constructs such as personal goal attainment (e.g. Gaudreau & Blondin, 2004), and (c) affective responses to sporting experiences (e.g. Crocker & Graham, 1995; Gaudreau & Blondin, 2004; Ntoumanis et al., 1999). For example, Gaudreau and Blondin (2004) examined athletes' self-reported profiles of what they labelled task-oriented (i.e. relaxation, support seeking, thought control, effort expenditure), distraction-oriented (i.e. distancing, mental distraction), and disengagement-oriented (i.e. disengagement, resignation, venting of unpleasant emotions) coping dimensions using the *Inventaire des Stratégies de Coping en Competition Sportive* (ISCCS; Gaudreau & Blondin, 2002). Results suggested that athletes who endorsed a coping profile that was high in task-oriented coping mechanisms (and low in the other categories) reported significantly higher levels of goal attainment, experience of control, positive affective states, and lower anger/dejection than athletes high in disengagement-oriented coping mechanisms (and low in the other categories).

Attachment theory offers useful conceptual avenues in relation to coping and dealing with stress that merit further exploration from sport psychologists. In the sections that follow I seek to discuss the links between attachment and coping and to briefly reflect upon the significance of such ideas for sport research. I begin with a conceptual and empirical discussion of how attachment has been related to coping and cognitive and emotional responses to threat, and discuss what this might mean in the context of sport. Following this, I have devoted attention to a body of research in the attachment literature suggesting that attachment may be a critical vulnerability factor in initial responses to the threat of pain. Subsequently, I use this body of literature to suggest parallels with athlete responses to the stresses that often surround athletic injury.

Attachment, cognitive and emotional responses to stressors, and coping

Torquati and Vazsonyi (1999) have hypothesised that one of the central predictions of attachment theory is that working models of attachment are likely to be activated in the context of *perceived threat*, potentially implicating them as significant in guiding cognitive, affective, and behavioural *responses* to threat (including appraisals and coping styles). One of the central ideas in Bowlby's (1973) theory is the notion that when individuals are *threatened* their attachment system is activated and they seek care and support from individuals who are perceived to represent a secure base. If the quest for care and support is satisfied the attachment system is 'toned down' and a sense of felt security is attained, allowing individuals to engage in exploratory behaviour and to function unimpeded. However, when attachment figures are perceived to be unavailable and unresponsive in the face of threat it is hypothesised that individuals develop alternative mechanisms, strategies,

and scripts that are designed to help them deal with the emotional consequences of threat in the perceived absence of support figures. It is the
development of such 'organisational rules' (Dewitte *et al.*, 2007, p. 1308) in
relation to the processing of and response to stressors that point to attachment
theory as a particularly useful framework for development of understanding in
this area.

Internal working models of attachment have been hypothesised to
encompass representations of the self, specific relationships, others, and the
social world in general (Bowlby, 1988) and it is suggested that these models
serve as interpretive schemata that function as a template for cognition,
affect, and behaviour in attachment-relevant situations or contexts. Torquati
and Vazsonyi (1999) have outlined that secure individuals benefit from 'a
positive perception of the social world in general and of attachment figures
in particular' (p. 550). Hypotheses surrounding the role of attachment characteristics in the appraisal of stress and coping styles suggest that secure
attachment styles correspond to stronger expectations regarding efficacious
behaviour from both the self and others in the face of threat. Secure individuals
are thought to anticipate comforting responses from attachment figures and
to believe in the utility of seeking proximity to such figures as a primary
source of coping when the attachment system is activated. Furthermore, it
has also been suggested (Torquati & Vazsonyi, 1999) that the enhanced levels
of self-efficacy associated with secure attachment styles may be linked to an
increased sense of control regarding the outcome of potentially threatening
or uncertain situations.

In contrast, insecure attachment styles have been linked to a contrasting
set of hypotheses. Florian *et al.* (1995) have suggested that insecurely
attached individuals, who grow up with a lack of certainty surrounding the
availability of their attachment figures (Ainsworth *et al.*, 1978), are likely to
develop a generalised belief in a 'non-supportive world' (p. 666). Insecure
attachment style has been linked to the anticipation or expectation of attachment figure insensitivity or inconsistency in the face of threat. As an attempt
to deal with the negative emotions aroused by anticipated attachment
figure insensitivity and/or to more closely monitor the availability of
perceived inconsistent attachment figures attachment theory predicts
(e.g. Main, 1990) that insecure individuals develop specific response patterns.
It is predicted that insecure-avoidant individuals develop an ability to sup-
press threat-related cues and attachment-relevant concerns in an apparent
deactivation of the attachment system, denying attachment needs and
adopting an excessive self-reliance in the face of threat (Shaver & Mikulincer,
2002). Insecure-anxious individuals adopt a hyper-vigilance towards threat
and a chronic accessibility of attachment-related thoughts in an attempt to
control the sense of uncertainty that surrounds attachment figure availability
(Dewitte *et al.*, 2007; Shaver & Mikulincer, 2002). Given the attachment
histories of individuals with such insecure models of attachment, these strategies are logical (and in some senses adaptive) attempts to deal with the

cognition and emotion aroused by attachment system activation in the face of threat.

The research in relation to attachment in this area has provided support for a link between attachment styles and specific individual tendencies to process and deal with perceived threat. However, such research has not always supported the predictions of attachment theory in the manner that has been hypothesised. For example, in an early study of attachment and attention in the face of a distressing separation, Main *et al.* (1985) identified that both insecure-avoidant *and* insecure-anxious children (assessed using the Strange Situation) looked away from attachment-related pictures. This suggested a tendency to dismiss attachment-related comfort as a coping mechanism in the face of distress. Furthermore, Kirsh and Cassidy (1997) attempted to explore selective attention in the face of threat, giving children a choice of simultaneously presented attachment-relevant positive or attachment-irrelevant neutral drawings to look at during distressing situations. Results again suggested that both insecure-avoidant *and* insecure-anxious children avoided looking at the attachment-relevant information. In the context of adult attachment there has also been a suggestion that both insecure-avoidant *and* insecure-anxious individuals are less inclined to process threatening information, seeming to ignore or avoid semantic representations of threat in comparison to secure individuals (e.g. Dewitte *et al.*, 2007; Zeijlmans Van Emmichoven *et al.*, 2003). For example, Zeijlmans Van Emmichoven *et al.* (2003) used the Stroop colour-naming task to examine attention allocation to threatening, positive, and neutral stimuli and discovered that individuals with both types of insecure attachment styles more quickly identified the colour of the stimulus word when it was threatening, whereas secure individuals experienced a delay in identification. The authors suggested that this may be evidence that secure individuals are more inclined to process threatening stimuli (i.e. they were more likely to pay attention to the threat word which caused delay in the identification of its colour) whereas both types of insecure individuals may be more likely to avoid or inhibit perceived threat.

The above findings associate both anxious *and* avoidant dimensions of attachment to initial attentional avoidance in the context of threat. This does not fit with the predictions outlined earlier proposing hyper-vigilance in the face of threat as a central feature of insecure-anxious individuals. To explain this discrepancy Dewitte *et al.* (2007) have hypothesised that a general dismissing style of attention in response to threat could assist in mood regulation for *both* types of insecure individuals (avoidant and anxious) as it serves to orient them away from (a) threatening stimuli per se, and/or (b) attachment-related stimuli (e.g. attachment figures or representations of social and emotional support from others) that are detected during threatening episodes. These are likely to be antecedents of anxious or negative mood states in insecure individuals because earlier attachment experiences have led them to anticipate rejection or ambiguity from others in the face of threat. Hence, there is a body of research suggesting that there may be a tendency for all insecure individuals to attempt to dismiss threat in general, and also to dismiss attachment-relevant stimuli in the face of threat. Such subconscious attentional reactions to initial encounters with threat may be important precursors of subsequent response patterns.

The above laboratory-based research is interesting in the sense that it provides an insight into some of the *instinctive* psychological reactions to threat that might develop in response to differential attachment histories. Some attachment theorists have argued that these initial subconscious cognitive reactions are influential because they often dictate subsequent conscious responses. For example, Mikulincer *et al.* (2002, p. 883) have suggested that 'a thought can become neurologically active and influence mental processes before it is recognized in one's stream of consciousness ... hence, the extent to which a thought influences performance on a cognitive task can serve as a measure of activation'. From this perspective, it might be suggested that differences in automatic cognitive reactions to threat in the laboratory are meaningful in the sense that they serve to orchestrate how subsequent cognition and behaviour unfolds in relation to a perceived threat. Research outside of the laboratory is likely to substantiate such claims, providing evidence that individuals' *actual behavioural tendencies* in relation to stress reactions and coping are also related to attachment characteristics.

Torquati and Vazsonyi (1999) have suggested that emotions themselves are likely to be significantly involved in dictating the coping process. Specifically, they have argued that particular types of emotion (e.g. anger, sadness, fear) may predict the type of coping strategy that is adopted or interfere with the act of solving the problem itself. Given that there may well be differences in both the intensity and types of emotions that individuals (with different attachment histories) experience in response to stressors it may be logical to predict that coping is linked to attachment styles. In support of this, Mikulincer and Florian (1995) examined self-reported attachment styles and coping styles in new military recruits and identified (a) that avoidant attachment style was associated with an enhanced perception of threat in relation to military training, (b) that enhanced perceptions of threat were linked to enhanced use of emotion-focused and distancing coping strategies, and (c) that avoidant recruits were less likely to rely on social support as a means of coping with perceived threat. Furthermore, Mikulincer *et al.* (1993) examined the attachment styles, perceptions of threat, and coping styles of Israeli college students who had been stationed in areas of high and low danger during the Gulf war. Their results supported some of the major conceptual predictions of attachment theory. For example, insecure-avoidant individuals reported higher levels of hostility, trauma-related avoidance, and distancing coping strategies in situations of high danger and secure individuals reported higher use of social support seeking in both high and low danger situations.

In a study of adolescent females Torquati and Vazsonyi (1999) studied the link between attachment characteristics, appraisals of threat, and coping responses in relation to interpersonal conflict. Results suggested that attachment was linked to both appraisals of distressing relational conflict and to styles of coping with such conflict. Securely attached individuals perceived greater control in relation to interpersonal conflict and insecurely attached individuals perceived such conflict to be a more significant threat. Furthermore, insecurely attached participants were more likely to use avoidant strategies to cope with interpersonal conflict across a range of close relationships. These findings have been supported in a number of other studies indicating that, in securely attached individuals, stress seems to activate increases in social communication and decreases in avoidance coping, reflecting a reliance and acceptance of social support as a primary coping response to stressors (e.g. Armsden & Greenberg, 1987; Howard & Medway, 2004; Shulman, 1993). Insecure attachment styles have been associated with avoidance of positive coping strategies, reflecting a lack of trust in the utility of others, a perception that the self is unworthy of such support, a lack of recognition of the need for others, and potential conflict about seeking help from others (e.g. Simpson & Rholes, 1994). Howard and Medway (2004) summarised such findings by suggesting that they 'highlight the central role that parents and caregivers play in inoculating individuals from stress and crisis during earlier times when children are likely to turn to them for guidance and support' (p. 399).

Implicating attachment in sport research

In a recent article in the sport psychology literature Forrest (2008) suggested researchers keep in mind the evidence from attachment research suggesting that the physiological and behavioural systems at the heart of individuals' attention regulation in response to distressing stimuli may well be shaped through repeated caregiver interactions (Hofer & Sullivan, 2001). Given that responses to distress are an integral aspect of sport involvement it is clear that attachment theory may have significant implications for sport coping. A key question to be addressed relates to whether or not the sorts of stressors encountered by athletes in the context of sport are likely to activate the attachment system, increasing the chances that cognitive, affective, and behavioural responses to encountered stressors are subject to influence from internal working models of attachment. Forrest (2008) has argued that Bowlby's (1969/1982) predictions suggest that the attachment system is likely to be activated in response to unfamiliar or strange stimuli (especially when attachment figures are not present), fatigue, hunger, pain, and other environmental stimuli that evoke perceptions of threat or fear. For Forrest (2008) there is no doubt that athletes are likely to encounter numerous stimuli that could serve to activate attachment-relevant processes:

> sport competition requires athletes to compete anywhere ... they must travel by air, rail, or bus, for longer than they are used to, experience

unfamiliar cultures, eat food with which they are unaccustomed ... athletes must handle changes in their own condition, such as feeling fatigued, sick, in pain ... a stress many athletes encounter is the 'threat to the self' ... performance pressure and the uncertainty of the outcome may be the largest sources of stress for athletes.

(pp. 247–8)

Hence, sport is rife with potential stimuli that could serve to activate the attachment system and it is imperative that sport researchers begin to examine the extent to which this assumption can be confirmed through empirical data.

On the one hand, if attachment characteristics are thought of as an individual difference variable that essentially reflects how caregivers have 'trained' infants' neurological apparatus to respond to threat and distress over the course of attachment histories (Fonagy & Target, 2002) it is possible to suggest that attachment styles would relate to *generalised differences* in sport coping styles. As discussed in the previous section, there are studies (e.g. Armsden & Greenberg, 1987; Howard & Medway, 2004; Mikulincer & Florian, 1995; Mikulincer *et al.*, 1993; Shulman, 1993) from the mainstream literature that have provided support for such generalised associations. However, the sport literature has provided mixed support for a stable, trait-like approach to coping styles. For example, of 64 reviewed studies in Nicholls and Polman's (2007) meta-analysis, 11 provided explicit support for the trait approach to coping whereas 46 provided support for a more dynamic, process approach, where coping mechanisms were identified to change in accordance with factors such as situational appraisal. The authors concluded that 'although there is partial evidence to support the trait theory of coping ... the majority of research suggests that coping is both recursive and dynamic ... this would indicate that athletes do not have preferred coping styles' (Nicholls & Polman, 2007, p. 16). Hence, research that seeks simply to relate stable differences in attachment characteristics to similar differences in trait-like coping characteristics (while potentially useful and interesting) may not be the most fruitful avenue for future research.

Hence, researchers might also consider the numerous complexities that are likely to be involved in integrating attachment ideas with sport coping research. For example, it is plausible that activation of the attachment system (and associated cognitive, affective, and behavioural processes in response to stress) may differ in strength and intensity in response to the various threats and stressors that athletes encounter. Particular stressors (e.g. interpersonal conflicts with coaches or teammates) may be more powerful in their activation of the attachment system than others and it may be that coping responses to *certain situations* are particularly likely to be governed by attachment-related processes. Researchers should consider that the attachment system may not be an equally powerful 'driver' of coping responses in *all* stressful situations. Forrest (2008) has suggested that there may be moments when 'sport-specific training may be pitted against the strength of attachment-related attentional tendencies' (p. 250), suggesting that the driving force behind coping responses in any given moment may depend upon the intensity with which instinctive attachment-related tendencies have been activated. Carefully designed studies will be required to explore such possibilities.

Researchers might also consider the benefit in adopting conceptualisations of attachment as a dynamic state of mind (e.g. Gillath & Shaver, 2007; Gillath *et al.*, 2006, 2009) when investigating its link with appraisal coping. Real-life events such as break-ups or the formation of romantic relationships (e.g. Feeney & Noller, 1992) and experimental priming techniques (e.g. Gillath *et al.*, 2009) have been demonstrated to evoke temporary (yet meaningful) fluctuations in attachment states of mind that have significant impact on behaviour. Carefully designed experiments would enable researchers to identify the extent to which encounters with *specific* sport-related stressors seem to activate *specific* attachment states of mind and result in temporary changes in coping mechanisms and threat appraisals. Such temporary fluctuations may have significant implications for performance and could also be constrained by generalised differences in attachment style.

There may also be significant *applied* implications to the consideration of athletes' attachment characteristics and the manner in which they respond to stressors in the context of sport. For example, one of Bowlby's (1969/1982) initial predictions was that attachment system activation is likely during encounters with strange, unfamiliar, or threatening situations, *particularly* when attachment figures are unavailable. In the 2010 soccer World Cup it was reported in the media that England coach Fabio Capello banned players from contact with wives and girlfriends during the course of team preparations and the tournament itself. It is interesting to speculate how athletes are likely to respond to factors such as a culturally unfamiliar environment, intense media pressure, significant threat to self-esteem, performance pressure, and coach stress when coaches enforce bans on contact with potentially significant attachment figures.

For example, Fraley and Shaver (1998) have predicted that *insecure-anxious* individuals are particularly likely to seek proximity to attachment figures during separations and to be emotionally destabilised by such episodes because their 'threshold' for emotional distress in response to separation has been identified to be lower (e.g. Feeney & Noller, 1992). Simpson *et al.* (1992) have suggested that when anxious individuals encounter distress they are likely to experience an intense psychological conflict. On the one hand, they have a strong motivation to alleviate their distress through comfort and close proximity to attachment figures and they are hypothesised to adopt a hyper-vigilant, excessive concern with attachment figure availability in response to threat. However, at the same time they can experience anger and resentment towards their partners for lack of availability and much-needed support. Furthermore, in situations of distress, they are likely to experience heightened negative emotional states due to a lack of belief in the efficacy of the self to control or cope with the situation. Enforced separation from attachment figures in such individuals may well serve to provoke a background psychological state that is not conducive to optimal performance, well-being, and coping with the rigours of competition.

Sport psychologists and coaches would benefit from an enhanced understanding of how factors such as enforced 'bans' on athletes' contact with potentially key attachment figures during stressful sporting situations impact upon states of mind, perception of threat, and coping responses. Initial priming studies in the attachment literature (Gillath *et al.*, 2009) have provided evidence that simply imagining that one is being separated from one's partner evokes a temporarily more intense insecure-anxious state of mind that may have significant effects on cognitive, affective, and behavioural responses. *Actual* enforced separations from important attachment figures during stressful situations may well produce similar fluctuations.

Attachment, pain, and athletic injury

In the following section special attention is devoted to the integration of literature on attachment, pain, and athletic injury. Injury is an integral part of the sporting experiences of most elite and recreational athletes. In studies of children who participate in sport, estimations have suggested that from 11 per cent to 22 per cent of children are injured each year while taking part in a form of organised sport (e.g. Backx *et al.*, 1991; Gallagher *et al.*, 1984; Helms, 1997; Jacobsson, 1986). Such generalised figures mask substantial differences in relation to factors such as sport type, with participation in non-contact activities such as weight training (1 per cent; Risser & Preston, 1989) reportedly resulting in a lower percentage of injured children than contact sports such as wrestling (70 per cent; Snook, 1982). In research with elite adult participants, Alonso *et al.* (2009) identified an injury rate of 97 injuries per 1,000 athletes (9.7 per cent) during the course of the 2007 World Athletics Championships. Of these injuries, 56 per cent were serious enough to prevent athletes from training and competing further in the games. Furthermore, Hootman *et al.*'s (2007) analyses of a 15-year (1988–9 through 2003–4) study of NCAA athlete injury rates across 15 college sports revealed an overall injury rate of 13.79 injuries per 1,000 athlete-exposures (one athlete exposure reflected one athlete participating in one game or training session); sport-specific injury rates varied from 35.9 injuries per 1,000 athlete-exposures for men's football games to 9.9 per 1,000 in men's basketball and 4.3 per 1,000 in women's softball. In many sports, a minority of athletes are also faced with the prospect of career-ending injuries. For example, Balendra *et al.* (2007) identified that from 1991 to 2005 there were 45 instances of serious injuries to British jockeys that directly resulted in career termination. Shankar *et al.*'s (2007) analysis of US high school and collegiate football injuries during 2005–6 identified a total injury occurrence of 517,726 in high school athletes and 3,459 in NCAA athletes. The proportion of these injuries that were identified as serious enough to end the athlete's season or career was 9.7 per cent ($n = 50,219$) in high school athletes and 7.3 per cent ($n = 252$) in collegiate athletes. Such data serve to highlight that athletes face a significant risk that they will experience sport-related injury at some point in their careers.

The sporting literature has examined athletes' psychological responses to sport injury in terms of both emotional and behavioural categories (Walker et al., 2007; Wiese-Bjornstal et al., 1995). From an emotional perspective, research has associated athletic injury experiences with a number of significant changes in mood, and emotional responses ranging from anger, frustration, and boredom to depression (Carson & Polman, 2008; McDonald & Hardy, 1990; Walker et al., 2007). For some athletes, studies have reported that the sense of loss associated with athletic injury is particularly strong and it is estimated that 10–20 per cent of athletes experience extreme negative emotional responses, including depression that often surpasses the levels required for clinical intervention (Brewer et al., 1995; Leddy et al., 1994). From a more positive perspective, there have also been suggestions that some of the emotional responses associated with athletic injury can ultimately have a positive influence on athletes in the longer term. Wiese-Bjornstal et al. (1998) have suggested that if athletes can learn to cope with the emotions and hardships associated with their recovery from injury then they may ultimately experience significant post-traumatic growth. In terms of behavioural responses to athletic injury, the research has tended to suggest that athletes who use psychological skills, adhere to programmes of rehabilitation, use social support, and invest significant effort in the rehabilitation process are more likely to recover effectively from athletic injury and to experience the process more positively (e.g. Ievleva & Orlick, 1991; Pearson & Jones, 1992; Walker et al., 2007).

Cognitive appraisal perspectives on athletic injury propose that it is athletes' *interpretation* of the injury that will ultimately dictate the nature of their cognitive, affective, and behavioural responses (Brewer, 1994; Wiese-Bjornstal et al., 1998). Gallagher and Gardner (2007) demonstrated that individual difference (e.g. personality, self-perceptions) *and* situational factors (e.g. family dynamics, social support provision) predicted variation in athletes' emotional responses to sports injury and identified that early maladaptive cognitive processes predicted negative affective processes at later stages in rehabilitation. Given that personality and individual difference factors have been implicated as potentially significant psychological antecedents to coping responses in athletic injury it may be productive for researchers to consider attachment characteristics as a significant developmental vulnerability factor.

Bowlby (1969/1982) put forward an evolutionary argument that attachment system activation would be particularly likely to occur when the organism is sick, in pain, hungry, or fatigued. It is logical to suggest that these physiological states render organisms more vulnerable to harm and that seeking proximity and security to attachment figures in such circum-stances would be a survival-related advantage. Accordingly, over the course of early development it is feasible to suggest that caregiver responses to expressions of the need for care and proximity during episodes where indi-viduals are injured, fatigued, or sick will give rise to specific expectations, patterns of emotion, and behaviour designed to help them deal most effec-tively with their vulnerability in the context of their care giving environment. If attachment figures have been consistently unavailable during episodes of physical vulnerability it is logical to suggest that specific response patterns would develop that, in the absence of the caregiver, are designed to help individuals deal with the emotion that such vulnerability evokes. The attachment literature has therefore predicted that attachment history may be a strong indicator of how individuals conceptualise, process, and deal with episodes of physical vulnerability (Meredith *et al.*, 2008).

There has been a particular focus in the attachment literature on the implications of attachment for experiences of chronic pain. Specifically, pain has been referred to as 'An unpleasant sensory or emotional experience associated with actual or potential tissue damage, or described in terms of such damage' (Merskey & Bogduk, 1994, p. 210), and chronic pain has gen-erally been defined as pain persisting for 3–6 months or more, with or without an obvious underlying pathology (e.g. Merskey & Bogduk, 1994; Zasler *et al.*, 2005). Given that chronic pain impacts upon all aspects of individuals' lives, it is a particularly significant stressor, and how individuals appraise and respond to such pain is of importance to their quality of life and clinical recovery. Theoretical conceptualisations of pain have suggested (a) that pain seems to exacerbate or activate particular personality factors that set in motion specific coping responses which subsequently dictate the degree of perceived disability and emotional experiences associated with the pain (Gatchel & Weisberg, 2000), and (b) that when demands placed on the indi-vidual by the pain are negatively perceived, exceeding the individual's per-ceived resources to cope with the pain, then negative responses are particularly likely to develop (Truchon, 2001).

Attachment theorists have argued that the theory offers a particularly useful framework in relation to the development of and adaptation to chronic pain, proposing attachment styles as important factors in vulner-ability. Some interesting studies have supported this suggestion. For example, Walsh *et al.* (2004) identified similar reactions to both separation and pain episodes in a sample of children, with children's distress, self-confidence, vulnerability, and avoidance reactions to pain being extremely similar to their reactions to separation. The researchers therefore suggested that 'an internal working model of attachment … organizes children's behaviors, thoughts and feelings in response to both separation experience and painful events' (Walsh *et al.*, 2004, p. 53). Furthermore, Eisenberger *et al.* (2003) utilised neuro-imaging in a sample of adults and identified that similar neu-rological activity underpinned responses to both physical pain and social rejection episodes. Such findings suggest that the underpinning neurological factors that dictate responses to attachment-related stimuli are also activated during episodes of pain and may well drive responses to such episodes.

There has been significant support for these predictions in the literature and research has generally suggested that insecurely attached individuals (a) appraise their pain as more threatening and view themselves as less capable of coping with it (e.g. Meredith *et al.*, 2005; Mikulincer & Florian, 1998), (b) report significantly more pain intensity and disability (e.g. McWilliams *et al.*, 2000), (c) are more likely to experience catastrophic thoughts and feelings (e.g. 'This is terrible and will never get better') in response to pain (e.g. McWilliams & Asmundson, 2007; Meredith *et al.*, 2006), and (d) to experience higher levels of anxiety and depression in response to pain (e.g. Ciechanowski *et al.*, 2003). In a recent review, Meredith *et al.* (2008) suggested that the evidence implicating attachment as a significant vulnerability factor in relation to pain coping responses is certainly significant. However, differences in how attachment has been conceptualised and measured in individual studies make it difficult to draw parallels. Furthermore, there has been very little research in the pain literature that has not relied upon self-report as an indicator of attachment characteristics.

Nevertheless, sport researchers with an interest in developing understanding in relation to how athletes cope with injury may find attachment theory a particularly useful framework. The body of research in relation to attachment and chronic pain suggests that compromised or vulnerable physiological states may be particularly likely to activate attachment-relevant processes. Depending upon injury severity, injured athletes' physical state is temporarily more vulnerable and their injuries can serve as a significant stressor in their lives. Furthermore, the sporting literature has already provided preliminary evidence that athletes prone to catastrophising (i.e. exaggerating the threat value of pain sensations, excessive focus on pain sensations, and lack of belief in ability to cope with pain) report experiences of pain as more negative, intense, and unbearable than those who do not catastrophise (e.g. Sullivan *et al.*, 2000). In a recent study of recreational athletes who had undergone reconstructive surgery for complete ACL (anterior cruciate ligament) ruptures, Tripp *et al.* (2003) identified that heightened catastrophising was linked to pain-related experiences in the 24-hour post-operative period. How athletes appraise and cope with injuries may have an important impact on their mental well-being and recovery process and it is therefore important that researchers and practitioners alike develop enhanced understanding of the factors that predict vulnerability to maladaptive injury responses. Given the apparent vulnerability that attachment characteristics appear to invoke with regard to pain-related cognition and experiences, it will be important to explore their role in relation to athletic injury.

In a recent clinical review of the aetiology of suicide in athletic populations Baum (2005) examined 71 cases of attempted or completed suicide. Her data identified that the most popular underpinning reason for suicidal attempts in athletes was sport injury, with individuals' cognitive and emotional responses to injury featuring heavily in the interpretation of their experiences. In the psychiatric literature, Dumais *et al.* (2005) have suggested that identifying why some individuals die by suicide whereas others facing seemingly the same set of circumstances (and with similar environmental support structures) do not is a question of enormous clinical relevance. In this vein, the identification of vulnerability factors such as attachment styles that might help us to predict the nature of athletes' catastrophic thinking, the likelihood of them drawing on social support, and subsequent behaviours in the context of athletic injury will be potentially significant.

Wiese-Bjornstal *et al.* (1998) have outlined that there can be positive benefits for injured athletes because by dealing with the emotional experience of serious injury they may experience significant personal growth, a sense of triumph, and a renewed belief in their ability to overcome adversity. The attachment literature has also hinted that attachment style may predict the degree of post-traumatic growth that individuals are able to experience in response to traumatic episodes in the course of their lives. For example, Salo *et al.* (2005) studied a sample of Palestinian former political prisoners who had been subject to traumatic and brutal periods of imprisonment during the Israeli/Palestinian conflict. Their results suggested that securely attached individuals (assessed using self-report measures) reported higher levels of post-traumatic growth in response to their harrowing experiences (e.g. personal strength, positive affiliation to others, and spiritual change), whereas insecure individuals reported higher levels of negative emotional responses in the aftermath. The researchers suggested that secure attachment style may play a protective role in relation to personal growth following stressful life episodes. They hypothesised that painful memories of traumatic episodes are likely to evoke powerful emotional responses and secure individuals may be more likely to utilise social support and to feel a sense of control over such emotional reactions, perhaps increasing the likelihood that they are able to integrate and make sense of their experiences. In contrast, insecure individuals are less likely to believe in the utility of others as a mechanism of dealing with their painful memories (perhaps resorting to defensive suppression as a means of dealing with them alone) and may lack belief in the self to deal with such feelings when confronted by them (perhaps being overwhelmed by them). Hence, the role of attachment style in relation to personal growth should also be kept in mind and researchers might consider its usefulness when exploring the issue of post-traumatic growth in response to sport injury experiences.

Conclusion

A central feature of attachment theory is the assumption that developmental history of caregiver responses in relation to infants' instinctive desire for care and protection when threatened, injured, sick, or afraid will give rise to the development of organisational schemata. These schemata provide guidance on how the individual should best attend to, appraise, and respond to threatening stimuli given their personal history of attachment experiences. The attachment literature has provided evidence that individuals' attachment characteristics are a significant vulnerability factor in relation to specific cognitive, affective, and behavioural responses to threat and physical vulnerability. Given the significant likelihood that individuals involved in sport will likely experience perceptions of threat, fear, and physical vulnerability it is logical to suggest that researchers might profit from exploring the extent to which attachment histories are associated with athletes' contextual responses to such issues in the context of sport. There are a number of reasons why an examination of the link between individual difference variables (such as attachment characteristics) linked heavily to developmental history and cognitive reactions to threat in sport is worthwhile. First, how athletes appraise and respond to threat and injury has been demonstrated to have a significant impact on their performance and well-being. It is therefore important to gain a fuller understanding of important underpinning antecedents. Second, implicating attachment characteristics in cognitive appraisal and reaction to threat in the context of sport implies that aspects of athletes' developmental histories may be partially responsible for contextual psychological responses. This may be important information for researchers, practitioners, and policy makers alike, as it would suggest that understanding and developing the psychological state of athletes in the present may well require attention to aspects of developmental history that are not directly related to the sporting context. Forrest (2008) has suitably summarised this argument,

> It is critical ... not to blur sport psychology's focus on performance with the time frame of that performance. Widening the time frame to investigate factors that may be rooted in the early attachment experiences of athletes may yield answers to the critical question of why some athletes are better able to regulate competitive stress and achieve performance-optimizing states.
>
> (p. 243)

As a final note, it is worth keeping in mind that research that has explicitly implicated attachment styles as important vulnerability factors in relation to cognitive reactions to threat, coping mechanisms, and pain response has tended to come almost exclusively from the social psychological tradition. Given that recent analyses (e.g. Roisman *et al.*, 2007) of the degree of convergence between the two measurement traditions have suggested trivial overlap, it will be important for researchers to examine the extent to which hypotheses linking attachment with threat responses and coping are verified when attachment is conceptualised according to the AAI tradition. Sport researchers will make useful contributions to the wider field by considering their measurement tools carefully.

6   Attachment and social relationships in sport

Introduction

The psychiatrist Harry Sullivan recognised the importance and inevitability of interpersonal relationships in human life. Specifically, he outlined how the field of psychology '*is* the field of interpersonal relations ... a personality can never be isolated from the complex of interpersonal relations in which the person lives and has his being' (1940, p. 10, italics added). For Sullivan, human beings have a fundamental *need* for interpersonal relations and nothing is a more significant determinant of psychological well-being and quality of experience than the nature of our connections to the people around us. The centrality of human relationships is obviously a defining feature of attachment theory and as such it is particularly important to explore how attachment characteristics are linked to the development and maintenance of significant human relationships through the lifespan.

By virtue of the fact that sport is often a microcosm of broader human existence, interpersonal relationships in sport are of critical import with regard to psychological functioning within sport and wider experiences of life itself. As such, there have been calls to recognise the significance of interpersonal relationship research within the sporting literature (e.g. Carr, 2009a; Jowett & Wylleman, 2006; Poczwardowski *et al.*, 2006; Smith, 2003; Wylleman, 2000). Jowett and Wylleman (2006) have identified that sport researchers

> are fortunate enough to have at our disposal such a large array of psychological theories about interpersonal relationships, their application in understanding relationships in sport and exercise would be paramount and could in turn bring about insights to the broader social psychological phenomena.
>
> (p. 122)

In this chapter I seek to provide an insight into how attachment theory has helped to stimulate important developments in social relationship research in the field of sport. The domain of social relationships in sport is the area of sport and exercise psychology that has been quickest to recognise the potential for theoretical integration with the attachment literature. Specifically, researchers have published data exploring the interface between attachment theory, sport friendships (e.g. Carr, 2009a, 2009b, Carr & Fitzpatrick, 2011), and coach–athlete bonds (e.g. Davis & Jowett, 2010) and such literature provides a useful platform from which to launch further discussion of the topic. The predominant aims of the chapter are therefore (a) to briefly review research in relation to friendship and coach–athlete relationships in the context of sport, (b) to explore how attachment theory has initially been implemented in these areas, and (c) to discuss how future research can further develop our understanding and build upon existing findings.

Friendship in sport

Weiss and her colleagues (e.g. Smith, 2003; Weiss & Smith, 1999, 2002; Weiss et al., 1996) have identified young people's peer relations in sport-related settings as a particularly important area for investigation:

> the sport context is riddled with examples of peer interactions that impinge upon children's enjoyment and attraction to physical activity … These include the social context surrounding arguments among or negative treatment from peers … and feelings of self-worth that emanate from peer evaluation.
>
> (Weiss et al., 1996, p. 348)

Studies targeting peer relationships in children and adolescents have focused upon issues such as peer acceptance, the perceived quality of mutual, dyadic friendships involving a degree of affection, or levels of popularity within a broader circle of peers to whom affective ties are not as strong (Newcomb & Bagwell, 1995). The perceived quality of dyadic friendships is the focus of the current discussion because it has framed much of the early research seeking to integrate attachment theory with peer relationships in sport. Research has consistently identified adolescents' friendship quality as a critical determinant of a variety of important outcomes such as general satisfaction with peer relations[1] (Ladd, 1999), emotional responses to peer relations (Hartup, 1989), peer acceptance (Parker & Asher, 1993) and rejection (Coie & Cillessen, 1993; Hartup, 1989; Ladd, 1999), self-esteem (Keefe & Berndt, 1996), social anxiety (La Greca & Moore Harrison, 2005) and achievement (Parker & Gottman, 1989).

In Weiss et al.'s (1996) qualitative work with children and adolescents a number of distinct dimensions emerged that help us to understand young people's friendship experiences in sport. Specifically, children and adolescents were found to experience a number of positive aspects of friendship from their involvement in sport, including companionship, self-esteem enhancement, intimacy, emotional support, and assistance in conflict resolution. Reported negative friendship dimensions included experiences of conflict and betrayal. In further research, Weiss and Smith (1999) expanded their earlier work (e.g. Weiss *et al.*, 1996) by developing and validating the Sport Friendship Quality Scale (SFQS) as a means of assessing children's and adolescents' perceptions of the quality of these important aspects of their sporting friendships. The SFQS is a self-report measure of perceived dimensions of friendship quality (e.g. companionship, emotional support, loyalty and intimacy, similarity, conflict resolution, and experiences of conflict) that reflects children's perceptions of a relationship experienced with a nominated best friend in sport.

These developments have stimulated a body of research that has sought to enhance understanding of the importance of friendship quality in sport contexts in relation to issues such as well-being, motivation, and involvement. For example, Weiss and Smith (2002) identified young people's perceptions of 'ability to resolve conflict' and 'companionship' with a nominated best friend in tennis as positively associated with commitment to the sport and levels of enjoyment. Ullrich-French and Smith (2006) showed that perceptions of positive dimensions of friendship quality were positively associated with enjoyment and levels of self-determined motivation in youth soccer. More recently, Ullrich-French and Smith (2009) identified that the likelihood of children remaining involved in soccer was significantly predicted by perceived positive soccer friendship quality reported a year earlier, with those reporting more positive friendship dimensions being more likely to have continued their involvement. Cox and Ullrich-French (2010) recently identified that youngsters involved in physical education (PE) who reported peer relationships characterised by more positive friendship quality and general peer acceptance were less likely to experience worry in PE, had higher perceptions of competence, and reported higher levels of involvement in physical activity. Hence, evidence is mounting in support of the important role that friendship quality plays in youth sport.

Another important area of research has centred on identification of the antecedents of friendship quality in youth sport. Some of this research has focused on context-specific variables that are likely to facilitate or impede the development of positive friendships. For example, Ommundsen *et al.* (2006) identified that perceptions of friendship quality were positively predicted by perceptions of the motivational climate created by coaches in the context of adolescent soccer. Specifically, a mastery-oriented motivational climate (emphasising features such as the encouragement of cooperative learning, all players having an important role regardless of ability, and effort being valued more highly than ability) positively predicted perceptions of friendship quality with a nominated best friend in soccer. In contrast, a performance-oriented environment (encouraging individual rivalry and promoting unequal recognition) negatively predicted friendship quality. Such findings suggest that the manner in which the sporting environment is constructed by coaches may provoke a social atmosphere that enhances or impedes positive friendship formation.

In addition to contextual predictors of friendship quality researchers have also devoted attention to more distal antecedents. Recent sporting literature (e.g. Carr, 2009a, 2009b; Carr & Fitzpatrick, 2011) has looked to young people's attachment relationships with parents as a potential predictor of their friendship quality. In the attachment literature West *et al.* (1998) have outlined that 'adolescents' success in creating new supportive relationships is critically influenced by the affectively charged pattern of attachment behaviors and beliefs about attachment carried forward from the attachment history with their parents' (p. 662). This perspective argues that it is logical to assume individuals with differing parental attachment histories may experience their friendships differently in the context of sport.

Adolescent attachment and sport friendship

Recognising the psychological importance of children's relationships with initial caregivers (typically parents), Bowlby (1973, 1980) hypothesised that the internal working models children construct as a consequence of initial attachment relationships will serve to marshal future patterns of cognition, affect, and behaviour. Bodies of attachment literature (e.g. George *et al.*, 1985, 1996; Main & Goldwyn, 1998; Main *et al.*, 1985) therefore afford particular importance to childhood relationships with *parents* in regulating later states of mind in relation to attachment and relationship formation. This is a conceptual reflection of the evolutionary importance afforded to the parent–child relationship in attachment theory (Bowlby, 1969/1982). Building upon this argument, I have (Carr, 2009b) hypothesised that adolescents' attachment relationships with key caregivers are likely to reflect the nature of internal working models that may well function as a psychological template during the construction of new close relationships in sport. Specifically, (a) adolescents whose early experiences enable them to develop a secure attachment model are more likely to develop internal working models of themselves and others that facilitate positive relationships with friends, (b) adolescents often develop a style of interaction with others that closely reflects the attachment relationship that they experience with caregivers (e.g. an individual whose mother is rejecting and withholds support and affection may come to respond in a similar manner towards their friends) (Weimer *et al.*, 2004; Youngblade & Belsky, 1992), and (c) adolescents can internalise complex patterns of emotional regulation developed in early attachment relationships and subsequently reproduce these strategies in their relationships with their friends (e.g. Contreras & Kerns, 2000; Contreras *et al.*, 2000). For example, insecure children may develop a self-protective distancing strategy with caregivers in order to avoid dealing with rejection and unavailability that they perceive as a likely occurrence. Subsequently, such children seek less intimacy, proximity, and social support from friendships in line with the framework of emotional responses to attachment relationships that they have developed (Weimer *et al.*, 2004).

In support of these predictions, one of my recent investigations (Carr, 2009b) identified that adolescents' self-reported levels of attachment security in relation to a nominated key caregiver significantly predicted their reports of sporting friendship quality with a nominated best friend in sports teams. Specifically, in this investigation the Adolescent Attachment Questionnaire (AAQ; West *et al.*, 1998) was employed to explore identified relationships between self-reported parental attachment and sport friendship quality. The AAQ is not a typological assessment of attachment and it taps adolescents' perceptions of relationship security with a nominated adult attachment figure on three continuous dimensions developed from Bowlby's ideas surrounding the key characteristics of attachment relations. The first subscale, *availability* (e.g. 'I'm confident that my Mum/Dad will listen to me'), is based upon Bowlby's (1973) contention that a secure attachment relationship involves an attachment figure that is perceived to be available and responsive to adolescents' attachment-related distress and anxiety. The second subscale, *angry distress* (e.g. 'I get annoyed at my Mum/Dad because it seems I have to demand his/her care and support'), is conceptually linked to Bowlby's (1973) contention that in less secure attachment bonds anger is likely to be directed towards attachment figures when attachment-related needs and desires are frustrated. The final subscale, *goal-corrected partnership* (e.g. 'I feel for my Mum/Dad when he/she is upset'), reflects Bowlby's (1969/1982) suggestion that secure attachment bonds are characterised by an increasing sense of empathy towards the attachment figure and that he or she is respected as a separate individual with needs and feelings. While this measure is obviously allied to the self-report tradition, West *et al.* (1998) have provided evidence in favour of the validity of the AAQ in relation to categorical assessment of attachment using the Adult Attachment Interview (AAI). Specifically, adolescents classified as securely attached according to the AAI endorse higher levels of *available responsiveness* and *goal-corrected partnership* subscales on the AAQ and those classified as insecurely attached on the AAI report lower levels of *goal-corrected partnership* and higher levels of *angry distress* on the AAQ.

My data (Carr, 2009b) suggested that self-reported features of attachment security with a key caregiver were positively related to a number of the features of positive sport friendship quality put forward by Weiss and Smith (1999). Specifically, the *goal-corrected partnership* scale of the AAQ was found to positively predict self-reported dimensions of friendship quality including *self-esteem support, companionship and pleasant play, loyalty and intimacy, things in common*, and *conflict resolution. Goal-corrected partnership* also predicted how strongly individuals appeared to be liked by other team mates with whom they were not considered to be best friends. It was interesting that the *goal-corrected partnership* subscale of the AAQ was identified as most strongly related to the sport friendship variables. Bowlby (1969/1982) identified what he termed *goal-corrected partnership* to be a central characteristic of a more secure attachment relationship with caregivers. He suggested that adolescents developing a secure working model of attachment come to receive and respond to their key attachment figures as separate individuals with needs, feelings, and goals to which the adolescent responds with care and empathy. Such a characteristic is less likely to be reflected in insecure attachment relationships because factors such as anger directed at attachment figures due to unavailability and a lack of responsiveness from caregivers to adolescents' own needs and goals lessen the likelihood of perceiving the attachment figure in an empathetic manner. Hence, such *goal-corrected partnership* has been predicted to be symptomatic of underlying working models of attachment. The fact that *goal-corrected partnership* was consistently identified as a positive predictor of more positive sport friendship characteristics in my study (Carr, 2009b) suggests that it reflects an aspect of a secure underlying model of attachment which extends influence on negotiation of relationships encountered in team sport contexts. Ultimately, the data suggested that *goal-corrected partnership* seems to ensure that youngsters are more sensitive to factors such as supporting the self-esteem of another person, loyalty, intimacy, and conflict resolution in the friendships that they forge in their sporting lives.

Developmental researchers (e.g. Allen & Land, 1999; Belsky & Cassidy, 1995) have suggested that the intense, intimate nature of the parental relationships conceptualised to underpin the formation of attachment styles is likely to differ somewhat from relations with friends. Hence, while parent–child attachment characteristics may 'guide' certain aspects of peer relations there may well be aspects of relationships with friends that are less likely to be underpinned by the 'cognitive maps' that attachment relationships with parents have sculpted. There were dimensions of attachment from the AAQ identified in my study (Carr, 2009b) as *less* influential in predicting sport friendship quality (i.e. the *angry distress* and *available responsiveness* subscales). It is important to note that such dimensions may be more likely to guide youngsters in the development of more intimate relationships (such as romantic relations) whereas *goal-corrected partnership* may be a feature of adolescent-parent attachment that is of consequence to sport friendships. Future research would be advised to investigate such issues further.

Actor and partner attachment characteristics as predictors of friendship perceptions

The above investigation (Carr, 2009b) was an important first step towards understanding the manner in which adolescents' internal working models of attachment relate to their friendship quality in the context of youth sport. However, it should be noted that this investigation was limited to exploring the hypothesis from an *intrapersonal* perspective (i.e. the influence of an adolescent's relationship security with a key caregiver on his or her *own* perception of relationship quality with a best friend). Recent research in the broader sphere of peer relationships has recognised that individual perceptions of dyadic peer relationships in adolescence are constructed as a consequence of both *intrapersonal* and *interpersonal* processes and should be considered as multilevel phenomena (e.g. Cillessen *et al.*, 2005). In the broader literature on attachment, researchers have provided evidence that models of attachment of *both* the self *and* one's partner are likely to predict the *self's* perception of the relationship and behaviour within it (Campbell *et al.*, 2001). For example, Campbell *et al.* (2001) videotaped dating couples who were waiting to engage in a task that was perceived to be stressful for the female member of the dyad. The researchers qualitatively examined each partner's behaviour during the waiting period as a function of their own attachment characteristics and those of their partner. Results identified that more avoidant individuals tended to behave more negatively towards their partners by distancing themselves, displaying more negative emotions, and being more aggressive towards their partner. This was evidence that their attachment style predicted their response to stressors in a relationship context. However, it was also the case that individuals with more avoidant *partners* (regardless of their own characteristics) also behaved more negatively towards their partners. The researchers suggested that their data indicate that in emotionally stressful situations avoidant individuals may transmit emotional and behavioural signals to partners that elicit some of the hostile behaviours they expect to find in others. In short, they may play a role in creating the characteristics they expect, ultimately confirming the working models of others they perceive as most likely.

It is worth noting that there is also a methodological impetus to attachment data that are part of such a multilevel investigation (Liu, 2009). Previous studies of dyadic relations have often attempted to analyse individual responses from each dyad member, assuming independent observations (e.g. 50 dyads might be analysed as 100 individual cases, predicting each *individual's* outcome variable from both her own predictor variable and that of her partner). However, Kashy and Kenny (2000) have outlined that ignoring the non-independent nature of dyadic data in this way poses significant threats to the accuracy of analyses (see Kenny *et al.*, 2006). Kenny and his colleagues have developed the 'Actor-Partner Interdependence Model' (APIM; Cook & Kenny, 2005; Kashy & Kenny, 2000; Kenny & Cook, 1999) as a promising method of tackling the issue of interdependence in dyadic research. The APIM enables researchers to distinguish between *partner effects* (i.e. the extent to which specified characteristics of the *self* are a function of specified characteristics of *one's partner* in a given dyad) and *actor effects* (i.e. the extent to which specified characteristics of the *self* are a function of other specified characteristics of the *self*).

In the youth sport friendship literature it may be interesting to explore the extent to which *individual* perceptions of friendship quality (which have been shown to be important predictors of a variety of critical outcomes) are constructed not only from variables that reside within the *self* but also from those that reside in one's *partner*. This would suggest that adolescents' perceptions of friendship quality may be constructed not only as a consequence of their own attachment characteristics but also of the attachment characteristics of their friend. To investigate this hypothesis, my colleague and I (Carr & Fitzpatrick, 2011) recently employed the multilevel modelling (MLM) procedures outlined by Kenny *et al.* (2006) in order to assess the effects of both actor *and* partner attachment characteristics on perceptions of dyadic sport friendship quality. We hypothesised that the attachment security (again assessed using the AAQ) of the self (i.e. *actor*) and of a nominated sporting best friend (i.e. *partner*) would influence the actor's perception of the friendship quality.

Our analyses identified actor effects for perceptions of *companionship and pleasant play, self-esteem enhancement and support, conflict resolution*, and *total positive friendship quality*, suggesting that when adolescents themselves report more secure relationships with caregivers then they were more likely to perceive friendships in sport as positive on a number of levels. This is in line with the earlier findings from my work reported above (Carr, 2009b). From a multidimensional perspective these findings implicate *actors'* attachment characteristics as particularly important in the prediction of *certain* dimensions of friendship quality and it is interesting to briefly speculate on such issues. For example, perceptions of *self-esteem enhancement and support* (e.g. 'My friend has confidence in me when we play cricket'; 'My friend gives me a second chance to perform skills') were most closely linked to actor attachment characteristics. Initially, it seems logical to expect responses to these *self-esteem enhancement and support* statements to depend quite heavily upon the *partner* in a given dyad (i.e. the statements seem to require a judgement about what the partner *does* or *believes* in the context of the relationship). However, the attachment literature (e.g. Cook, 2000; Duchesne & Larose, 2007; Sroufe & Waters, 1977) has suggested that one of the central features of working models of attachment is the development of strong subconscious beliefs in relation to (a) the perceived worthiness of the self in the eyes of others, and (b) the support likely to be received from others. If this assumption is accurate, it may be that young athletes have constructed strong internal expectations (based upon earlier attachment experiences) in relation to the support and self-esteem enhancement that they believe relationship partners are *likely* to express towards them. This internal expectation may be powerful enough to influence their perceptions of this dimension of friendship quality more strongly than any characteristics the partner possesses.

The *things in common* dimension of perceived friendship quality was significantly predicted by *partner* (but not actor) attachment characteristics. This suggested that *certain aspects* of perceived friendship quality may be particularly susceptible to *partner* influence. Closer examination of the items that constitute this subscale of the SFQS reveals that it taps into perceptions that one shares 'common interests', has 'similar values', and 'thinks the same way' as one's friendship partner. Our findings suggest that the construction of such perceptions in the context of a dyadic sporting friendship may be more heavily dependent upon the *partner's* attachment characteristics than the actor's. This is logical because for adolescents to develop the perception that a friend *shares* their interests, values, and ways of thinking it may be necessary for *their friend* to possess certain cognitive and emotional characteristics. The attachment literature has suggested that key features of constructs such as *empathy* involve factors such as *perspective-taking* (i.e. a cognitive ability related to taking other people's point of view) and *empathic concern* (i.e. the tendency to feel sympathy or concern for other people). There has been evidence in support of the claim that insecure attachment bonds and poor care experiences with parents are linked with hindered perspective-taking and empathic concern (e.g. Britton & Fuendeling, 2005; Reti *et al.*, 2002). It may be that the partner effect in relation to *things in common* in our study can be explained by the fact that decreased attachment security in relation to parental relationships reflects less-developed cognitive and emotional capacities in relation to such empathic features and this seems to be *felt* by relationship partners in sport friendships, hindering their construction of a perception that common values, interests, and ways of being are shared.

Perceptions of sporting friendships are complex in the sense that they are ultimately *individual* perceptions. However, they are individual perceptions of a relationship that takes place *with* another person. Our data supported the idea that such perceptions should be thought of as a 'co-coordinated and emergent musicality' (Pincus *et al.*, 2007, p. 635) constructed partially as a consequence of ingrained, subconscious beliefs about relationships that individuals essentially 'bring with them' and partly as a function of interactions with relationship partners (through which partner characteristics are inevitably 'transmitted' and 'received').

Future research avenues in the integration of sport friendships and attachment

The above discussions suggest that the integration of attachment theory and sport friendship research is potentially profitable. However, there is still much to be learned in what is a relatively fledgling area of research within the field of sport psychology itself. While the above data suggest that adolescents' working models of attachment may well be 'active' in the context of their sporting friendships (and hence may influence friendship development), little is known about how the sporting context itself enhances or dampens this process. For example, the broader motivational climate within which sporting friendships are situated could create a contextual barrier to the expression, manifestation, or activation of deep-rooted internal models of attachment that children have constructed through parental relations, rendering them less likely (a) to be 'active' in the sporting context, and (b) to 'exert an influence on' sporting friendships. Ommundsen *et al.* (2005) have identified that performance-oriented motivational climates seem to inhibit positive friendship quality by creating a competitive sporting environment which encourages the perception that team mates are rivals and dampens the likelihood of intimacy and closeness in sporting relations. It is possible that such an environment would dampen the likelihood that internal models of attachment would be called upon for 'guidance' in the context of sporting relations.

From an applied intervention perspective, there are also potentially useful implications to the idea that young people's working models of attachment may be 'active' in the context of sport. This suggests that such working models may therefore be 'accessible' to interventions, raising the possibility that not only could such active models of attachment exert an influence on how sporting relationships are experienced but also that they could themselves be 'reworked' (e.g. in children with maladaptive beliefs about relationships) through the medium of *sporting* relationships. There has been a long-standing faith in the contexts of sport and physical activity in the usefulness of sport as a tool for the positive development of disaffected youth (e.g. Bailey *et al.*, 2009; Theodoulides & Armour, 2001). However, the evidence base for how such interventions are able to assist in positive youth development has been sparse and little is known about the mechanisms that underpin any identified positive influence (Bailey *et al.*, 2009). There has been a suggestion that one of the central factors for positive youth development in the context of sport-related interventions is the formation of supportive and caring relationships (Fraser-Thomas *et al.*, 2005; Petitpas *et al.*, 2008). Petitpas *et al.* (2008) have suggested that positive development is most likely when young people are 'surrounded by external assets, including a positive community environment with caring adult mentors' (p. 61). Attachment theory may provide a particularly useful theoretical direction to our efforts to understand the mechanisms underpinning aspects of positive youth development in the context of sport. It may be that internal working models of attachment are not only active but also 'open to influence' from relationships developed in the context of sport and physical activity. Future research would make an interesting contribution by exploring whether sporting relationships could offer any benefit with respect to reworking maladaptive aspects of individuals' internal models of attachment.

Coach–athlete relationships and attachment

Above I discussed the possibility that sporting relationships might have the potential to 'rework' models of attachment in the context of intervention. This idea necessitates careful consideration of (a) *how* and (b) *if* sporting relationships can be considered to possess the characteristics necessary to impact upon or rework models of attachment. Recent work in the context of coach–athlete relationships has been useful in helping us to understand that coach–athlete relationships themselves might be considered to possess some of the fundamental functions of an attachment bond.

Poczwardowski *et al.* (2006) have suggested that coach–athlete dyads are a particularly fruitful area for research in sport social relationships. Recent work (e.g. Jowett & Cockerill, 2003; Poczwardowski *et al.*, 2002; Wylleman, 2000) has put forward coach–athlete dyadic relationships as a central influence on the quality of both coaches' and athletes' experiences and sporting performance. For example, Jowett (Jowett, 2003; Jowett & Clark-Carter, 2006; Jowett & Cockerill, 2002, 2003; Jowett & Meek, 2000; Jowett & Ntoumanis, 2004) has recognised the importance of a number of critical interpersonal relationship characteristics in the coach–athlete dyad. Her '3 Cs' model (see for example Jowett, 2003; Jowett & Cockerill, 2002), integrating ideas from dyadic relationship models (e.g. Berscheid *et al.*, 1989; Kiesler, 1997; Newcomb, 1953), has identified the higher-order factors of *closeness* (including polar dimensions of *closeness* such as feelings of trust/distrust in the other, a liking/disliking of the other, feelings of attachment/isolation, feelings of respect/disrespect, and emotional closeness/emotional distance), *co-orientation* (including communicational dimensions such as self-disclosure, information exchange, shared understanding, acceptance, and connection/disconnection), and *complementarity* (including behavioural interactions such as helping transactions, instructional or emotional support, and power balance) as a fundamental way of conceptualising coach–athlete dyadic relations. Jowett's work has provided an interesting insight into how the 3Cs characterise coach–athlete dyadic relations and she has provided evidence to suggest that when the 3Cs are experienced positively the coach–athlete relationship has adaptive consequences for those involved. Negative experiences of the 3Cs have been implicated in less adaptive coach–athlete relationships (e.g. Jowett, 2003).

There has been a call from coach–athlete relationship researchers (e.g. Jowett & Wylleman, 2006) to embrace a diversity of theoretical approaches in the quest to shed further light on research questions in a complex area. However, the integration of the area with attachment theory has been slow to develop. Recently, one study was conducted that highlighted the promise for theoretical integration between attachment theory and coach–athlete relationship research. Specifically, Davis and Jowett (2010) examined athletes' perceptions of the attachment style that characterised their relationship with coaches. This was measured by adapting the Experiences in Close Relationships Scale (ECR; Brennan *et al.*, 1998) to refer specifically to coach–athlete relationships. The ECR is a self-report measure that taps two dimensions of attachment insecurity: avoidance and anxiety (low levels of both dimensions typically infer more secure attachment). The authors also checked the extent to which the coach–athlete relationships concerned were considered 'attachment bonds' by athletes through responses to an adapted version of the Components of Attachment Questionnaire (CAQ; Parish, 2000). The CAQ assesses the extent to which a specific relationship is reported to satisfy the fundamental functions of an attachment bond forwarded by adult attachment researchers (e.g. Hazan & Shaver, 1987);

proximity maintenance (when the individual feels the need to be close to the attached person), safe haven (when the attachment figure acts as a source of comfort and security), and secure base (when the attachment figure provides a secure platform from which the individual can explore outside of the relationship).

Exploring their data, the authors suggested that as the measures of central tendency for the CAQ subscales of proximity seeking, safe haven, and secure base were above the midpoint, the coach–athlete bonds could be considered as 'attachment relationships'. Subsequently, this gave them confidence to further explore how the self-reported quality of these attachment relationships (measured on the ECR) was linked to reports of satisfaction with the coach–athlete relationship and with sport in general. Results suggested that both avoidant and anxious dimensions of attachment were negatively linked to dimensions of satisfaction, with particularly strong associations identified for the avoidant dimension. The authors suggested:

> that especially avoidant athletes who have a discomfort with closeness, distrust their coach, and remain both behaviourally and emotionally disconnected with their coach may be less likely to experience satisfaction with aspects of sport and aspects of the athletic relationship. Based on this finding, it is possible that attachment avoidance presents athletes with greater levels of dysfunctionality than does anxious attachment.
>
> (Davis & Jowett, 2010, p. 127)

The above investigation provides interesting data that is encouraging with regard to the potential that attachment theory holds to enhance our understanding of coach–athlete relationship research and the potential of sporting relationships to serve as attachment bonds.

Can the coach be considered an attachment figure?

It is important to recognise that Davis and Jowett (2010) considered the coach–athlete relationship as an 'attachment bond' based upon athletes' self-reports of the relationship fulfilling the basic attachment functions tapped by the CAQ. Their data identified that the sample means for these attachment functions (assessed on a 7-point scale) were 4.44 (proximity seeking, $SD =$ 1.11), 3.87 (safe haven, $SD = 1.15$), and 5.02 (secure base, $SD = 1.13$) and this was interpreted as 'suggesting that the current sample of athletes viewed their coach as fulfilling the basic attachment functions' (p. 121). It is worth keeping in mind that such statistics suggest that athletes' responses fluctuated around the midpoint of the CAQ subscales and at first glance it seems optimistic to suggest that this reflects *strong* endorsement of attachment functions (perhaps bringing into question the extent to which the relationships can be considered attachment bonds). However, these CAQ scores compare favourably to those identified by Parish and Eagle (2003) in a study of the attachment functions satisfied by clients' relationships with their therapist over a course of long-term psychoanalytic therapy. A significant point of departure was that Parish and Eagle's (2003) investigation *also assessed* participants' CAQ ratings in relation to an identified *primary attachment figure* (in addition to ratings of the therapeutic relationship), enabling them to verify that scores in relation to the therapist were *comparable* to relationships considered by the individual to be of primary importance in attachment terms. It may be useful for future studies in coach–athlete relationship research to explore the level of satisfaction of attachment functions with the coach *in comparison* to individuals considered to be of primary importance in individuals' attachment hierarchies. This may serve to further support the argument that such relationships should be considered attachment bonds.

Furthermore, it would also be interesting to *qualitatively* explore differences relating to what individuals have in mind when they report coaches to satisfy attachment functions such as proximity seeking ('I look forward to seeing my coach'), safe haven ('I feel very safe with my coach'), and secure base ('My coach provides me with a sense of security'). It may be that when we unravel the finer details of how individuals *interpret* such statements in relation to the *coach–athlete relationship* (as opposed to their relationships with identified *primary attachment figures*) we identify distinct differences in the way they interpret the meaning of a 'sense of security' in the context of the coach–athlete relationship. This would help us to further confirm that the coach–athlete relationship is used to satisfy attachment functions in a manner that seems emotionally similar to other established attachment bonds.

My argument above centres upon the extent to which coach–athlete relationships might be considered attachment bonds. Recent lines of research in the attachment literature have shed light on the extent to which self-reports of various relationship referents as attachment figures (i.e. with measures such as the CAQ that assess reported satisfaction of basic attachment functions) seem to be mirrored by subconscious responses to threat. Maier *et al.* (2004) have outlined that subliminal priming methods make many of the unconscious processes predicted by attachment theory (such as the tendency to seek contact with attachment figures when threatened) accessible to researchers and have supported the use of such methods in attachment research. Mikulincer and his colleagues (e.g. Mikulincer *et al.*, 2000, 2002) have utilised this paradigm to investigate activation of the attachment system in adults, reasoning that detection of threat on an unconscious level should automatically heighten cognitive accessibility of thoughts related to attachment figures.

Mikulincer *et al.* (2002) argued that unconscious detection of threat should initially activate the attachment system (and hence representations of those considered to be attachment figures) in *all* humans (regardless of attachment security). This is because Bowlby (1969/1982) proposed that the attachment system serves an *innate* protective function and there are survival-related advantages to the unconscious activation of thoughts about attachment figures upon the detection of threat.

Mikulincer and his colleagues (Mikulincer *et al.*, 2000) investigated activation of the attachment system in a subliminal priming paradigm and explored how threatening and non-threatening primes were related to the cognitive accessibility of thoughts related to attachment figures. In essence, they explored whether the subliminal presentation of threat (theorised to automatically enhance individuals' sensitivity to those considered to be attachment figures) would amplify the extent to which attachment-related thoughts influenced information processing. A series of experiments focused upon the accessibility of the names of people whom participants had indicated served attachment functions through self-report measures similar to the CAQ. Specifically, they asked participants to provide the names of (a) individuals they felt served attachment functions (i.e. proximity-seeking, safe-haven, and secure-base functions), (b) individuals that were considered close but did not serve attachment functions, (c) individuals they knew but with whom they were not close, and (d) individuals that they did not know at all. Participants then completed a lexical decision task (they were required to identify whether a series of words, some of which were the names they had previously identified, that flashed onto the screen were recognisable words or nonsense letter strings) under conditions of threat or non-threat primes (prior to identifying each word or non-word participants were subliminally primed with either a threatening word such as 'failure' and 'death' or a non-threatening word such as 'hat'), with the relative accessibility of the names of attachment figures, close others, known others, and unknown others being examined. Results revealed that subliminal priming (20-ms exposure) with threat words compared to neutral words led to significantly faster identification of individuals reported to serve attachment functions. This was not the case for close others who did not serve attachment functions, known others, or unknown others, and the effect was independent of attachment style characteristics (again supporting the hypothesis that attachment system activation in the face of threat may occur in all individuals). In a further experiment, Stroop colour-naming task results revealed that individuals were slower to name the colour of the printed names of attachment figures following threat primes. Again, this effect was independent of attachment style and was not identified in the names of close others, known others, or unknown others. The researchers suggested that heightened accessibility in response to threat therefore depends upon the extent to which a person has been 'neurologically internalised' as serving attachment functions.

What is particularly interesting about such approaches to exploring attachment figures is that they enable researchers to examine the extent to which various relationship referents elicit responses that are *unconscious* indicators of attachment figure status. This is important as it provides preliminary evidence that such figures have been internalised as sources of safety and security in the face of threat. It may be that through such experimental paradigms researchers will be able to further corroborate the findings of Davis and Jowett (2010) by examining unconscious responses to representations of coaches in the context of threat primes, particularly in comparison to other significant attachment figures.

How might 'secure' coach–athlete bonds be constructed?

There are further discussions to be had and work to be done in relation to whether coach–athlete relationships can be conceptually considered to be attachment bonds. However, if such sporting relationships are to be considered attachment bonds (and if their attachment-related qualities have an influence on broader psychological and social outcomes in the context of sport) then it will befit researchers to investigate the mechanisms that might serve to bring about the development of secure attachment relationships in the context of the coach–athlete bond. Recent work in the coach–athlete relationship literature may help to shed light on such issues. For example, Lorimer and Jowett (2009) examined the empathic accuracy of coach–athlete dyads from a selection of team and individual sports. Their study was grounded on the assumption that getting empathically alongside athletes and understanding 'what makes them tick' is often cited as one of the most critical elements of the coaching process (Jones & Cassidy, 2004; Jones *et al.*, 2004). Accordingly, Lorimer and Jowett (2009) video-recorded the unstructured dyadic interactions between coach–athlete dyads over the course of a typical training session and asked members of each dyad to independently report on what both they and their partner had been thinking and feeling during the array of interactions that had taken place. Interesting findings included the fact that coaches of athletes in individual sports were more empathically accurate in their perceptions of athletes' thoughts and feelings than coaches of athletes in team sports. Furthermore, increased length of training sessions was also found to increase coaches' sense of empathic accuracy with regard to their athletes.

The above findings raise interesting points for discussion in relation to whether or not issues such as empathic accuracy might be important ingredients in the construction of a more *secure* coach–athlete relationship. As discussed earlier in this chapter, the attachment literature has highlighted issues such as *empathic concern* and *perspective-taking* to be central features in the construction of secure attachment relationships (e.g. Britton & Fuendeling, 2005; Reti *et al.*, 2002) and it may be that coaches who are able to draw upon such psychological resources in the context of the coach–athlete bond are more likely to facilitate the development of attachment security within the relationship. Furthermore, confirmation of this above argument would also bring about discussions of the personal and environmental factors that might predispose individual dyads to variation in relation to factors such as empathic accuracy. To this end, researchers might look to constructs such as attachment styles of dyad members to help explain such variation. For example, in the attachment literature there has been evidence that adult attachment styles predispose individuals to differing degrees of accuracy in terms of their emotional perception. Feeney *et al.* (1994a) identified that males with insecure self-reported attachment styles were less likely to emotionally decode their romantic partner's non-verbal behaviour in a naturalistic setting. Furthermore, Kafetsios (2000) employed both laboratory and naturalistic assessments to explore the relationship between self-reported attachment style and the recognition of emotion in partners' facial expressions. Results identified that secure attachment style was positively related to such emotional accuracy. Such findings hint at the existence of attachment style differences in relation to important perceptual abilities that are likely to underpin empathic accuracy in coach–athlete dyads. It will be interesting to explore whether the existence of empathic accuracy in coach–athlete dyads (a) is predicted by the existing attachment characteristics of dyad members, and (b) leads to the construction of more or less secure contextual attachment relationships. Such research would also provide important information about how pre-existing attachment styles are inevitably involved in the construction of context-specific attachment bonds in relationships such as coach–athlete dyads.

Such issues are likely to be more complex than the above paragraph suggests. Simpson *et al.* (1999) have outlined how the notion of empathic accuracy itself has very different connotations in the minds of those with differing attachment styles – particularly insecure-anxious individuals. Bowlby (1973) predicted that ultimately insecure-anxious individuals 'have no confidence that [attachment figures] will ever be truly available and dependable. Through their eyes the world is seen as comfortless and unpredictable' (p. 204). In response to such chronic uncertainty, such individuals have been proposed (a) to develop heightened and easily activated attachment behaviour (particularly in situations where there is perceived inaccessibility to attachment figures), (b) to closely monitor their attachment figure and any signs that will help them gain information about the likelihood of his/her proximity and availability in the future, and (c) as a result of (a) and (b) above, to be less psychologically available to focus resources on task engagement and pursuit in the short and long term. In relation to constructs such as empathic accuracy, Simpson *et al.* (1999) identified that insecure-anxious individuals were more likely to display greater empathic accuracy (they were acutely sensitive to and aware of their partner's emotional state, particularly to potential cues related to interpersonal rejection) and also to be emotionally and psychologically destabilised by negative cues they detected. In the context of the coach–athlete relationship these arguments raise important questions such as (a) whether insecure-anxious individuals might be ultimately hindered (because they allocate psychological resources away from performance) in the sporting context by hyperactive empathic judgement, (b) whether such individuals' empathic accuracy is biased towards information that links to their concern with potential rejection, and (c) how such individuals ultimately interpret and manage the emotional fall-out that results from their empathic judgements. These sorts of questions will have important implications for the functioning of coach–athlete dyads and for the broader development of athletes in psychological and performance contexts.

Conclusion

This chapter sought to review and discuss the literature that has begun to explore the interface between attachment theory and social relationships in the context of sport. Two bodies of developing literature were discussed, focusing upon sporting friendships and the coach–athlete relationship. Both bodies of literature provide an initial suggestion that attachment theory is likely to enhance our understanding of sporting relationships. However, one of the most significant points to note is that the two emerging bodies of research adopt different approaches to their use of attachment theory. My work on attachment and sport friendships (e.g. Carr, 2009a, 2009b; Carr & Fitzpatrick, 2011) views indicators of attachment security in the adolescent-parent attachment bond as a likely *reflection* of adolescents' internal organisation in relation to attachment. This assumption is based on attachment theorists' (e.g. George *et al.*, 1985, 1996; Main & Goldwyn, 1998; Main *et al.*, 1985) argument that particular importance should be afforded to childhood relationships with *parents* in regulating adolescent and adult states of mind in relation to attachment. Subsequently, I have sought to explore the extent to which these parental attachment characteristics seem to overlap with the close friendships that unfold in the context of sport. It should be noted that I have not specifically considered sport friendships *themselves* to be attachment bonds (although this does not preclude the idea that they could be). Kobak (1994) has outlined that while it is highly likely that individuals will enter new relationships equipped with *pre-existing* working models that will influence how the relationship plays out, it is also important not to neglect the fact that new relationships may well serve to 'update' and 'rework' this internal organisation. This idea fits with Bowlby's suggestion that working models are controlled and modified with experience. One might expect, with more sophisticated levels of cognitive development and a wider array of relationships, that individuals develop flexibility with respect to how internal models are employed and differentiated in various relationships. It will be interesting for researchers to explore the extent to which sporting friendships are involved in a reciprocal 'reworking' of individuals' internal organisation in relation to attachment. This will likely require the use of more sophisticated research designs that move beyond cross-sectional examination.

In contrast to my approach, Davis and Jowett's (2010) work in the context of coach–athlete relationships has been less concerned with tapping into the working models that coaches and athletes 'bring with them' to the sporting context. Rather, they have conceptualised the coach–athlete relationship itself as an attachment bond in its own right, providing evidence that the attachment characteristics of this single relationship are likely to underpin significant contextual responses. However, because more general internal organisations in relation to attachment were not assessed outside of the context of the coach–athlete relationship it is difficult to be certain whether the attachment characteristics of this relationship are a product of the specific relationship interactions alone or of broader internal working models individuals had previously developed. Again, further research is needed in order to unravel these complexities.

The initial research in the domain of attachment theory and sport relationships is encouraging and will hopefully stimulate new developments and understanding in relation to the complexities inherent in the social aspect of sport involvement. However, it should also be noted that this research has been heavily allied to the self-report tradition situated in the social psychological school of thought. Further developments in this field are encouraged to embrace other methodological and paradigmatic stances.

Note

1 In this sentence I take 'friendship' to refer to a deeper and more intimate connection and 'peer relationships' to refer to more superficial interactions which have lesser affective ties (Newcomb & Bagwell, 1995).

7 Attachment, exercise, and health

Introduction

Repetti *et al.* (2002) have suggested that while 'good health begins early in life … poor health also begins early in life' (p. 330). In support of this, the attachment literature suggests that individuals' fundamental familial relationships help to construct a sense of emotional security and psychological well-being that will ultimately enable them to acquire behaviours that help to effectively self-regulate mental and physical health as independence from caregivers is attained. This chapter discusses the interface between attachment theory, mental and physical health, and exercise. It begins by exploring the general links between attachment and mental and physical health and then discusses potential links with exercise.

Attachment and mental health

There is ample evidence in the literature that emotional nurturance in relation to central familial caregivers is independently associated with mental health. Repetti *et al.*'s (2002) influential review identified that critical aspects of caregiver relationships such as emotional neglect, unresponsive or rejecting parenting, lack of parental availability, warmth, and support, and children's feelings of a lack of acceptance have all been linked both to internalised mental health problems such as anxiety disorders, depression, and suicide risk (e.g. Chorpita & Barlow, 1998; Kaslow *et al.*, 1994) and to externalised issues such as aggressive, hostile behaviour and delinquency (e.g. Barber, 1996; Rothbaum & Weisz, 1994).

Researchers have interpreted and explained specific links between attachment characteristics and mental health in accordance with the underpinning school of thought in relation to the measurement and conceptualisation of attachment they employ (as discussed in Chapter 2). For example, Cole-Detke and Kobak (1996) used Main's (1990) model of attachment and the AAI assessment method to explore the links between attachment and eating disorders. Accordingly, these researchers looked to psychodynamic and clinical explanations for identified association. Conceptually, it was suggested that insecure-dismissing individuals tend to perceive attachment figures as ignoring or rejecting of their attachment signals. Subsequently, such individuals develop defensive strategies that centre on *deactivation* of the attachment system by actively diverting their attention away from attachment cues and dampening their outward expression of distress (Main, 1990). Such defensive strategies are designed to reduce potential conflict with attachment figures. However, the intra-psychic conflict that such individuals face is related to the fact that their goal of gaining access to attachment figures is biologically determined (and in some senses inescapable) and while their attempts to deactivate the attachment system are in some senses adaptive, disengagement from this biological goal can never be fully accomplished (Main, 1990). Hence, there may be subsequent distortion or subconscious transformation of the suppressed attachment desires. In some individuals this transformation may be expressed in the form of an eating disorder. For example, research has identified that bulimic females recall relationships with paternal caregivers as lacking in care, warmth, and emotional acceptance, leaving them feeling that they had failed their fathers and frustrating their instinctive attachment-related needs in relation to him (Becker *et al.*, 1987; Steiger *et al.*, 1989). It is hypothesised that while such daughters may deactivate their efforts to meet their attachment needs from their fathers they are subconsciously diverting their attention towards the improvement of their physical appearance in an effort to enhance their acceptability to him. Cole-Detke and Kobak (1996) have suggested that 'ironically, these daughters may be trying to improve the father–daughter relationship by deactivating the attachment system and focusing on appearance' (p. 288).

An interesting paper in the clinical literature explored attachment states of mind as measured by the AAI in samples of non-psychotic inpatients and matched controls. Specifically, Fonagy *et al.* (1996) were interested in how individuals' attachment classification in relation to their AAI narratives related to their mental health status with respect to Axis I (e.g. depression, anxiety disorders, anorexia nervosa) and Axis II (e.g. borderline personality disorder) disorders in the DSM-III manual. In addition to paying attention to the predominant AAI categories outlined in Chapter 2 of this book, the researchers also paid attention to issues such as sub-classification of the insecure-preoccupied interviews (i.e. a distinction can be made in the AAI between a *fearful* or an *angry* preoccupation with childhood experiences). Furthermore, distinctions were also made in relation to whether individuals appear to have *resolved* their negative feelings in relation to mourning or loss of attachment figures and traumatic events and incidents that formed part of their childhood. Data suggested that psychiatric patients could be readily distinguished from their matched counterparts as a function of the qualitative differences inherent in their AAI narratives. For example, there were clear and distinct patterns of difference that included psychiatric patients exhibiting obviously lower levels of recalled positive experiences (e.g. of parental love and non-rejection) and positive states of mind during recollection (a coherent narrative and transcript) coupled with higher levels of recalled negative experience (e.g. parental neglect and rejection) and states of mind (incoherent and emotionally charged narratives). For example, depressed patients consistently reported lower expectations of their attachment figures, lower idealisation of these figures during childhood, and higher levels of unresolved anger in relation to childhood attachment experiences with them. This is consistent with classic psychodynamic explanation for depression, which views it as unresolved anger with attachment figures which is ultimately turned against the self. The researchers concluded that their data provide 'overwhelming support for the association of psychiatric disorder with unresolved difficult early relationships, in line with the predictions of attachment theory' (Bowlby, 1980, 1988; Fonagy *et al.*, 1996, p. 28).

Outside of the psychodynamic literature the social psychological school of thought has also provided compelling evidence in favour of an association between attachment and mental health. Bifulco and her colleagues (e.g. Bifulco *et al.*, 2002a, 2002b) have explored the relation between attachment styles identified using the ASI (see Chapter 2 for a brief description of this interview) and clinical depression. Results from a large-scale study of GP patients from the UK identified a positive association between all of the various types of insecure attachment styles identified by the ASI (i.e. insecure-enmeshed, fearful, angry-dismissive, and withdrawn-avoidant) and depression over a 12-month period. However, the researchers also identified that differentiating the *various forms* of insecure attachment provides useful information about the level of risk associated with 12-month depression. Specifically, while all insecure individuals carried greater risk of depression, *insecure angry-dismissive* individuals (i.e. a type of insecurity where individuals use anger and hostility as a general style for dismissing others in attachment relationships) showed the highest level of risk. Again, the researchers argued that such anger has been hypothesised to underpin experiences of helplessness and guilt in relation to earlier experiences of attachment relationships and forms a central feature of such individuals' feelings in relation to attachment figures. It therefore surfaces when new attachment relationships form during adulthood and tends to characterise individuals' feelings and behaviour in the context of such relations. This finding tends to support Fonagy *et al.*'s (1996) work with the AAI and psychiatric patients described above. As Bifulco *et al.* (2002a) suggest, Bowlby identified 'functional' anger (i.e. anger expressed with the purpose of maintaining the bond when the close other has been neglectful or inattentive) and 'dysfunctional' anger (i.e. the principal aim of which is malice or revenge) in the context of attachment bonds. The latter was suggested to become so intense and persistent that it often alienates the close other and is destructive in the context of the attachment bond (Bowlby 1973). Insecure angry-dismissive individuals in the context of the ASI are thought to experience heightened levels of such anger as a central feature of their attachment relationships.

In the self-report tradition, Birnbaum *et al.* (1997) examined the relationship between self-reported attachment styles (e.g. secure, avoidant, anxious-ambivalent) and individuals' self-reported mental health (i.e. anxiety, depression, behavioural control, positive affect) in samples of individuals who were either married or undergoing legal proceedings for divorce. Results identified that divorcing participants reported greater levels of mental distress than married ones. However, this effect was only found to be the case for individuals with avoidant or anxious-ambivalent attachment styles. There was no difference in mental distress between married and divorcing participants with a secure attachment style. The researchers further identified that this effect was likely explainable through differences in appraisal and coping mechanisms that securely and insecurely attached individuals employ during crises such as divorce proceedings.

Attachment and physical health

There has also been a large body of literature in support of the notion that attachment experiences are also linked to individuals' physical health status. For example, Felitti *et al.* (1998) studied a large sample of over 13,000 adults and identified that exposure to a dysfunctional family environment during childhood was linked to an increased risk of heart disease, chronic lung disease, cancer, skeletal fractures, and liver disease in adulthood. Furthermore, Orth-Gomer *et al.* (1993) identified that the self-reported levels of emotional support from attachment figures in a longitudinal study of over 700 Swedish men were associated with incidence of coronary heart disease. Specifically, men who went on to contract coronary heart disease over a six-year period were less likely to have reported a positive quality of emotional support from their attachment figures. Longitudinal and follow-up designs have provided evidence to indicate that deficient nurturing experiences during childhood, characterised by neglecting and rejecting parents, are associated with an array of physical health problems, including higher levels of physical complaints and general illness several years later (e.g. Gottman *et al.*, 1996) and obesity in early adulthood (e.g. Lissau & Sorensen, 1994).

It is interesting to speculate as to why attachment-related characteristics would be significantly linked to physical health. It is far beyond the scope of this chapter to thoroughly review such literature. However, in this section I offer a brief discussion of hypotheses that have been put forward in relation to this issue. Previous studies have explored the intriguing possibility that socialisation experiences have significant physiological influences that are linked to physical health status. For example, laboratory studies have identified links between dysfunction of the immune system and variables such as loneliness (e.g. Glaser *et al.*, 1985), bereavement (e.g. Irwin *et al.*, 1987), and relationship conflict (e.g. Kiecolt-Glaser *et al.*, 1993). Accordingly, Repetti *et al.* (2002) have suggested that much of the risk that early family experiences cause in relation to physical health can be explained in the development of dysfunctional biological responses in relation to stress. It is argued that the effects of such dysfunctional biological responses are likely to be cumulative over the course of the lifespan, which may explain why a number of the negative physical health effects are not experienced until many years later.

One hypothesis has centred on differences in sympathetic-adrenomedullary (SAM) functioning in children who are exposed to less supportive or unloving family experiences. For example, Repetti *et al.* (2002) have suggested that repeated exposure to stress in the context of the family environment may lead to chronic SAM activation in children, which in turn may produce higher levels of cumulative stress or wear and tear on the cardiovascular system. In support of this hypothesis, Woodall and Matthews (1989) identified that boys from families who were less loving and supportive exhibited stronger heart rate responses to laboratory-induced stressors than boys from supportive, loving family backgrounds.

A second hypothesis has focused upon the serotonergic system. Specifically, dysfunction in the serotonergic system has been associated with an array of health issues such as depression, anxiety, suicide, and even substance abuse. The most promising lines of research that have linked deficiencies in nurturing experiences to serotonergic dysfunction have been found in the literature on primates. For example, studies have identified that monkeys raised in unloving, cold rearing conditions develop long-term differences in relation to their serotonergic functioning (e.g. Kraemer & Clarke, 1990). Furthermore, in some fascinating work Suomi (1991, 1997) has identified that maternal care may even moderate the effects of genetics on serotonergic function. Specifically, Suomi (1999) compared monkeys with two forms of the 5-HTT allele – a specific gene related to serotonin transport (the short form of the allele relates to decreased serotonergic functioning and the long form to normal functioning). Monkeys were either raised by their peers (a factor that has consistently been shown to lead to anti-social and aggressive long-term behaviour in monkeys) or their mothers. Results identified that in monkeys raised by their peers those with the short form of the 5-HTT allele developed serotonergic and behavioural dysfunction whereas those with the long form developed normally in both respects. In monkeys raised by their mothers, those with the short form of the allele did not develop abnormally (in terms of serotonergic function or behaviourally), suggesting that maternal care had somehow prevented genetic expression of this biological deficit.

Attachment and health behaviour

A final important correlate of attachment in the health literature has been its relationship with health behaviour. For example, in a longitudinal study of young children, Lewis *et al.* (1984) identified that boys who had been identified as insecure (either anxious or ambivalent) at 12 months were more likely to present with somatic physical complaints at age 6 years than boys who had been classified as securely attached. Furthermore, Tonge (1994) outlined how children with separation anxiety are more likely to present with somatic symptoms that are medically unexplainable. Such data are interesting and point to theoretical possibilities suggesting that insecurely attached children may (a) be hyper-aware of bodily sensations that are both medically significant or benign, (b) be overly threatened by such bodily sensations, (c) appraise illness per se as more threatening, and (d) appraise themselves as less able to cope with the threat of illness. In adult samples Hazan and Shaver (1990) have also linked insecure attachment styles to higher levels of psychosomatic complaints and physical illness.

Scharfe and Eldredge (2001) hypothesised that attachment would be conceptually likely to underpin individuals' (college students') health behaviour for a number of reasons. For example, they argued that Bowlby (1973) proposed securely attached individuals (as a result of their exposure to positive care experiences) as more likely to view the self as *worthy of care* and also to think of *others* as willing and able to care for them. Accordingly, such internal representations are more likely to result in secure individuals (a) being more willing to care for themselves and (b) possessing a greater expectation of care from others. Translating such assumptions into the domain of physical health, Scharfe and Eldredge (2001) hypothesised that secure individuals may therefore be prone to lead more healthy lifestyles and to be psychologically suited to caring for the self. Insecure individuals were thought more likely to engage in unhealthy behaviours. Specifically, the researchers aimed to test the hypothesis 'that individuals of differing attachment patterns attend to their health in much the same way as they attend to their relationships' (p. 297), suggesting that securely attached individuals would be more likely to engage in health promoting behaviours and avoid risky behaviours. Insecurely attached individuals were hypothesised to be more likely to engage in risky behaviours and less likely to be concerned with health promotion.

Scharfe and Eldredge's (2001) results revealed some interesting findings. It is important to note that they employed a four-category attachment style model assessed through self-report measures (i.e. secure, fearful-avoidant, dismissive-avoidant, anxious-ambivalent; see Chapter 2). First, they supported their general hypotheses by identifying main effects for secure attachment on health *promotion* behaviours (e.g. exercise, good eating habits, dental care, and good hygiene) with higher attachment security predicting more positive health promotion. There was also positive association between insecure fearful-avoidant attachment and health *risk* behaviours (e.g. lack of exercise, drug taking, excessive alcohol consumption, poor dietary habits). Such findings support the contention that attachment variables may reflect important personality constructs when seeking to understand health behaviour.

However, a more powerful effect also emerged in relation to an interaction between romantic relationship status (single versus committed) and attachment scores. Specifically, there was a significant interaction between levels of attachment security and relationship status, with secure attachment being *negatively* related to *risky* health behaviour in individuals who were in committed relationships but *positively* related to health risk behaviour in single individuals. The researchers explained this interaction by suggesting that single college students with high levels of secure attachment are likely to expose themselves to significant risks in the typical college environment (i.e. an environment where drugs, alcohol, and sex are perhaps more freely available) because they deploy their high levels of social confidence towards building the supportive social relationships they need and desire on the college campus. This may well mean they are *more* likely to expose themselves to health risks than secure individuals who are part of a committed romantic relationship. However, there was also evidence that they were exposing themselves to risky health behaviours safely. For example, for single participants, security was associated with a higher number of casual sex encounters but also with a higher level of condom use. This suggested that although such individuals were more likely to engage in multiple sexual encounters they were also more likely to do so safely. It is interesting to speculate as to whether secure attachment would predict such sensible measures in the context of other potentially risky health behaviours.

Exercise

In the section that follows I seek to briefly review the literature in relation to exercise and public health. Subsequently, I discuss some of the interesting implications that arise when considering the interface between attachment literature and exercise.

Exercise and health

Public health policies now advance scientifically supported guidelines and campaigning in relation to important health-related behaviours such as tobacco consumption and diet. Researchers have suggested that if such guidelines were widely and consistently adopted then there is little doubt that they would result in a significant reduction in some of the major threats to contemporary public health such as cancer and heart disease (Friedenreich & Orenstein, 2002). Similarly, there is an escalating body of literature linked to the protective effect of a physically active lifestyle in relation to major public health threats. For example, in relation to cancer Thune and Furberg (2001) suggested that 'Even a small protective effect of physical activity on cancer risk may be of considerable importance for public health as the population ages and a sedentary lifestyle increases worldwide' (p. S535). Meta-analyses provide support for a protective effect:

> The evidence for a beneficial effect of physical activity on cancer incidence is accumulating rapidly and can be classified as 'convincing' for colon and breast and 'probable' for prostate [cancer].
> (Friedenreich & Orenstein, 2002, p. 3461S)

Physical activity has also been linked to protection from forms of dementia associated with the ageing process. For example, Rovio *et al.*'s (2005) longitudinal examination of a large sample of participants through middle age and into old age revealed that a higher level of physical activity at middle age was associated with a decreased risk of dementia and Alzheimer's disease in later life, especially among genetically susceptible individuals. Lautenschlager *et al.* (2008) conducted a randomised control trial on a sample of elderly individuals with initial memory problems and identified that those assigned to a home-based physical activity programme demonstrated improved Alzheimer's-related cognitive function scores over the course of the study in comparison to a control group. Recent reviews of the literature in relation to physical activity and forms of dementia have suggested that there is 'enough evidence to support the hypothesis that an active and socially integrated lifestyle seems to protect against Alzheimer's disease and dementia' (Fratiglioni *et al.*, 2004, p. 351).

Additionally, the literature related to physical activity and mental health (see Biddle, 2000 for a review) also suggests that a physically active lifestyle is associated with a wealth of important outcome variables related to mental health. For example, Hassmen *et al.* (2000) identified that individuals who exercised between two and three times a week experienced significantly less depression, anger, and stress than those who exercised less frequently or not at all. Schmitz *et al.* (2004) studied health-related quality of life and physical activity in the German National Health Interview and Examination Survey from 1997 to 1999 and identified that physical activity was associated with higher health-related quality of life in people who suffered from affective, anxiety, and substance dependent disorders. Examining 11 clinical intervention studies, Stathopoulou *et al.* (2006) identified a large combined effect size in relation to the efficacy of exercise as a treatment for depression in comparison to control conditions. The researchers concluded that 'exercise can be a powerful intervention for clinical depression' (p. 188).

Hence, the evidence in favour of the health-related benefits linked to a physically active lifestyle is accumulating rapidly. Significant questions remain open for investigation, such as issues related to physical activity dosage, mediating and moderating variables, and investigation of the specific mechanisms underlying the effects of physical activity on important outcome variables. Additionally, researchers (e.g. Haskell *et al.*, 2007) have also suggested that the majority of the population does not meet recommended guidelines for physical activity, prompting researchers to investigate how behaviour change occurs and how it is maintained. Exploring the potential role of attachment in the development of the exercise literature may be a useful development.

Exercise as a moderator

Attachment security has been put forward as a significant personality factor that has the potential to impact health-related variables (Feeney, 2000;

Scharfe & Eldredge, 2001). If attachment as an individual difference factor is likely to predispose individuals to different quality experiences in relation to health behaviour and the broader condition of their physical and mental health then it will be important to identify whether particular lifestyle factors serve to moderate such effects. In their discussion of exercise, personality, mental and physical health De Moor *et al.* (2006) suggested that one method by which exercise might exert its influence on mental and physical health is by moderating the effects of personality.

From a neurophysiological perspective there are various reasons to suggest that exercise might offer a protective effect that would counter the biological dysfunction that has been hypothesised to increase the likelihood that individuals with insecure attachment histories will experience both physical and mental health problems. For example, in the sections above I discussed the hypothesis (Repetti *et al.*, 2002) that increased experiences of attachment-related distress in insecure individuals may be related to the development of a chronically overactive SAM that may, over time, result in cumulative damage to important bodily systems. The physiological literature has provided interesting data to suggest that exercise may offer protective effects in this regard. For example, laboratory studies have identified that experimentally induced chronic social and physical stress in rats is significantly linked to excessive SAM functioning that seems to have particularly detrimental effects on factors such as blood pressure (e.g. Mormede, 1997). However, exercise seems to blunt these detrimental effects. Cox *et al.* (1985) conducted a study with a sample of rats that were engineered to exhibit borderline hypertension in the laboratory environment. They identified that daily exposure to stress (the threat of electric shock treatment) over a long-term period resulted in significant hypertension and related irreversible damage to the rats' major organs and blood pressure. However, such stress-induced damage (that was hypothesised to result partially from chronic overreaction of the SAM induced by stress exposure) was blunted when the daily stress that the rats experienced was supplemented by daily physical exercise in the form of swimming. Such findings offer interesting physiological evidence that physical activity might attenuate the damage that has been linked to a stress-induced overactive SAM.

Additionally, the exercise literature is replete with studies supporting the suggestion that physical activity seems to offer anti-depressive effects in patients with mild to moderate forms of depressive illness (e.g. De Moor *et al.*, 2006; Doyne *et al.*, 1983; Freemont & Craighead, 1987; Martinsen, 1990; Martinsen *et al.*, 1985) and there have been animal studies to suggest that exercise is associated with positive benefits to the serotonergic system (e.g. Brown *et al.*, 1979; Dey, 1994; Dey *et al.*, 1992). Furthermore, many of the important psychological factors that have been positively associated with secure attachment and negatively linked to insecurity, such as self-esteem (Griffin & Bartholomew, 1994) and self-concept (Mikulincer, 1995), have also been linked to exercise (e.g. Ekeland *et al.*, 2005; Fox, 1992; Gruber,

1986). Hence, there is reason to believe that exercise is a lifestyle factor that has the potential to influence many of the neuro-physiological and psychological systems that have also been linked to individuals' attachment characteristics. This makes exercise an important candidate for the role of an environmental buffer of the potential negative effects of insecure attachment on aspects of health.

There is a wealth of exciting potential for future research to investigate such hypotheses. For example, it will be important to explore the *mechanisms* by which exercise might buffer some of the potential negative concomitants of insecure attachment characteristics. Ford and Collins (2010) have provided interesting recent evidence that factors such as self-esteem may play a significant role in moderating both psychological and physiological responses to stressful social experiences. Specifically, they argued that stressful social experiences (e.g. rejection, loss) are likely to evoke physiological (e.g. hypothalamic-pituitary-adrenal and SAM responses, which trigger the release of a cascade of stress hormones) and psychological (e.g. anxiety, loss of control, impaired self-regulation) responses and patterns that have developed in order to assist optimal response to such threat. The attachment literature (as has been discussed) suggests that such responses are likely to be more sensitive and potentially chronic in individuals with insecure attachment histories. Ford and Collins (2010) identified in an experimental investigation of college students exposed to experiences of rejection that self-esteem may be a critical moderator of stress responses in such situations. They identified that students with higher self-esteem exhibited lower levels of negative self-appraisal, self-blaming, physiological stress hormone responses, and derogation of the rejecting individual than students with lower self-esteem. One explanation the researchers offered for their findings was that self-esteem may calibrate the threshold individuals use to detect negative or threatening social situations that would activate their instinctive physiological and psychological threat responses. Accordingly, it is interesting to speculate as to whether interventions targeting self-esteem enhancement would result in more positive responses to stress in individuals theoretically prone to chronically overactive stress response systems (i.e. individuals with particular attachment histories). Furthermore, it would be interesting to explore whether exercise could offer a potential route to such self-esteem alteration in such individuals or whether exercise targets self-esteem in a different manner.

Attachment characteristics as an indirect influence on exercise behaviour

De Moor *et al.* (2006) have also suggested that an additional plausible scenario is that personality variables such as attachment history may well exert both direct and indirect influences on exercise behaviour through multiple means. This is also an important consideration and it may be useful to explore the specific mechanisms by which such an influence might be exerted. In the sections that follow I offer some thoughts on these issues and discuss how attachment characteristics might be theorised to underpin important variables linked to exercise behaviour.

Role modelling

Parental and peer influence have been explored in the sport, exercise, and health literature in a number of ways. From one perspective, there have been investigations exploring a *role modelling* hypothesis, suggesting that children *reproduce* their parents' or peers' behaviours via mechanisms central to social learning (e.g. Bandura, 1986). Support for this hypothesis has been mixed. Some studies have supported a correlation between parent/peer levels of physical activity (e.g. Bois *et al.*, 2005; Freedson & Evenson, 1991; Moore *et al.*, 1991; Vilhjalmsson & Thorlindsson, 1998) or health behaviour (e.g. Barnes & Welte, 1986; Krohn *et al.*, 1985) and those of the child, whereas others have provided no support for a link (Brustad, 1993; Dempsey *et al.*, 1993; Jago *et al.*, 2010; Kimiecik & Horn, 1998). Bois *et al.* (2005) have suggested that much of the inconsistency in the literature can be attributed to methodological differences between studies (e.g. studies have relied upon objective activity data, children's self-reports, and parents' self-reports as indicators of activity levels) and this seems a plausible explanation. For example, Gustafson and Rhodes (2006) reviewed 24 studies investigating the parental role modelling hypothesis and found that in 18 studies the methods used were not objective measures of child and parent physical activity and in 12 studies the methods employed did not even report the validity of physical activity assessment methods employed.

However, additional explanations exist for the lack of a consistently identified association between the physical activity levels of young people and their parents or peers. One explanation that has been put forward is the suggestion that role modelling in relation to physical activity is likely to be heavily dependent upon the specific quality of the peer or parental relationship in question. From this perspective, it is unwise to assume that because a relationship is parental- or peer-based it will necessarily follow that youngsters will be inclined to model the physical activity or health-related behaviours of the significant other. For example, Vilhjalmsson and Thorlindsson's (1998) study of over 1,000 Icelandic adolescents suggested that role modelling in relation to physical activity behaviour was dependent upon the degree of emotional closeness that adolescents reported with the relationship referent concerned. Specifically, adolescents' physical activity behaviour was more likely to correlate with a significant other when they reported a higher degree of emotional closeness to them. Vilhjalmsson and Thorlindsson's (1998) study supports earlier work in a health behaviour context. Foshee and Bauman (1992) identified that for adolescents with a parent who smokes, smoking behaviour increases as attachment to that parent increases, whereas for adolescents with a parent who does not smoke, smoking decreases as attachment to that parent increases. In short, role modelling of health behaviours in adolescents was more likely when the relationship between the parties was an emotionally close attachment. Such findings support Bandura's (Bandura & Walters, 1963) initial predictions that modelling is likely to be dependent upon the quality of the relationship within which it takes place.

Future work in the field of sport, exercise, and health would make a useful contribution to the literature by further examining the extent to which attachment characteristics within a given relationship predict the likelihood of social learning or modelling in relation to positive and negative health behaviours. The above reported studies were hindered by relatively crude assessments of whether the relationships were considered to be 'attachment' bonds (i.e. they relied on single-item assessments of emotional closeness and feelings of attachment to the other) and future work might be advised to employ a more thorough assessment of whether a relationship should be considered an attachment bond using developments in the attachment literature. For example, Mikulincer *et al.*'s (2002) investigation identified attachment figures using the WHOTO (and inventory to assess the attachment functions of significant others, it is called the WHOTO because of the frequency of references to 'who to' in the items; Fraley & Davis, 1997). Participants were asked to list the names of individuals they felt best served the attachment-related functions of proximity seeking (e.g. 'Who is the person you most like to spend time with?'), safe haven (e.g. 'Who is the person you would count on for advice?'), and secure base (e.g. 'Who is the person you can always count on?'). Alternatively, attachment figures have also been differentiated in accordance with their place in an *attachment hierarchy* (e.g. Ainsworth, 1982; Kobak, 1994; Kobak *et al.*, 2007; Main *et al.*, 1985), a collection of others that are consciously looked to to fulfil attachment needs yet are arranged in a clear preferential order with regard to the pervasiveness of the attachment functions they serve or with whom the individual would most like to meet his or her attachment needs (Trinke, 1995; Trinke & Bartholomew, 1997). Such distinctions have been captured using measurement tools such as the Attachment Network Questionnaire (Trinke & Bartholomew, 1997). It would be interesting to explore the relationship between the attachment-related quality of a given relationship and the likelihood of health-related modelling.

Relationships with exercise and health providers

In the context of adherence to exercise and health-related behavioural change interventions, researchers have suggested that one of the most significant factors is the level of interpersonal support and communication individuals receive. Such support may come from a number of sources (e.g. health care provider, home, fellow participants) and also may be emotional, instructional, or informational in nature (Culos-Reed *et al.*, 2000). In a discussion of the particular significance of the practitioner–patient relationship during health behaviour change programmes, Culos-Reed *et al.* (2000) suggested that this relationship has the potential to enhance individuals' adherence to behavioural interventions by allowing individuals to develop (a) a sense of collaboration with the provider whereby they develop a feeling that they have a 'partner' with whom they are able to solve problems and work through worries or concerns, and (b) a feeling that they are supported as they progress through the intervention.

In the health literature attachment theory has provided a framework for a small body of work to explore the relationship between attachment characteristics and individuals' relationships with health providers. For example, Ciechanowski *et al.* (2001) examined adherence to diabetic self-management regimens in the context of a four-category model of attachment (i.e. self-reported levels of secure, fearful-avoidant, dismissive-avoidant, and anxious-ambivalent attachment styles). Specifically, they reasoned patients' levels of satisfaction and participation in the patient–provider relationship could be understood in the context of their working model of attachment. It was hypothesised that insecure dismissive-avoidant individuals (who have experienced consistently rejecting and emotionally unresponsive early childhoods and have subsequently become compulsively 'self-reliant' with a 'negative view of others') would possess mental characteristics particularly incompatible with a collaborative patient–provider relationship during the course of diabetic self-management regimens and would as such be more likely to exhibit poor adherence. Data supported this hypothesis with dismissing individuals demonstrating poorer levels of glucose control over the course of the investigation in comparison to other attachment styles. Furthermore, the researchers also identified that the poor adherence to diabetes self-management in these dismissing individuals could be attenuated when care providers were reported to exhibit particularly strong communication skills, suggesting that there may be important skills that care providers can employ that will offset the negative impact that patients with dismissive models of attachment can bring to the adherence process. It will be important for research in the context of exercise to examine whether provider–client relationships follow similar patterns in relation to attachment characteristics.

Exercise and cohesion

Chapter 4 of this book discussed some of the potential links that attachment theory might have with group cohesion. The exercise literature has provided evidence that cohesion is significantly linked to exercise behaviour. For example, Fraser and Spink (2002) examined group cohesion, social support, and exercise compliance in a sample of women involved in a clinical exercise group (i.e. they had been referred by healthcare professionals to participate in the group to attenuate high risk of illness or to rehabilitate following illness). Results suggested that higher scores on the support provision 'reliable alliance' (i.e. the perception that one has a reliable alliance with one's fellow group members) and higher perceptions of the cohesion dimension 'individual attraction to the group-task' (i.e. individuals' perceptions of *personal involvement with and attraction to* the group in relation to *task cohesion*) were associated with attendance at a higher proportion of classes. With respect to cohesion, the researchers argued that they likely identified a dimension of task cohesion (as opposed to social cohesion) to be related to compliance as participants had been explicitly instructed to exercise for health reasons and this objective was potentially more salient than social reasons. Furthermore, both cohesion and social support factors made independent contributions to the prediction of compliance, suggesting unique influences on the outcome variable.

A study by Midtgaard *et al.* (2006) also explored group cohesion in a sample of Danish cancer patients involved in group exercise programmes. Exercise has been highlighted as a significant factor in improvement of cancer patients' physical performance (e.g. Segal *et al.*, 2001) and quality of life (e.g. Courneya & Friedenreich, 1999). Longitudinal qualitative data throughout the programme identified that the development of group cohesion during the course of the programme enabled patients to develop alternative forms of motivation for their involvement in the group (i.e. at the beginning they were very task oriented but developed stronger social incentives as cohesion increased), to escape their worries and concerns about cancer as they began to genuinely enjoy being part of the group, and to obtain valuable support from others in the group as cohesion developed and they constructed genuine affection for each other. Each member's battle against cancer became a group concern and the authors noted that 'Individuals shared the same opponent and the group, as well as the physical activity, became the solution, as well as the social mediator' (Midtgaard *et al.*, 2006, p. 31).

Attachment characteristics may have important implications in the context of group exercise interventions. For example, Rom and Mikulincer (2003) identified that cohesion may serve as an important moderator of the link between self-reported insecure-anxious attachment and individuals' levels of productivity within the group context (i.e. individual productivity and contribution to group tasks and goals). Specifically, the negative relationship that levels of insecure-anxious attachment shared with productivity was attenuated when there was a high level of cohesion within the group (i.e. the aggregated perceptions of group cohesion across all members). The researchers suggested that a high level of cohesion within a group context may serve to activate a sense of attachment security that serves to dampen the typical negative emotional strategies employed by insecure-anxious individuals, freeing up their psychological resources and allowing them to better focus on individual and group productivity. Feeney (2000) has argued that Bowlby's predictions suggest that ill-health is particularly likely to activate individuals' predominant attachment characteristics. This is suggested to result in these attachment characteristics having a powerful influence over the manner in which individuals respond during periods of ill-health. When individuals are part of group contexts that are connected to their experience of illness it may be particularly likely that negative patterns of thinking and emotion linked to attachment patterns will interfere with their functioning in group contexts and inhibit the development of quality of life that such groups often provide. The development of cohesion in group exercise contexts may be an important buffer for individuals with negative attachment styles (e.g. insecure-anxious) and researchers could make an important contribution to the literature by exploring such hypotheses further.

Conclusion

The interface between attachment, exercise, and health is both interesting and extremely complex. However, there are potentially important benefits to developing our understanding and empirical knowledge in relation to the links between important personality variables such as attachment characteristics and lifestyle factors with significant health implications such as exercise. In this chapter I sought to facilitate the development of discussion and debate surrounding the links between these important fields of research. Initially, the literature surrounding attachment and health was examined and subsequently ideas were offered in relation to the potential implications of attachment for bodies of literature in exercise and health. Potential links that were discussed included the role of exercise as a moderator of the effects of attachment on health-related variables, the role of attachment in provider–client relationships, and the role of attachment in the development of cohesion in group exercise settings.

Concluding thoughts

Introduction

In this final section I offer some concluding thoughts that aim to summarise, draw from, and extend some of the overriding issues and themes that are reflected in the previous seven chapters. These thoughts centre around (a) the notion of emerging schools of thought in relation to attachment and the significance of this issue for sport, exercise, and wellness, (b) the idea that attachment theory may well be a 'bridge' across disciplines, giving rise to important moral and ethical questions, and (c) the idea of attachment as a 'grand theory' and the significance of this notion for the sport and exercise context.

Emerging 'schools of thought' in attachment research: implications for sport, exercise, and wellness

In Chapter 2 I attempted to outline how attachment research has developed into distinct 'schools of thought' that broadly reflect either (a) social psychological, or (b) psychodynamic and clinical ways of thinking. As I have developed this book I have become acutely aware that my discussions of the interface between attachment literature and ideas from sport, exercise, and wellness have much more strongly reflected a social psychological way of thinking. This is largely explainable by the fact that sport and exercise psychology remains dominated by a social psychological paradigm and the ideas with which I have sought to integrate attachment literature have been grounded in this approach. As such, in attempting to integrate ideas from attachment theory with these popular frameworks I have found myself thinking according to the norms, language, and traditions that underpin them. In many ways I believe that I have predominantly sketched out a vision for the integration of attachment theory and sport-related literature that is couched in social psychological 'language' and 'ways of thinking'.

However, it would be an oversight to finish this book without referring readers once again to the material discussed in Chapter 2. It is important to recognise that alternative ways of conceptualising, studying, and approaching the research questions we formulate as we begin to integrate attachment theory with our ideas from sport-related contexts could play a crucial role not only in extending our lines of enquiry along pre-existing avenues of social psychological research, but also in helping us to adopt different ways of conceptualising and thinking about sport and exercise psychology itself. Rainer Martens (2007) has forcefully suggested that

> the prevailing paradigm of social psychology, which many of us in sport psychology have borrowed, is inadequate for understanding human behaviour … I believe that a radical new paradigm is needed … a scientific revolution … I have doubts about the snapshot model of linear causation … and that the categories of ANOVA can provide a useful model of what goes on in the personal and social world of sport.
>
> (pp. 32–3)

While I am not as strong a critic of the social psychological way of thinking in the contexts of sport and exercise as Martens (indeed I believe it has made, and can continue to make, a significant contribution to knowledge), it is important that the field take every opportunity to embrace new ways of thinking and to develop alternative ways of understanding personal and social experiences in sport. To this end, the integration of attachment theory offers an excellent opportunity for sport-related researchers to explore new avenues. The psychodynamic and clinical tradition within the attachment literature provides a wealth of ideas, methods, and concepts that could serve as a refreshing lens through which to view many of the issues sport and exercise psychology has typically viewed through a social psychological lens. I would encourage future researchers to think carefully about embracing this school of thought in their attempts to integrate attachment theory. Such attempts may ultimately help to enrich the paradigmatic assumptions that sport researchers entertain.

Embracing the psychodynamic and clinical traditions in the context of sport and exercise might most obviously be reflected in the adoption of measurement tools that have been developed within this school of thought. For example, by undergoing training in assessment tools such as the Adult Attachment Interview (AAI; George *et al.*, 1985) or the Adult Attachment Projective (AAP; George & West, 2001, 2003) and employing them in the context of the sport-related literature researchers will be helping to diversify the ways in which we think about attachment in the context of our research. However, perhaps of more significance than the simple employment of such measurement tools will be an explicit recognition of the assumptions in which they are grounded. Ultimately, when we tap attachment-related constructs via measures that have been developed within the psychoanalytical and clinical traditions we are perhaps (and this was debated in Chapter 2) concerned with theorised dimensions of the mind (e.g. subconscious layers of the psyche) that we would not 'access' or 'entertain' with social psychological measures. Accordingly, the use of such tools and their under-pinning assumptions would require sport researchers to consider how such assumptions can be integrated into and extend our current frameworks of thinking.

Ethical implications

I believe it is important to briefly discuss some of the ethical issues that arise from the ideas that have been discussed in this book. For example, in Chapter 6 I outlined how early research in the context of youth sport (e.g. Carr, 2009b; Carr & Fitzpatrick, 2011) is beginning to suggest that individuals' working models of attachment may well be 'active' within the sporting context. As such, these models may well have the potential to partially dictate the manner in which sport relationships are negotiated. It follows that if internal working models of attachment are in play within the contextual relationships that individuals experience in their sporting lives then the link that they share with sport relationships may be reciprocal. That is, internal working models of attachment not only have the potential to influence the experience of sporting relationships but sporting relationships themselves may have the capacity to amend and rework models of attachment. Given that initial research (e.g. Davis & Jowett, 2010) in the context of the coach–athlete bond is suggesting that this relationship may well meet many of the functions necessary to be considered an 'attachment relationship', it is plausible that such relationships have the capacity to impact internal working models of attachment.

In light of the above, questions will ultimately arise in relation to the potential benefits of sporting relationships for the explicit purpose of reworking maladaptive internal working models of attachment as part of the use of sport-related interventions in the context of positive youth development. This idea is undoubtedly exciting, potentially significant, and would serve to further demonstrate the significant impact of sport in young people's lives. However, in utilising attachment theory to this end researchers should also be aware that the boundaries between sport and exercise psychology and domains such as the therapeutic setting are inevitably blurred. Discussions about whether the study of sport relationships *can* and *should* extend into such uncharted research territory will undoubtedly need to take place.

Attachment theory: a 'grand theory'

Waters (2000) has written of the distinction between research paradigms and theories. He suggests that paradigms 'provide a general framework and approach that organizes how broad areas of theory and research should proceed, what the key questions should be, and what the answers will be like' (p. 1). Theories, in contrast, are suggested as being more closely tied to specific content, organising data, helping to shape hypotheses, and evolving according to empirical verification. However, the notion of *grand theory* has been put forward as something that seems to sit somewhere in the grey area between paradigm and theoretical framework. Waters (2000, p. 1) has labelled grand theories as 'ambitious efforts to integrate diverse phenomena under a relatively small set of general postulates'. Most grand theories fail to stand the test of time and do not tend to achieve the broad and integrative objectives for which they have been designed.

Attachment theory has been labelled as one of the last surviving grand theories not to have been completely dismissed, replaced, or extensively reworked (Mercer, 2011). Waters (2000) suggested that attachment should be considered a grand theory because it (a) specifically defines a broad spectrum of key phenomena, (b) is grounded in evolutionary principles, (c) helps in understanding a range of dimensions of human experiences, (d) is relevant through the lifespan, (e) provides a developmental analysis, (f) appeals to individual difference and normative ways of thinking, (g) draws upon the notions of stability *and* change, and (h) provides prescriptive guidance on what makes a good human relationship. Clearly, such objectives are a testament to the broadly integrative ideas in attachment theory. Furthermore, Bowlby's attempts to provide such an integrative framework for our understanding of cognition, emotion, behaviour, and relationships suggests that he saw each of these aspects of human experience as best understood in the context of the others (as opposed to separately analysed components).

Recognising attachment theory in this way, as a grand theory with broadly integrative goals, it is possible to appreciate the broad scope of the potential interface between attachment and sport, exercise, and wellness. For example, point (f) in the above paragraph suggests that attachment theory has particular appeal to 'individual difference' ways of thinking. One of the central ideas that has characterised the pages of this book is the idea that attachment offers us an insight into important individual differences that seem to serve as an organising force in relation to an array of cognitive, emotional, and behavioural experiences. As such, it is unsurprising that social and personality psychologists have been keen to tap into these individual differences and how they relate to meaningful differences in individuals' social worlds. This book has highlighted that such individual differences in relation to attachment can be identified and are indeed related to 'meaningful differences' in psychological and social experiences, many of which are closely linked to the contexts of sport, exercise, and wellness. For those adopting an individual difference approach to sport and exercise, ideas and concepts have been discussed in relation to attachment styles as distal predictors of patterns of stress and coping in sport, achievement goals, cognitive and emotional reactions to injury, perceptions of cohesion, and perceived sport friendship quality. There is a wealth of research questions to explore in relation to this dimension of attachment theory.

In an early theoretical paper Bowlby (1940) discussed his position on attachment by advocating that 'like nurserymen, psychoanalysts should study the nature of the organism, the properties of the soil, and their inter-action' (p. 23). One interpretation of this comment (and I believe there are different interpretations to be made) is that in many ways it reflects the interactional approach that has characterised much of the sport and exercise psychology literature to date. That is, we should be mindful that individual differences in attachment might be seen to reflect the 'nature of the organism' but that the characteristics of the sport-related context within which the individual is embedded reflect 'the properties of the soil'.

In addition to a simplistic individual difference approach, this book has provided numerous insights into how the properties of the sport or exercise context might be seen to interact with attachment-related individual differ-ences in order to regulate critical aspects of their experiences. For example, in Chapter 4 we discussed the idea that a cohesive environment may well serve to dampen the heightened concerns about rejection and self-worth in the eyes of others that often characterise the social experiences of insecurely attached individuals, allowing them to engage in group processes with a greater sense of psychological comfort. In Chapter 6 we discussed the idea that a performance-oriented motivational climate might be seen as a con-textual block in relation to the employment of internal working models of attachment within sporting friendships. In Chapter 7 we discussed the idea that some of the psychological and physiological correlates of chronic stress that have been associated with maladaptive attachment styles might be buffered by exercise as a lifestyle factor. Hence, there are additional research avenues related to the development of our understanding of how the properties of sport-related contexts *interact* with individual differences rooted in attach-ment. These avenues of research may have enormous potential for applied intervention as they unfold and can also help us to better understand the reciprocal relationship between attachment-related individual differences and the sporting context.

It was also noted above that attachment theory draws upon notions of both stability *and* change (point g). In Chapter 1 of this book I suggested that:

> Key questions centre around (a) the degree of *stability* of initial attach-ment patterns developed with primary caregivers through the lifespan, (b) if it is accepted that individuals can develop *multiple* models of attachment in relation to *multiple others*, what is the degree of 'primacy' that early attachment to 'primary' caregivers would occupy within such a network of attachment models, and (c) if individuals do develop 'sec-ondary' models of attachment, *how* are such models combined with primary models?

To this end, there are opportunities for sport-related researchers to explore and contribute to these important research questions. For example, in Chapter 6 I discussed the idea (e.g. Davis & Jowett, 2010) that individuals might construct models of attachment within the sporting context (e.g. in relationships with coaches). However, it will be both important and interesting to explore (a) the stability of attachment characteristics within such relationships (and indeed whether such stability is meaningful in regulating psychological well-being and performance), (b) the relationship of such context-specific attachment models to other (perhaps more primary) models of attachment (e.g. this might include an assessment of their place in an attachment hierarchy), (c) whether such context-specific models of attachment hold any agency with respect to the 'reworking' of more primary, pre-existing attachment models, and (d) the role of more primary, pre-existing models of attachment in the construction of context-specific attachment bonds in sport.

In point (e), Waters (2000) suggested that attachment theory is particularly open to a developmental perspective. Again, this notion offers useful insight to sport psychologists. In Chapter 6 I presented my own research in the context of sport friendships that drew heavily upon the idea that adolescents' attachment relationships with their parents can provide us with a significant insight into the likely internal working models of attachment that they have constructed as a consequence of this critical bond. My research suggested that how adolescents experience their sporting friendships is likely to be influenced by the affectively charged patterns of cognition and emotion that they bring forward from earlier parental relationships. In this sense, attachment theory is a useful lens, through which to develop understanding in relation to important 'psychological threads' that can be traced backed to early relationships yet still hold significance in the context of new relationships experienced within sporting environments.

In point (h) Waters (2000) suggested that attachment theory also offers prescriptive guidance on what makes a decent human relationship. Early research in the sporting context has suggested that the attachment characteristics of context-specific relationships seem to have a link to wider psychological experiences. For example, Davis and Jowett (2010) identified that more secure coach–athlete bonds were linked to wider experiences of sport satisfaction and to satisfaction within the relationship. Hence, it may be important to discuss and think about the manner in which differing attachment relationships are constructed in the context of sport and the factors involved in this process. To this end, Chapter 3 of this book put forward self-determination theory as a potentially fruitful framework, suggesting that basic psychological need satisfaction may be a critical element in the construction of relationships that are felt to be secure attachment bonds (e.g. La Guardia *et al.*, 2000). Given the popularity of this framework in the context of sport-related research, sport researchers may have much to offer in relation to this aspect of attachment research.

My point above is that attachment theory can be seen to be a broadly integrative framework in a number of senses. Accordingly, it also provides broadly integrative possibilities for the world of sport, exercise, and wellness. However, in addition to the above, the theory might also be used as a framework (a) for the integration of relatively fragmented areas of research in sport, exercise, and physical activity, and (b) for the integration of sport-related research with a diverse range of other sub-disciplines within psychology. That is, perhaps an additional benefit of such a 'grand theory' can be found in its potential to stimulate an integration of key ideas and frameworks within and between fields, providing an overriding sense of coherence to previously disjointed areas of research. The content presented in this book is in many ways an argument that attachment theory might serve as an organisational force for a diverse array of ideas. Waters (2000) has nicely articulated that we can take something from the fact that attachment theory is a 'surviving' grand theory:

> Grand theory remains an attractive goal, but in an era of specialization and domain specific theory, many have concluded that it is unattainable or even discredited as a way of organizing and guiding empirical research. Nonetheless, measured from Bowlby's (1958) paper ... modern attachment theory has entered its fifth decade and seems likely to reach its silver anniversary more coherent and productive than ever.
>
> (p. 3)

Moving forward with attachment theory in sport, exercise, and wellness

Researchers have suggested that one of the reasons for the above notions of durability and robustness in relation to attachment theory is its simultaneous openness to revisions and further integrations. As discussed in Chapter 1 of this book, Ainsworth (1993) has recognised that the genius of attachment theory:

> lies in the way he [Bowlby] has integrated a collection of concepts together to form a coherent and comprehensive theory that is still open ended and subject to revision/extension through the research for which it has provided a useful guide.
>
> (p. 476)

Furthermore, as Waters and Cummings (2000) have outlined: 'Maintaining the coherence and empirical underpinnings of attachment theory is a continuous process of updating key ideas in light of advances in theory, data, and other areas of psychology' (p. 164). It has been my intention in this book to stimulate the sort of thinking, debate, and discussion that can serve to ensure that the field of sport and exercise psychology can itself contribute ideas, advances, and data that will ultimately help to evolve and update these assumptions further.

References

Abercrombie, M.L.J. (1984). Group analysis and higher education. In T.E. Lear (Ed.), *Spheres of group analysis*. Naas, Co. Kildare: The Leinster Leader.

Ablard, K., & Parker, W. (1997). Parents' achievement goals and perfectionism in their academically talented children. *Journal of Youth and Adolescence*, 26, 651–67.

Ahrens, R. (1954). Beitrag zur entwicklung des physiognomie – und mimikerkennes. *Zeitschrift fur Experimentelle und Angewandte Psychologie*, 11, 412–54.

Ainsworth, M.D.S. (1963). The development of infant–mother interaction among the Ganda. In B.M. Foss (Ed.), *Determinants of infant behavior* (pp. 67–104). New York: Wiley.

——(1982). Attachment: Retrospect and prospect. In C.M. Parkes & J. Stevenson-Hinde (Eds.), *The place of attachment in human behavior* (pp. 3–30). New York: Basic Books.

——(1990). Epilogue. In M.T. Greenberg, D. Cicchetti, & E.M. Cummings (Eds.), *Attachment in the pre-school years: Theory, research, and intervention* (pp. 463–88). Chicago: University of Chicago Press.

——(1993). Some considerations regarding theory and assessment relevant to attachments beyond infancy. In M.T. Greenberg, D. Cicchetti, & E.M. Cummings (Eds.), *Attachment in the pre-school years: Theory, research, and intervention* (pp. 463–8). Chicago: University of Chicago Press.

Ainsworth, M.D.S., Blehar, M.C., Waters, E., & Wall, S. (1978). *Patterns of attachment: A psychological study of the strange situation*. Hillsdale, NJ: Erlbaum.

Allen, J.P., & Land, D. (1999). Attachment in adolescence. In J. Cassidy & P.R. Shaver (Eds.), *Handbook of attachment: Theory, research, and clinical applications* (pp. 319–35). New York: Guilford.

Alonso, J.M., Junge, A., Renstrom, P., Engebretson, L., Mountjoy, M., & Dvorak, J. (2009). Sport injuries surveillance during the 2007 IAAF World Athletics Championships. *Clinical Journal of Sports Medicine*, 19, 26–32.

Ames, C. (1984). Competitive, cooperative, and individualistic goal structures: A motivational analysis. In R.E. Ames and C. Ames (Eds.), *Research on motivation in education, vol. 1: Student motivation* (pp. 177–207). New York: Academic Press.

——(1992). Classrooms: Goals, structures, and student motivation. *Journal of Educational Psychology*, 84, 261–71.

Ames, C., & Archer, J. (1987). Mothers' beliefs about the role of effort and ability in school learning. *Journal of Educational Psychology*, 79, 409–14.

——(1988) Achievement goals in the classroom: Students' learning strategies and motivation processes. *Journal of Educational Psychology*, 80, 260–7.

Andersen, S.M., & Berk, M.S. (1998). Transference in everyday experience: Implications of experimental research for relevant clinical phenomena. *Review of General Psychiatry*, 2, 81–120.

Andersen, S.M., & Glassman, N.S. (1996). Responding to significant others when they are not there: Effects on interpersonal inference, motivation and affect. In R.M. Sorrentino & E.T. Higgins (Eds.), *Handbook of motivation and cognition* (vol. 3, pp. 262–321). New York: Guilford.

Anshel, M.H., & Anderson, D. (2002). Coping with acute stress in sport: Linking athletes' coping style, coping strategies, affect and motor performance. *Anxiety, Stress, and Coping*, 15, 193–209.

Anshel M.H., & Delany, J. (2001). Sources of acute stress, cognitive appraisals, and coping strategies of male and female child athletes. *Journal of Sport Behavior*, 24, 329–53.

Anshel, M.H., Jamieson, J., & Raviv, S. (2001). Coping with acute stress among male and female Israeli athletes. *International Journal of Sport Psychology*, 32, 271–89.

Armsden, G.C., & Greenberg, M.T. (1987). The inventory of parent and peer attachment: Individual differences and their relationship to psychological well-being in adolescence. *Journal of Youth and Adolescence*, 16, 427–54.

Atkinson, J. (1957). Motivational determinants of risk-taking behavior. *Psychological Review*, 64, 359–72.

Ayers, T.S., Sandler, I.N., West, S.G., & Roose, M.W. (1996). A dispositional and situation assessment of children's coping. Testing alternative models of coping. *Journal of Personality*, 64, 923–58.

Babcock, J., Jacobson, N.S., Gottman, J.M., & Yerington, T.P. (2000). Attachment, emotional regulation, and the function of marital violence: Differences between secure, preoccupied, and dismissing violent and nonviolent husbands. *Journal of Family Violence*, 15, 391–408.

Backx, F.J.G., Beijer, H.J.M., & Bol, E.E. (1991). Injuries in high risk persons and high risk sports: A longitudinal study of 1818 school children. *American Journal of Sports Medicine*, 19, 124–30.

Bailey, R., Armour, K., Kirk, D., Jess, M., Pickup, I., & Sandford, R. (2009). The educational benefits claimed for physical education and school sport: An academic review. *Research Papers in Education*, 24, 1–27.

Baldwin, M.W. (1995). Relational schemas and cognition in close relationships. *Journal of Social and Personal Relationships*, 12, 547–52.

Baldwin, M.W., & Fehr, B. (1995). On the instability of attachment style ratings. *Personal Relationships*, 2, 247–61.

Baldwin, M.W., Keelan, J.P.R., Fehr, B., Enns, V., & Koh Rangarajoo, E. (1996). Social-cognitive conceptualization of attachment working models: Availability and accessibility effects. *Journal of Personality and Social Psychology*, 71, 94–109.

Balendra, G., Turner, M., & McCrory, P. (2007). Career-ending injuries to professional jockeys in British horse racing. *British Journal of Sports Medicine*, 42, 22–4.

Bandura, A. (1986). *Social foundations of thought and action: A social-cognitive theory.* Englewood Cliffs, NJ: Prentice Hall.

Bandura, A., & Walters, R.H. (1963). *Social learning and personality development.* New York: Holt, Rinehart, & Winston.

Barber, B.K. (1996). Parental psychological control: Revisiting a neglected construct. *Child Development*, 67, 3296–319.

Barkoukis, V., Thogerson-Ntoumanis, C., Ntoumanis, N., & Nikitaras, N. (2007). Achievement goals in physical education: Examining the predictive ability of five different dimensions of motivational climate. *European Physical Education Review*, 13, 267–85.

Barnes, G.M., & Welte, J.W. (1986). Patterns and predictors of alcohol use among 7–12th grade students in New York State. *Journal of Studies on Alcohol*, 47, 53–62.

Bartholomew, K. (1990). Avoidance of intimacy: An attachment perspective. *Journal of Social and Personal Relationships*, 7, 147–78.

Bartholomew, K., & Horowitz, L.M. (1991). Attachment styles among young adults: A test of a four-category model. *Journal of Personality and Social Psychology*, 61, 226–44.

Barthomolew, K., & Moretti, M. (2002). The dynamics of measuring attachment. *Attachment and Human Development*, 4, 162–5.

Bartholomew, K., & Shaver, P.R. (1998). Methods of assessing adult attachment: Do they converge? In J.A. Simpson and W.S. Rholes (Eds.), *Attachment theory and close relationships* (pp. 25–45). New York: Guilford Press.

Baum, A.L. (2005). Suicide in athletes: A review and commentary. *Clinical Sports Medicine*, 24, 853–69.

Becker, B., Bell, M., & Billington, R. (1987). Object relations ego deficits in bulimic college women. *Journal of Clinical Psychology*, 43, 92–5.

Belsky, J., & Cassidy, J. (1995). Attachment theory and evidence. In M. Rutter & D. Hay (Eds.), *Development through life* (pp. 373–402). London: Blackwell.

Belsky, J., Campbell, S.B., Cohn, J.F., & Moore, G. (1996). Instability of infant–parent attachment security. *Developmental Psychology*, 32, 921–4.

Bernier, A., & Dozier, M. (2002). Assessing adult attachment: Empirical sophistication and conceptual bases. *Attachment & Human Development*, 4, 171–9.

Berscheid, E., Snyder, M., & Omoto, A.M. (1989). Issues in studying close relationships: conceptualising and measuring closeness. In C. Hendric (Ed.), *Close relationships* (pp. 63–91). Newbury Park, CA: SAGE.

Biddle, S. (2000). Exercise, emotions, and mental health. In Y. Hanin (Ed.), *Emotions in sport*. Champaign, IL: Human Kinetics.

——(2001). Enhancing motivation in physical education. In G. Roberts (Ed.), *Advances in motivation in sport and exercise*. Champaign, IL: Human Kinetics.

Biederman, J., Hirshfield-Becker, D., Rosenbaum, J., Herot, C., Friedman, D., Snidman, N. *et al.* (2001). Further evidence of association between behavioral inhibition and social anxiety in children. *American Journal of Psychiatry*, 158, 1673–9.

Bifulco, A., Moran, P.M., Ball, C., & Bernazzi, O. (2002a). Adult attachment style 1: Its relationship to clinical depression. *Social Psychiatry and Psychiatric Epidemiology*, 37, 50–9.

Bifulco, A., Moran, P.M., Ball, C., & Lillie, A. (2002b). Adult attachment style 2: Its relationship to psychosocial depressive vulnerability. *Social Psychiatry and Psychiatric Epidemiology*, 37, 60–67.

Birnbaum, G., Orr, I., Mikulincer, M., & Florian, V. (1997). When marriage breaks up does attachment style contribute to coping and mental health? *Journal of Social and Personal Relationships*, 14, 643–54.

Bischof, M. (1975). A systems approach toward the functional connections of attachment and fear. *Child Development*, 46, 801–7.

Blanchard, C., & Vallerand, R.J. (1996). Perceptions of competence, autonomy, and relatedness as psychological mediators of the social factors-contextual motivational relationship. Unpublished manuscript, Université du Quebec à Montreal.

Bois, J.E., Sarrazin, P.G., Brustad, R.J., Cury, F, & Trouilloud, D.O. (2005). Elementary schoolchildren's perceived competence and physical activity involvement:

The influence of parents' role modeling behaviors and perceptions of their child's competence. *Psychology of Sport and Exercise*, 6, 381–97.

Bonito, J.A. (2002). The analysis of participation in small groups: Methodological and conceptual issues related to interdependence. *Small Group Research*, 33, 412–38.

Borman, E., & Cole, H. (1993). A comparison of three measures of adult attachment. Poster presented at the meeting of the Society for Research in Child Development, New Orleans, April.

Bowlby, J. (1940). The influence of early environment in the development of neurosis and neurotic character. *International Journal of Psycho-Analysis*, 21, 1–25.

——(1951). Maternal care and mental health. *World Health Organization Monograph* (Serial No. 2). Geneva, World Health Organization.

——(1958). The nature of the child's tie to his mother. *International Journal of Psycho-Analysis*, 39, 1–23.

——(1968). Effects on behaviour of disruption of an affectional bond. In J.M. Thoday & A.S. Parker (Eds.), *Genetic and environmental influences on behaviour*. Edinburgh: Oliver & Boyd.

——(1969/1982). *Attachment and loss, vol. 1: Attachment*. New York: Basic Books.

——(1973). *Attachment and loss, vol. 2: Separation: Anxiety and anger*. New York: Basic Books.

——(1975). Attachment theory, separation anxiety and mourning. In S. Arieti (Ed.), *American handbook of psychiatry* (2nd Ed.). New York: Basic Books.

——(1977). The making and breaking of affectional bonds. *British Journal of Psychiatry*, 130, 201–10.

——(1979/2005). *The making and breaking of affectional bonds*. New York: Routledge (1st Ed. 1979, 2nd Ed. 2005).

——(1980). *Attachment and loss, vol. 3: Loss: Sadness and depression*. New York: Basic Books.

——(1988). *A secure base: Parent–child attachment and healthy human development*. New York: Basic Books.

Brawley, L.R., Carron, A.V., & Widmeyer,W.N. (1987). Assessing the cohesion of teams: Validity of the Group Environment Questionnaire. *Journal of Sport and Exercise Psychology*, 9, 275–94.

Brazelton, T.B. (1977). Implications of infant development among Mayan Indians of Mexico. In P.H. Leiderman, S.R. Tulkin, & A. Rosenfeld (Eds.), *Culture and infancy: Variations in the human experience* (pp. 151–88). New York: Academic Press.

Brennan, K.A., Clark, C.L., & Shaver, P.R. (1998). Self-report measurement of adult attachment: An integrative overview. In J.A. Simpson & W.S. Rholes (Eds.), *Attachment theory and close relationships* (pp. 46–76). New York: Guilford.

Bretherton, I. (1985). Attachment theory: Retrospect and prospect. In I. Bretherton & F. Waters (Eds.), *Growing points of attachment theory and research: Monographs of the Society for Research in Child Development*, 50(1–2), 3–35.

——(1987). New perspectives on attachment relations: Security, communication and internal working models. In J. Osofsky (Ed.), *Handbook of infant development* (pp. 1061–100). New York: Wiley.

——(1992). The origins of attachment theory: J. Bowlby and M.D.S. Ainsworth. *Developmental Psychology*, 28, 759–75.

Brewer, B.W. (1994). Review and critique of models of psychological adjustment to athletic injury. *Journal of Applied Sport Psychology*, 6, 87–100.

Brewer, B.W., Linder, D.E., & Phelps, C.M. (1995). Situational correlates of emotional adjustment to athletic injury. *Clinical Journal of Sport Medicine*, 5, 241–5.

Britton, P.C., & Fuendeling, J.M. (2005). The relations among the varieties of adult attachment and the components of empathy. *Journal of Social Psychology*, 145, 519–30.

Brown, B.S., Payne, T., Kim, C., Moore, G., Krebs, P., & Martin, W. (1979). Chronic response of rat brain norepinephrine and serotonin levels to endurance training. *Journal of Applied Physiology*, 46, 19–23.

Brustad, R.J. (1993). Who will go out to play? Parental and psychological influences on children's attraction to physical activity. *Journal of Sport and Exercise Psychology*, 14, 59–77.

Byng-Hall, J. (1995). Creating a secure family base: Some implications of attachment theory for family therapy. *Family Process*, 34, 45–58.

Cadorette, I., Blanchard, C., & Vallerand, R.J. (1996). Programme d'amaigrissement: Influence du centre de conditionnement physique et du style de l'entraîneur sur la motivation des participants. [Weight loss programme: Effects of the fitness centre and the instructor on participants' motivation.] Paper presented at the SQRP conference, Trois-Rivieres, Quebec.

Campbell, L., Simpson, J.A., Kashy, D.A., & Rholes, W.S. (2001). Attachment orientations, dependence, and behaviour in a stressful situation: An application of the Actor–Partner Independence Model. *Journal of Social and Personal Relationships*, 18, 821–43.

Carr, S. (2006). An examination of multiple goals in children's physical education: Motivational effects of goal profiles and the role of perceived climate in multiple goal development. *Journal of Sports Sciences*, 24, 281–97.

——(2009a). Implications of attachment theory for sport and physical activity research: Conceptual links with achievement goal and peer relationship models. *International Review of Sport and Exercise Psychology*, 2, 95–115.

——(2009b). Adolescent–parent attachment characteristics and quality of youth sport friendship. *Psychology of Sport and Exercise*, 10, 653–61.

Carr, S. and Weigand, D.A. (2001). Parental, peer, teacher, and sporting hero influence on the goal orientations of children in physical education. *European Physical Education Review*, 7, 305–28.

Carr, S., & Fitzpatrick, N. (2011). Experiences of dyadic sport friendships as a function of self and partner attachment characteristics. *Psychology of Sport and Exercise*, 12, 383–91.

Carr, S., Weigand, D.A., & Hussey, W. (1999). The relative influence of parents, teachers, and peers on children and adolescents' achievement and intrinsic motivation and perceived competence in physical education. *Journal of Sport Pedagogy*, 5, 28–50.

Carr, S., Weigand, D.A., & Jones, J. (2000). The relative influence of parents, peers, and sporting heroes on the goal orientations of children and adolescents in sport. *Journal of Sport Pedagogy*, 6, 34–55.

Carron, A.V. (1982). Cohesiveness in sport groups: Interpretation and considerations. *Journal of Sport Psychology*, 4, 123–38.

——(1988). *Group dynamics in sport*. London, Canada: Spodym.

Carron, A.V., & Ball, J.R. (1978). Cause–effect characteristics of cohesiveness and participation motivation in intercollegiate hockey. *International Review of Sport Sociology*, 12, 49–60.

Carron, A.V., & Chelladurai, P. (1981). The dynamics of group cohesion in sport. *Journal of Sport Psychology*, 3, 123–39.

Carron, A.V., & Spink, K.S. (1993). Team building in an exercise setting. *The Sport Psychologist*, 7, 8–18.

——(1995). The group size–cohesion relationship in minimal groups. *Small Group Research*, 26, 86–105.

Carron, A.V., Brawley, L.R., & Widmeyer, W.N. (1998). The measurement of cohesiveness in sport groups. In J.L. Duda (Ed.), *Advances in sport and exercise psychology measurement* (pp. 213–26). Morgantown, WV: Fitness Information Technology.

Carron, A.V., Colman, M.M., Wheeler, J., & Stevens, D. (2002). Cohesion and performance in sport: A meta analysis. *Journal of Sport and Exercise Psychology, 24,* 168–88.

Carron, A.V., Shapcott, K.M., & Burke, S.M. (2007). Group cohesion in sport and exercise: Past, present and future. In M. Beauchamp & M. Eys (Eds.), *Group dynamics in exercise and sport psychology: Contemporary themes* (pp. 117–35). New York: Routledge.

Carson, F., & Polman, R.C. (2008). ACL injury rehabilitation: A psychological case study of a professional rugby union player. *Journal of Clinical Sport Psychology, 2,* 71–90.

Carver, C.S., Scheier, M.F., & Weintraub, J.K. (1989). Assessing coping strategies: A theoretically based approach. *Journal of Personality and Social Psychology, 56,* 267–83.

Cassidy J. (1999). The nature of a child's ties. In J. Cassidy and P.R. Shaver (Eds.), *Handbook of attachment: Theory, research and clinical applications* (pp. 3–20). New York: Guilford Press.

Cassidy, J., & Berlin, L.J. (1994). The insecure/ambivalent pattern of attachment: Theory and research. *Child Development, 65,* 971–81.

Chatzisarantis, N.L.D., & Hagger, M.S (2007). Intrinsic motivation and self-determination in exercise and sport: Reflecting on the past and sketching the future. In M.S. Hagger and N.L.D. Chatzisarantis (Eds.), *Intrinsic motivation and self-determination in exercise and sport* (pp. 281–96). Champaign, IL: Human Kinetics.

Chatzisarantis, N.L., Hagger, M., Biddle, S.J.H., Smith, B., & Wang, J.C.K. (2003). A meta-analysis of perceived locus of causality in exercise, sport, and physical education contexts. *Journal of Sport and Exercise Psychology, 25,* 284–306.

Chorpita, B.F., & Barlow, D.H. (1998). The development of anxiety: The role of control in the early environment. *Psychological Bulletin, 124,* 3–21.

Ciechanowski, P.S., Katon, W.J., Russo, J., & Walker, E.A. (2001). The patient–provider relationship: Attachment and adherence to treatment in diabetes. *American Journal of Psychiatry, 158,* 29–35.

Ciechanowski, P.S., Sullivan, M., Jensen, M., Romano, J., & Summers, H. (2003). The relationship of attachment style to depression, catastrophizing and health care utilization in patients with chronic pain. *Pain, 104,* 627–37.

Cillessen, A.H.N., Lu Jiang, X., West, T.V., & Laszkowski, D.K. (2005). Predictors of dyadic friendship quality in adolescence. *International Journal of Behavioural Development, 29,* 165–72.

Cohen, J. (1992). A power primer. *Psychological Bulletin, 112,* 155–9.

Coie, I.D., & Cillessen, A.H.N. (1993). Peer rejection: Origins and effects on children's development. *Current Directions, 2,* 89–92.

Cole-Detke, H., & Kobak, R. (1996). Attachment processes in eating disorder and depression. *Journal of Consulting and Clinical Psychology, 64,* 282–90.

Colin, V. (1987). Infants' preferences between parents before and after moderate stress activates behavior. Paper presented at the meeting of the Society for Research in Child Development, Baltimore.

Collins, N.L., & Read, S.J. (1990). Adult attachment, working models, and relationship quality in dating couples. *Journal of Personality and Social Psychology, 58,* 644–63.

——(1994). Cognitive representations of attachment: The structure and function of working models. In K. Bartholomew & D. Perlman (Eds.), *Attachment processes in adulthood* (pp. 53–92). London: Jessica Kingsley.

Conroy, D.E., Elliot, A.J., & Hofer, S.M. (2003). A 2 × 2 achievement goals questionnaire for sport: Evidence for factorial invariance, temporal stability, and external validity. *Journal of Sport and Exercise Psychology*, 25, 456–76.

Contreras, J.M., & Kerns, K.A. (2000). Emotion regulation processes: Explaining links between parent–child attachment and peer relationships. In K.A. Kerns, J.M. Contreras, & A.M. Neal-Barnett (Eds.), *Family and peers: Linking two social worlds* (pp. 1–25). Westport, CT: Praeger.

Contreras, J.M., Kerns, K.A., Weimer, B.L., Gentzler, A.L., & Tomich, P.L. (2000). Emotion regulation as a mediator of associations between mother–child attachment and peer relationships in middle childhood. *Journal of Family Psychology*, 14, 111–24.

Cook, W.L. (2000). Understanding attachment security in family context. *Journal of Personality and Social Psychology*, 78, 285–94.

Cook, W.L., & Kenny, D.A. (2005). The Actor–Partner Interdependence Model: A model of bidirectional effects in developmental studies. *International Journal of Behavioural Development*, 29, 101–9.

Courneya K.S., & Friedenreich C.M. (1999) Physical exercise and quality of life following cancer diagnosis: A literature review. *Annals of Behavioral Medicine*, 21, 171–9.

Cox, A., & Ullrich-French, S. (2010). The motivational relevance of peer and teacher relationship profiles in physical education. *Psychology of Sport and Exercise*, 11, 337–44.

Cox, R.H., Hubbard, J.W., Lawler, J.E., Sanders, B.J., & Mitchell, V.P. (1985). Exercise training attenuates stress-induced hypertension in the rat. *Hypertension*, 7, 747–51.

Craik, K. (1943). *The Nature of Explanation*. Cambridge: Cambridge University Press.

Creasey, G. (2002). Associations between working models of attachment and conflict management behavior in romantic couples. *Journal of Counseling Psychology*, 49, 365–75.

Crocker, P.R.E., & Graham, T.R. (1995). Coping by competitive athletes with performance stress: Gender differences and relationships with affect. *The Sport Psychologist*, 9, 325–38.

Crowell, J.A., Treboux, D., & Waters, E. (2002). Stability of attachment representations: The transition to marriage. *Developmental Psychology*, 38, 467–79.

Culos-Reed, S., Rejeski, J., Mcauley, E., Ockene, J., & Roter, D. (2000). Predictors of adherence to behaviour change interventions in the elderly. *Controlled Clinical Trials*, 21, 200S–205S.

Cury, F., Da Fonseca, D., Rufo, M., & Sarrazin, P. (2002). Perceptions of competence, implicit theory of ability, perception of motivational climate and achievement goals: A test of the trichotomous conceptualisation of achievement motivation in the physical education setting. *Perceptual and Motor Skills*, 95, 233–44.

Dale, G.A. (2000). Distractions and coping strategies of elite decathletes during their most memorable performances. *The Sport Psychologist*, 14, 17–41.

Davila, J., Burge, D., & Hammen, C. (1997). Why does attachment style change? *Journal of Personality and Social Psychology*, 73, 826–38.

Davila, J., Karney, T.R., & Bradbury, T.N. (1999). Attachment change processes in the early years of marriage. *Journal of Personality and Social Psychology*, 76, 783–802.

Davis, L., & Jowett, S. (2010). Investigating the interpersonal dynamics between coaches and athletes based on fundamental principles of attachment. *Journal of Clinical Sport Psychology*, 4(1), 112–132.

De Moor, M., Beem, A., Stubbe, J., Boomsma, D., & De Geus, E. (2006). Regular exercise, anxiety, depression, and personality: A population based study. *Preventative Medicine*, 42, 273–9.

De Wolff, M.S., & van Ijzendoorn, M.H. (1997). Sensitivity and attachment: A meta-analysis on parental antecedents of infant attachment. *Child Development*, 68, 571–91.

Deci, E.L., & Ryan, R.M. (1980). The empirical exploration of intrinsic motivational processes. In L. Berkowitz (Ed.), *Advances in experimental social psychology* (vol. 13, pp. 39–80). New York: Academic Press.

——(1985). *Intrinsic motivation and self-determination in human behavior.* New York: Plenum.

——(1985b). The General Causality Orientations Scale: Self-determination in personality. *Journal of Research in Personality*, 19, 109–34.

——(1990). A motivational approach to the self: Integration in personality. In R. Dienstbier (Ed.), *Nebraska Symposium on motivation* (vol. 38). Lincoln: University of Nebraska Press.

——(2008). Self-determination theory: A macrotheory of human motivation, development, and health. *Canadian Psychology*, 49, 182–5.

Deci, E.L., Koestner, R., & Ryan, R.M. (1999). A meta-analytic review of experiments examining the effects of extrinsic rewards on intrinsic motivation. *Psychological Bulletin*, 125, 627–68.

Dempsey, J.M., Kimiecik, J.C., & Horn, T.S. (1993). Parental influence on children's moderate to vigorous physical activity participation: An expectancy-value approach. *Pediatric Exercise Science*, 5, 151–67.

Dewitte, M., Koster, E.H.W., De Houwer, J., & Buysse, A. (2007). Attentive processing of threat and adult attachment: A dot-probe study. *Behaviour Research and Therapy*, 45, 1307–17.

Dey, S. (1994). Physical exercise as a novel antidepressant agent: Possible role of serotonin receptor subtypes. *Physiology and Behavior*, 55, 353–9.

Dey, S., Singh, R., & Dey, P. (1992). Exercise training: Significance of regional alterations in serotonin metabolism of rat brain in relation to antidepressant effect of exercise. *Physiology and Behavior*, 52, 1095–9.

Doyne, E.J, Chambless, D.L., & Beutler, L.E. (1983). Aerobic exercise as a treatment for depression in women. *Behavioral Therapy*, 14, 434–40.

Duchesne, S., & Larose, S. (2007). Adolescent parental attachment and academic motivation and performance in early adolescence. *Journal of Applied Social Psychology*, 37, 1501–21.

Duda, J.L. (1992). Motivation in sport settings: A goal perspective approach. In G. Roberts (Ed.), *Motivation in sport and exercise*. Champaign, IL: Human Kinetics.

——(1993). Goals: A social cognitive approach to the study of achievement motivation sport. In R.N. Singer, M. Murphy, & L.K. Tennant (Eds.), *Handbook on research in sport psychology* (pp. 421–36). New York: Macmillan.

——(1996). Maximising motivation in sport and physical education among children and adolescents: The case for greater task involvement. *Quest*, 48, 290–302.

——(2005). Motivation in sport: The relevance of competence and achievement goals. In A.J. Elliot & C.S. Dweck (Eds.), *Handbook of competence motivation* (ch. 18). New York: Guilford Press.

——(2007). Motivation in sport settings: A goal perspective approach. In D. Smith & M. Bar-Eli (Eds.), *Essential readings in sport and exercise psychology* (ch. 9). Champaign, IL: Human Kinetics.

Duda, J.L., & Hall, H.K. (2001). Achievement goal theory in sport: Recent extensions and future directions. In R. Singer, H. Hausenblas, & C. Janelle (Eds.), *Handbook of research in sport psychology* (2nd Ed.) (pp. 417–34). New York: John Wiley & Sons.

Duda, J.L., & Whitehead, J. (1998). Measurement of goal perspectives in the physical domain. In J. Duda (Ed.), *Advances in sport and exercise psychology measurement*. Morgantown, WV: FIT Press.

Dumais, A., Lesage, A., Alda, M., Rouleau, G., Dumont, M., Chawky, N. *et al.* (2005). Risk factors for suicide completion in major depression: A case-controlled study of compulsive and aggressive behaviours in men. *American Journal of Psychiatry*, 162, 2116–24.

Dweck, C.S. (1986). Motivational processes affecting learning. *American Psychologist*, 41, 1040–8.

Dweck, C.S., & Elliott, E. (1983). Achievement motivation. In E. Heatherington (Ed.), *Handbook of child psychology* (vol. 4). New York: Wiley.

Dweck, C.S., & Leggett, E.L. (1988). A social-cognitive approach to motivation and personality. *Psychological Review*, 95, 256–73.

Edmunds, J., Ntoumanis, N., & Duda, J.L. (2008). Testing a self-determination theory based teaching-style intervention in the exercise domain. *European Journal of Social Psychology*, 38, 375–88.

Eisenberger, N.I., Lieberman, M.D., & Williams, K.D. (2003). Does rejection hurt? An fMRI study of social exclusion. *Science*, 302, 290–2.

Ekeland, E., Heian, F., & Hagan, K.B. (2005). Can exercise improve self-esteem in children and young people? A systematic review of randomised control trials. *British Journal of Sports Medicine*, 39, 792–8.

Elliot, A.J. (1997). Integrating the 'classic' and 'contemporary' approaches to achievement motivation: A hierarchical model of approach and avoidance achievement motivation. In M.L. Maehr & P.R. Pintrich (Eds.), *Advances in motivation and achievement* (vol. 10, pp. 143–79). Greenwich, CT: JAI Press Inc.

——(2005) A conceptual history of the achievement goal construct. In A.J. Elliot & C.S. Dweck (Eds.), *Handbook of competence and motivation*. New York: Guilford Press.

Elliot, A.J., & Church, M. (1997). A hierarchical model of approach and avoidance achievement motivation. *Journal of Personality and Social Psychology*, 72, 218–32.

Elliot, A.J., & Conroy, D.E. (2005). Beyond the dichotomous model of achievement goals in sport and exercise psychology. *Sport and Exercise Psychology Review*, 1, 17–25.

Elliot, A.J., & Dweck, C.S. (2005). Competence as the core of achievement motivation. In A.J. Elliot & C. Dweck (Eds.), *Handbook of competence and motivation*. New York: Guilford Press.

Elliot, A.J., & Harackiewicz, J.M. (1996). Approach and avoidance achievement goals and intrinsic motivation: A mediational analysis. *Journal of Personality and Social Psychology*, 70, 461–75.

Elliot, A.J., & McGregor, H.A. (2001). A 2 × 2 achievement goal framework. *Journal of Personality and Social Psychology*, 80, 501–19.

Elliot, A.J., & Reis, H.T. (2003). Attachment and exploration in adulthood. *Journal of Personality and Social Psychology*, 85, 317–31.

Elliot, E.S., & Dweck, C.S. (1988). Goals: An approach to motivation and achievement. *Journal of Personality and Social Psychology*, 54, 5–12.

Evans, N.J., & Jarvis, P.A. (1980). Group cohesion: A review and reevaluation. *Small Group Research*, 11, 359–70.

Eys, M.A., Hardy, J., Carron, A.V., & Beauchamp, M.R. (2003). The relationship between task cohesion and competitive state anxiety. *Journal of Sport and Exercise Psychology*, 25, 66–76.

Fanshawe, J.P., & Burnett, P.C. (1991). Assessing school-related stressors and coping mechanisms in adolescents. *British Journal of Educational Psychology*, 61, 92–8.

Farroni, T., Johnson, M., Menon, E., Zulian, L., Faraguna, D., & Csibra, G. (2005). Newborns' preference for face relevant stimuli: Effects of contrast polarity. *Proceedings of the National Academy of Sciences*, 102, 17245–50.

Feeney, J.A. (1999). Adult romantic attachment and couple relationships. In J. Cassidy & P.R. Shaver (Eds.), *Handbook of attachment, theory, research, and clinical applications* (pp. 355–77). New York: Guilford Press.

——(2000). Implications of attachment style for patterns of health and illness. *Child: Care, Health, and Development*, 26, 277–88.

Feeney, J.A., & Noller, P. (1992). Attachment style and romantic love: Relationship dissolution. *Australian Journal of Psychology*, 44, 69–74.

Feeney, J.A., Noller, P., & Callan, V.J. (1994a). Attachment style, communication and satisfaction in the early years of marriage. In K. Bartholomew & D. Perlman (Eds.), *Advances in personal relationships: Adult attachment relationships* (vol. 5, pp. 269–308). London: Jessica Kingsley.

Feeney, J.A., Noller, P., & Hanrahan, M. (1994b). Assessing adult attachment: Developments in the conceptualization of security and insecurity. In M.B. Sperling & W.H. Berman (Eds), *Attachment in adults: Clinical and developmental perspectives* (pp. 128–52). New York: Guilford.

Felitti, V.J., Anda, R.F., Nordenberg, D., Williamson, D.F., Apitz, A.M., Edwards, V. et al. (1998). Relationship of childhood abuse and household dysfunction to many of the leading causes of death in adults. *American Journal of Preventive Medicine*, 14, 245–58.

Fiedler, F.E. (1967). *A theory of leadership effectiveness*. New York: McGraw-Hill.

Figueirido, B., Bifulco, A., Pachecho, A., Costa, R., & Magarinho, R. (2006). Teenage pregnancy, attachment style and depression: A comparison of teenage and adult pregnant women in a Portuguese series. *Attachment and Human Development*, 8, 123–8.

Florian, V., Mikulincer, M., & Bucholtz, I. (1995). Effects of adult attachment style on the perception and search for social support. *Journal of Psychology*, 129, 665–76.

Fonagy, P., & Target, M. (2002). Early intervention and the development of self-regulation. *Psychoanalytic Inquiry*, 22, 307–35.

Fonagy, P., Leigh, T., Steele, M., Steele, H., Kennedy, R., Mattoon, G. et al. (1996). The relation of attachment status, psychiatric classification, and response to psychotherapy. *Journal of Consulting and Clinical Psychology*, 64, 22–31.

Ford, M., & Collins, N.L. (2010). Self-esteem moderates neuroendocrine and psychological responses to interpersonal rejection. *Journal of Personality and Social Psychology*, 98, 405–19.

Forrest, K. (2008). Attachment and attention in sport. *Journal of Clinical Sport Psychology*, 2, 242–58.

Foshee, V., & Bauman, K. (1992). Parental and peer characteristics as modifiers of the bond–behaviour relationship: An elaboration of control theory. *Journal of Health and Social Behaviour*, 33, 6–76.

Fox, K.R. (1992). Physical education and the development of children's self esteem. In N. Amstrong (Ed.), *New directions in physical education, 2: Towards a national curriculum*. Champaign, IL: Human Kinetics.

Fraley, R.C., & Brumbaugh, C.C. (2004). A dynamical systems approach to understanding stability and change in attachment security. In W.S. Rholes & J.A. Simpson (Eds.), *Adult attachment: Theory, research, and clinical implications* (pp. 86–132). New York: Guilford Press.

Fraley, R.C., & Davis, K.E. (1997). Attachment formation and transfer in young adults' close friendships and romantic relationships. *Personal Relationships*, 4, 131–44.

Fraley, R.C., & Shaver, P.R. (1998). Airport separations: A naturalistic study of adult attachment dynamics in separating couples. *Journal of Personality and Social Psychology*, 75, 1198–212.

Fraley, R.C., & Waller, N.G. (1998). Adult attachment patterns: A test of the typological model. In J.A. Simpson & W.S. Rholes (Eds.), *Attachment theory and close relationships* (pp. 77–114). New York: Guilford.

Fraley, R.C., Waller, N.G., & Brennan, K.A. (2000). An item response theory analysis of self-report measures of adult attachment. *Journal of Personality and Social Psychology*, 78, 350–65.

Fraser, S.N., & Spink, K.S. (2002). Examining the role of social support and group cohesion in exercise compliance. *Journal of Behavioral Medicine*, 25, 233–49.

Fraser-Thomas, J.L., Côté, J., & Deakin, J. 2005. Youth sport programs: An avenue to foster positive youth development. *Physical Education and Sport Pedagogy*, 10, 19–40.

Fratiglioni, L., Paillard-Borg, S., & Winblad, B. (2004). An active and socially integrated lifestyle in late life might protect against dementia. *Lancet*, 3, 343–53.

Frederick, C.M., & Ryan, R.M. (1995). Self-determination in sport: A review using cognitive evaluation theory. *International Journal of Sport Psychology*, 26, 5–23.

Frederick-Recascino, C.M. (2004). Self-determination theory and participation motivation research in the sport and exercise domain. In E.L. Deci & R.M. Ryan (Eds.), *Handbook of self-determination research* (ch. 13). Rochester, NY: University of Rochester Press.

Freedson, P.S., & Evenson, S. (1991). Familial aggregation in physical activity. *Research Quarterly for Exercise and Sport*, 62, 384–9.

Freemont, J., & Craighead, L.W. (1987). Aerobic exercise and cognitive therapy in the treatment of dysphoric moods. *Journal of Cognitive Therapy and Research*, 2, 241–51.

Freud, S. (1912/1963). The dynamics of transference. In *Therapy and technique* (pp. 105–15). New York: Macmillan.

——(1940) *An Outline of Psychoanalysis*. New York: Norton

Friedenreich, C., & Orenstein, M. (2002). Physical activity and cancer prevention: Etiological evidence and biological mechanisms. Paper presented at the International Research Conference on Food, Nutrition & Cancer, Washington, DC, 11–12 July.

Fuller, T.L., & Fincham, F.D. (1995). Attachment style in married couples: Relation to current marital functioning, stability over time, and method of assessment. *Personal Relationships*, 2, 17–34.

Gallagher, B.V., & Gardner, F.L. (2007). An examination of the relationship between early maladaptive schemas, coping, and emotional response to athletic injury. *Journal of Clinical Sports Psychology*, 1, 47–67.

Gallagher, S.S., Finison, K., Guyer, B., & Goodenough, S. (1984). The incidence of injuries among 87,000 Massachusetts children and adolescents: Results of the 1980–81 statewide childhood injury presentation program surveillance system. *American Journal of Public Health*, 8, 318–24.

Gatchel, R.J., & Weisberg, J.N. (Eds.) (2000). *Personality characteristic of patients with pain*. Washington, DC: American Psychological Association.

Gaudreau, P., & Blondin, J.-P. (2002). Development of a questionnaire for the assessment of coping strategies employed by athletes in competitive sport settings. *Psychology of Sport and Exercise*, 3, 1–34.

Gaudreau, P., & Blondin, J.-P. (2004). Different athletes cope differently during a sport competition: A cluster analysis of coping. *Personality and Individual Differences*, 36, 1865–77.

George, C., & West, M. (2001). The development and preliminary validation of a new measure of adult attachment: The adult attachment projective. *Attachment and Human Development*, 3, 30–61.

——(2003). The adult attachment projective: measuring individual differences in attachment security using projective methodology. In Hilsenroth, M.J. (Ed.), *Comprehensive handbook of psychological assessment, vol. 2: Personality assessment*. New York: John Wiley & Sons.

George, C., Kaplan, N., & Main, M. (1985). Adult Attachment Interview. Unpublished manuscript, Department of Psychology, University of California at Berkeley.

——(1996). Adult Attachment Interview (3rd Ed.). Unpublished manuscript, Department of Psychology, University of California, Berkeley.

Gillath, O., & Shaver, P.R. (2007). Effects of attachment style and relationship context on selection among relational strategies. *Journal of Research in Personality*, 41, 968–76.

Gillath, O., Hart, J., Noftle, E.E., & Stockdale, G.D. (2009). Development and validation of a state adult attachment measure (SAAM). *Journal of Research in Personality*, 43, 362–73.

Gillath, O., Mikulincer, M., Fitzsimons, G.M., Shaver, P.R., Schachner, D.A., & Bargh, J.A. (2006). Automatic activation of attachment-related goals. *Personality and Social Psychology Bulletin*, 32, 1375–88.

Glaser, R, Kiecolt-Glaser, J.K, Speicher, C.E, & Holliday, J.E. (1985). Stress, loneliness and changes in herpes virus latency. *Journal of Behavioral Medicine*, 8, 249–60.

Goldfarb, W. (1943). The effects of early institutional care on adolescent personality. *Journal of Experimental Education*, 14, 441–7.

Gottman, J.M., & Katz, L.F. (1989). Effects of marital discord on young children's peer interaction and health. *Developmental Psychology*, 25, 373–81.

Gottman, J.M., Katz, L.F., & Hooven, C. (1996). Parental meta-emotion philosophy and the emotional life of families: Theoretical models and preliminary data. *Journal of Family Psychology*, 10, 243–68.

Goudas, M., Biddle, S.J.H., & Fox, K.R. (1994). Achievement goal orientations and intrinsic motivation in physical testing with children. *Pediatric Exercise Science*, 6, 159–67.

Gould, D., Eklund, R.C., & Jackson, S.A. (1993). Coping strategies used by US Olympic wrestlers. *Research Quarterly for Exercise and Sport*, 64, 83–93.

Green, J.D., & Campbell, W.K. (2000). Attachment and exploration in adults: Chronic and contextual variability. *Personality and Social Psychology Bulletin*, 26, 452–61.

Griffin, D.W., & Bartholomew, K. (1994). Models of the self and other: Fundamental dimensions underlying measures of adult attachment. *Journal of Personality and Social Psychology*, 67, 430–45.

Gruber, J. (1986). Physical activity and self esteem development in children: A metaanalysis. In G. Stull & H. Eckern (Eds.), *Effects of physical activity on children*. Champaign, IL: Human Kinetics.

Gustafson, S.L., & Rhodes, R.E. (2006) Parental correlates of physical activity in children and early adolescents. *Sports Medicine*, 36, 79–97.

Hagger, M., & Chatzisarantis, N. (2007). *Intrinsic motivation and self-determination in exercise and sport*. Champaign, IL: Human Kinetics.

Hamilton, C.E. (2000). Continuity and discontinuity of attachment from infancy through adolescence. *Child Development*, 71, 690–4.

Hammond, J.R., & Fletcher, G.J.O. (1991). Attachment styles and relationship satisfaction in the development of close relationships. *New Zealand Journal of Psychology*, 20, 56–62.

Harackiewicz, J., Barron, K., & Elliot, A. (1998). Rethinking achievement goals: When are they adaptive for college students and why? *Educational Psychologist*, 33, 1–21.

Hardy, J., Eys, M.E., & Carron, A.V. (2005). Exploring the potential disadvantages of high cohesion in sports teams. *Small Group Research*, 36, 166–87.

Hardy, L., Jones, G., & Gould, D. (1996). *Understanding psychological preparation for sport: Theory and practice of elite performers*. Chichester, Wiley.

Harlow, H.E. (1958). The nature of love. *American Psychologist*, 13, 673–85.

Hartup, W.W. (1989). Behavioral manifestations of children's friendships. In T.J. Bemdt & G.W. Ladd (Eds.), *Peer relationships in child development* (pp. 46–70). New York: Wiley.

Harwood, C., & Hardy, L. (2001). Persistence and effort in moving achievement goal research forward: A response to Treasure and colleagues. *Journal of Sport and Exercise Psychology*, 23, 330–45.

Harwood, C., Hardy, L., & Swain, A. (2000). Achievement goals in sport: A critique of conceptual and measurement issues. *Journal of Sport and Exercise Psychology*, 22, 235–55.

Harwood, C., Spray, C., & Keegan, R. (2008). Achievement goal theories in sport. In T.S. Horn (Ed.), *Advances in sport psychology* (3rd Ed.) (pp. 157–85). Champaign, IL: Human Kinetics.

Haskell, W.L., Lee, I.M., Pate, R.R., Powell, K.E., Blair, S.N., Franklin, B.A. *et al.* (2007). Physical activity and public health: Updated recommendation for adults from the American College of Sports Medicine and the American Heart Association. *Circulation*, 116, 1081–93.

Hassmen, P., Koivula, N., & Uutela, A., 2000. Physical exercise and psychological well-being: A population study in Finland. *Preventative Medicine*, 30, 17–25.

Hazan, C., & Shaver, P.R (1987). Romantic love conceptualized as an attachment process. *Journal of Personality and Social Psychology*, 2, 511–24.

——(1990). Love and work: An attachment-theoretical perspective. *Journal of Personality and Social Psychology*, 59, 270–80.

——(1994a). Attachment as an organizational framework for research on close relationships. *Psychological Inquiry*, 5, 1–22.

——(1994b). Deeper into attachment theory. *Psychological Inquiry*, 5, 68–79.

Helms, P.J. (1997). Sports injuries in children: Should we be concerned? *Archives of Disease in Childhood*, 77, 161–3.

Hersey, P., & Blanchard, K.H. (1969). *Management and organizational behaviour*. Englewood Cliffs, NJ: Prentice Hall.

Hesse, E. (1999). The Adult Attachment Interview: Historical and current perspectives. In J. Cassidy & P.R. Shaver (Eds.), *Handbook of attachment: Theory, research, and clinical applications* (pp. 395–433). New York: Guilford.

Hofer, M.A., & Sullivan, R.M. (2001). Toward a neurobiology of attachment. In C.A. Nelson & M. Luciana (Eds.), *Handbook of developmental cognitive neuroscience*. Cambridge, MA: MIT Press.

Hogg, M.A. (1992). *The social psychology of group cohesiveness: From attraction to social identity.* New York: New York University Press.

——(1993). Group cohesiveness: A critical review and some new directions. *European Review of Social Psychology,* 4, 85–111.

Holt, N.L., & Dunn, J.G.H. (2004). Longitudinal idiographic analyses of appraisal and coping responses in sport. *Psychology of Sport and Exercise,* 5, 213–22.

Holt, N.L., & Hogg, J.M. (2002). Perceptions of stress and coping during preparations for the 1999 women's soccer world cup finals. *The Sport Psychologist,* 16, 251–71.

Holtzworth-Munroe, A., Stuart, G., & Hutchinson, G. (1997). Violent versus non-violent husbands: Differences in attachment patterns, dependency, and jealousy. *Journal of Family Psychology,* 11, 314–31.

Hootman, J.M., Dick, R., & Agel, J. (2007). Epidemiology of collegiate injuries for 15 sports: Summary and recommendations for injury prevention initiatives. *Journal of Athletic Training,* 42, 311–19.

Howard, M.S., & Medway, F.J. (2004). Adolescents' attachment and coping with stress. *Psychology in the Schools,* 41, 391–402.

Hunt, J. (1941). The effects of infant feeding frustration on adult hoarding of the albino rat. *Journal of Abnormal and Social Psychology,* 36, 338–60.

Ievleva, L., & Orlick, T. (1991). Mental links to enhanced healing: An exploratory study. *The Sport Psychologist,* 5, 25–40.

Irwin, M., Daniels, M., Smith, T., Bloom, E., & Weiner, H. (1987). Impaired natural killer cell activity during bereavement. *Brain, Behaviour, and Immunity,* 1, 98–104.

Jacobsen, T., Edelstein, W., & Hoffman, V. (1994). A longitudinal study of the relation between representations of attachment in childhood and cognitive functioning in childhood and adolescence. *Developmental Psychology,* 30, 112–24.

Jacobsson, B. (1986). Sports accidents among children and teenagers: A one-year study of incidence and severity in a Swedish rural municipality. *Scandinavian Journal of Sports Sciences,* 8, 75–9.

Jacobvitz, D., Curran, M., & Moller, N. (2002). Measurement of adult attachment: The place of self-report and interview methodologies. *Attachment and Human Development,* 4, 207–15.

Jago, R., Brockman, R., Fox, K.R., Cartwright, K., Page, A.S., & Thompson, J.L. (2009). Friendship groups and physical activity: Qualitative findings on how physical activity is initiated and maintained among 10–11-year-old children. *International Journal of Behavioural Nutrition and Physical Activity,* 6, 23–32.

Jago, R.P., Fox, K.R., Page, A.S., Brockman, R., & Thompson, J.L. (2010). Parent and child physical activity and sedentary time: Do active parents foster active children? *BMC Public Health,* 10, 194–203.

Jang, G.J., & Chung, K.A. (2009). A study on infant temperament and mother–infant attachment of breastfeeding mothers. *Korean Journal of Women's Health Nursing,* 15, 224–30.

Janik, V.M., & Slater, P.J.B. (1998). Context-specific use suggests that bottlenose dolphin signature whistles are cohesion calls. *Animal Behaviour,* 56, 829–38.

Johnson, M., Dziurawiec, S., Ellis, H., & Morton, J. (1991). Newborns' preferential tracking of face-like stimuli and its subsequent decline. *Cognition,* 40, 1–19.

Jones, R., & Cassidy, T. (2004). *Understanding sports coaching: The social, cultural and pedagogical foundations of coaching practice.* London: Routledge.

Jones, R., Armour, K., & Potrac, P. (2004). *Sports coaching cultures.* London: Routledge.

Jowett, S. (2003). When the honeymoon is over: A case study of a coach–athlete relationship in crisis. *The Sport Psychologist*, 17, 444–60.

Jowett, S., & Clark-Carter, D. (2006). Perceptions of empathic accuracy and assumed similarity in the coach–athlete relationship. *British Journal of Social Psychology*, 45, 617–37.

Jowett, S., & Cockerill, I.M. (2002). Incompatibility in the coach–athlete relationship. In I.M. Cockerill (Ed.), *Solutions in sport psychology* (pp. 16–31). London: Thomson Learning.

——(2003). Olympic medallists' perspective of the athlete–coach relationship. *Psychology of Sport and Exercise*, 4, 313–31.

Jowett, S., & Meek, G.A. (2000). The coach–athlete relationship in married couples: An exploratory content analysis. *The Sport Psychologist*, 14, 157–75.

Jowett, S., & Ntoumanis, N. (2004). The coach–athlete relationship questionnaire (CART-Q): Development and initial validation. *Scandinavian Journal of Medicine and Science in Sports*, 14, 245–57.

Jowett, S., & Wylleman, P. (2006). Interpersonal relationships in sport and exercise settings: Crossing the chasm. *Psychology of Sport and Exercise*, 7, 119–23.

Julian, J., Bishop, D., & Fiedler, F.E. (1966). Quasitherapeutic effects of intergroup competition. *Journal of Personality and Social Psychology*, 3, 321–7.

Kafetsios, K. (2000). Attachment, positive and negative emotions in close relationships. Paper presented at the 10th International Conference in Personal Relationships, University of Queensland, Brisbane, July.

Kaplan, A., Gheen, M., & Midgley, C. (2002). Classroom goal structure and students' disruptive behaviour. *British Journal of Educational Psychology*, 72, 191–211.

Kaplan, N. (1987). Individual differences in six-year-olds' thoughts about separation: Predicted from attachment to mother at one year of age. Unpublished doctoral dissertation, University of California, Berkeley.

Kashy, D.A., & Kenny, D.A. (2000). The analysis of data from dyads and groups. In H.T. Reis & C.M. Judd (Eds.), *Handbook of research methods in social and personality psychology* (pp. 451–77). Cambridge: Cambridge University Press.

Kaslow, M.H., Deering, C.G., & Racusia, G.R. (1994). Depressed children and their families. *Clinical Psychological Review*, 14, 39–59.

Kavussanu, M., & Roberts, G.C. (1996). Motivation in physical activity contexts: The relationship of perceived motivational climate to intrinsic motivation and self-efficacy. *Journal of Sport and Exercise Psychology*, 18, 264–80.

Keefe, K., & Berndt, T.J. (1996). Relations of friendship quality to self-esteem in early adolescence. *Journal of Early Adolescence*, 16, 110–29.

Kenny, D.A., & Cook, W. (1999). Partner effects in relationship research: Conceptual issues, analytic difficulties, and illustrations. *Personal Relationships*, 6, 433–88.

Kenny, D.A., & Lavoie, L. (1985). Separating individual and group effects. *Journal of Personality and Social Psychology*, 48, 339–48.

Kenny, D.A., Kashy, D.A., & Cook, W. (2006). *Dyadic data analysis*. New York: Guilford Press.

Kiecolt-Glaser, J.K., Malarkey, W.B., Chee, M., Newton, X, Cacioppo, J.T., Mao, H. et al. (1993). Negative behavior during marital conflict is associated with immunological down-regulation. *Psychosomatic Medicine*, 55, 395–409.

Kiesler, D.J. (1997). *Contemporary interpersonal theory research and personality, psychopathology, and psychotherapy*. New York: Wiley.

Kimiecik, J.C., & Horn, T.S. (1998). Parental beliefs and children's moderate-to-vigorous physical activity. *Research Quarterly for Exercise and Sport*, 69, 163–75.

Kirsh, S.J., & Cassidy, J. (1997). Preschoolers attention to and memory for attachment-relevant information. *Child Development*, 68, 1143–53.

Klein, M. (1932). *The psycho-analysis of children*. London: Hogarth Press.

Klint, K.A., & Weiss, M.R. (1986). Dropping in and dropping out: Participation motives of current and former youth athletes. *Canadian Journal of Applied Sport Sciences*, 11, 106–114.

Kobak, R. (1994). Adult attachment: A personality or relationship construct? *Psychological Inquiry*, 5, 42–4.

——(2009). Defining and measuring of attachment bonds: Comment on Kurdek (2009). *Journal of Family Psychology*, 23, 447–9.

Kobak, R., Rosenthal, N., Zajac, K., & Madsen, S.D. (2007). Adolescent attachment hierarchies and the search for an adult pair-bond. *New Directions for Child and Adolescent Development*, 117, 57–72.

Korfmacher, J., Adam, E., Ogawa, J., & Egeland, B. (1997). Adult attachment: Implications for the therapeutic process in a home visitation intervention. *Applied Developmental Science*, 1, 43–52.

Kraemer, G., & Clarke, A. (1990). The behavioral neurobiology of self-injurious behavior in rhesus monkeys. *Progress in Neuro-Psychopharmacology and Biological Psychiatry*, 14, 5141–68.

Krohn, M.D., Skinner, W.F., Massey, J.L., & Akers, R.L. (1985). Social learning theory and adolescent cigarette smoking: A longitudinal study. *Social Problems*, 32, 455–71.

Krohne, H.W., & Hindel, C. (1988). Trait anxiety, state anxiety, and coping behavior as predictors of athletic performance. *Anxiety Research*, 1, 225–34.

Ladd, G.W. (1999). Peer relationships and social competence during early and middle childhood. *Annual Review of Psychology*, 50, 333–59.

La Greca, A.M., & Moore Harrison, H. (2005). Adolescent peer relations, friendships, and romantic relationships: Do they predict social anxiety and depression? *Journal of Clinical Child and Adolescent Psychology*, 34, 49–61.

La Guardia, J.G., Ryan, R.M., Couchman, C.E., & Deci, E.L. (2000). Within-person variation in security of attachment: A self-determination theory perspective on attachment, need fulfillment, and well being. *Journal of Personality and Social Psychology*, 79, 367–84.

Lamb, M.E. (1976). The role of the father: An overview. In M.E. Lamb (Ed.), *The role of the father in child development*. New York: Wiley.

——(1977). The development of mother–infant and father–infant attachments during the second year of life. *Developmental Psychology*, 13, 637–48.

Lautenshlager, N., Cox, T., Flicker, L., Foster, J., van Bockxmeer, F., Xiao, J. et al. (2008). Effect of physical activity on cognitive function in older adults at risk of Alzheimer's disease: A randomized trial. *Journal of the American Medical Association*, 300, 1027–37.

Lazarus, R.S. (1999). *Stress and emotion: A new synthesis*. New York: Springer.

——(2000). How emotions influence performance in competitive sports. *The Sport Psychologist*, 14, 229–52.

Lazarus, R.S., & Folkman, S. (1984). *Stress, appraisal and coping*. New York: Springer.

Leddy, M.H., Lambert, M.J., & Ogles, B.M. (1994). Psychological consequences of athletic injury among high-level competitors. *Research Quarterly for Exercise and Sport*, 64, 349–54.

Lewis, M., Feiring, C., McGuffog, C., & Jaskir, J. (1984). Predicting psychopathology in six-year-olds from early social relations. *Child Development*, 55, 123–36.

Lissau, I., & Sorensen, T.I.A. (1994). Parental neglect during childhood and increased risk of obesity in young adulthood. *Lancet*, 343, 324–7.

Liu, M. (2009). The intrapersonal and interpersonal effects of anger on negotiation strategies: A cross-cultural investigation. *Human Communication Research*, 35, 148–69.

Lorenz, K.Z. (1935). Der kumpan in der umwelt des vogels. *Journal of Ornithology* (Leipzig), 83. (English translation in C. Schiller (Ed.) (1957). *Instinctive behaviour*. New York: International Universities Press.)

Lorimer, R., & Jowett, S. (2009). Empathic accuracy in coach–athlete dyads who participate in team and individual sports. *Psychology of Sport and Exercise*, 10, 152–8.

Lusseau, D., & Newman, M.E.J. (2004). Identifying the role that animals play in their social networks. *Proceedings of the Royal Society B: Biological Sciences*, 271, S477–S481.

McCarthy, G. (1998). Attachment representations and representations of the self in relation to other: A study of preschool children in inner-city London. *British Journal of Medical Psychology*, 71, 57–72.

McClelland, D.C. (1951). *Personality*. New York: Dryden Press.

McDonald, S.A., & Hardy, L. (1990). Affective response patterns of the injured athlete: An exploratory analysis. *The Sport Psychologist*, 4, 261–74.

McWilliams, L.A., & Asmundson, G.J.G. (2007). The relationship of adult attachment dimensions to pain-related fear, hypervigilance, and catastrophizing. *Pain*, 127, 27–34.

McWilliams, L.A., Cox, B.J., & Enns, M.W. (2000). Impact of adult attachment styles on pain and disability associated with arthritis in a nationally representative sample. *Clinical Journal of Pain*, 16, 360–4.

Madigan, S., Bakermans-Kranenburg, M.J., van Izjendoorn, M.H., Moran, G., Pederson, D.R., & Benoit, D. (2006). Unresolved states of mind, anomalous parental behaviour, and disorganised attachment: A review and meta-analysis of a transmission gap. *Attachment and Human Development*, 8, 89–111.

Maehr, M.L. (1989). Thoughts about motivation. In C. Ames and R. Ames (Eds.), *Research on motivation in education* (vol. 3, pp. 299–315). New York: Academic Press.

Maehr, M., & Midgley, C. (1991) Enhancing student motivation: A schoolwide approach. *Educational Psychologist*, 26, 399–427.

Maier, M.A., Bernier, A., Pekrun, R., Zimmermann, P., & Grossmann, E. (2004). Attachment working models as unconscious structures: An experimental test. *International Journal of Behavioural Development*, 28, 180–9.

Main, M. (1985). An adult attachment classification system: Its relation to infant–parent attachment. Paper presented at the biennial meeting of the Society for Research in Child Development, Toronto.

Main, M. (1990). Cross-cultural studies of attachment organization: Recent studies, changing methodologies and the concept of conditional strategies. *Human Development*, 33, 48–61.

——(1996). Introduction to the special section on attachment and psychopathology: 2. Overview of the field of attachment. *Journal of Consulting and Clinical Psychology*, 64, 237–43.

Main, M., & Cassidy, J. (1988). Categories of response to reunion with the parent at age 6: Predictable from infant attachment classifications and stable for a 1-month period. *Developmental Psychology*, 24, 415–26.

Main, M., & Goldwyn, R. (1998). Adult Attachment Interview scoring and classification system. Unpublished manuscript, University of California at Berkeley.

Main, M, & Solomon, J. (1986). Discovery of an insecure-disorganized/disoriented attachment pattern. In T.B. Brazelton and M.W. Yogman (Eds.), *Affective development in infancy* (pp. 95–124) Norwood, NJ: Ablex.

——(1990) Procedures for identifying infants as disorganized/disoriented during the Ainsworth Strange Situation. In M.T. Greenberg, D. Cicchetti, & E.M. Cummmgs (Eds.), *Attachment in the preschool years: Theory, research, and intervention* (pp. 121–60). Chicago: University of Chicago Press.

Main, M., Kaplan, N., & Cassidy, J. (1985). Security in infancy, childhood, and adulthood: A move to the level of representation. *Monographs of the Society for Research in Child Development*, 50(1–2, Serial No. 219).

Martens, R. (2007). About smocks and jocks. In D. Smith & M. Bar-Eli (Eds.), *Essential readings in sport and exercise psychology* (pp. 32–7). Champaign, IL: Human Kinetics.

Martinsen, E.W. (1990). Benefits of exercise for the treatment of depression: A review. *Sports Medicine*, 9, 380–9.

Martinsen, E.W., Sandwik, L., & Kolbjornsrud, O.B. (1985). Aerobic exercise in the treatment of nonpsychotic mental disorders: An explanatory study. *Nordic Journal of Psychiatry*, 43, 411–15.

Marvin, R.S., & Stewart, R.S. (1990). A family systems framework for the study of attachment (pp. 51–86). In M.T. Greenberg, D. Cicchetti, & E.M. Cummings (Eds.), *Attachment in the preschool years: Research and intervention*. Chicago: University of Chicago Press.

Mercer, J. (2011). Attachment and its vicissitudes: Toward an updated theory. *Theory & Psychology*, 21, 25–45.

Meredith, P.J., Ownsworth, T., & Strong, J. (2008). A review of the evidence linking adult attachment theory and chronic pain: A conceptual model. *Clinical Psychology Review*, 28, 407–29.

Meredith, P.J., Strong, J., & Feeney, J.A. (2005). Evidence of a relationship between adult attachment variables and appraisals of chronic pain. *Pain Research and Management*, 10, 191–200.

——(2006). The relationship of adult attachment to emotion, catastrophizing, control, threshold and tolerance, in experimentally induced pain. *Pain*, 120, 44–52.

Merskey, H., & Bogduk, N. (Eds.) (1994). *Classification of chronic pain: Descriptions of chronic pain syndromes and definitions of pain terms* (2nd Ed.). Seattle: IASP Press.

Midtgaard, J., Rorth, M., Stelter, R., & Adamsen, L. (2006). The group matters: An exploratory study of group cohesion and quality of life in cancer patients participating in physical activity intervention during treatment. *European Journal of Cancer Care*, 15, 25–33.

Mikulincer, M. (1995). Attachment style and the mental representation of the self. *Journal of Personality and Social Psychology*, 69, 1203–15.

——(1997). Adult attachment style and information processing: Individual differences in curiosity and cognitive closure. *Journal of Personality and Social Psychology*, 72, 1217–30.

——(1998a). Adult attachment style and affect regulation: Strategic variations in self-appraisals. *Journal of Personality and Social Psychology*, 75, 420–35.

——(1998b). Attachment working models and the sense of trust: An exploration of interaction goals and affect regulation. *Journal of Personality and Social Psychology*, 81, 1209–24.

Mikulincer, M., & Florian, V. (1995). Appraisal and coping with a real-life stressful situation: The contribution of attachment styles. *Personality and Social Psychology Bulletin*, 21, 408–16.

——(1998). The relationship between adult attachment styles and emotional and cognitive reactions to stressful events. In J.A. Simpson & W.S. Rholes (Eds.), *Attachment theory and close relationships* (pp. 143–65). New York: Guilford Press.

Mikulincer, M., & Shaver, P.R. (2007). Boosting attachment security to promote mental health, prosocial values, and inter-group tolerance. *Psychological Inquiry*, 18, 139–56.

Mikulincer, M., Birnbaum, G., Woddis, D., & Nachmias, O. (2000). Stress and accessibility of proximity-related thoughts: Exploring the normative and intraindividual components of attachment theory. *Journal of Personality and Social Psychology*, 78, 509–23.

Mikulincer, M., Florian, V., & Weller, A. (1993). Attachment strategies, and post-traumatic psychological distress: The impact of the Gulf War in Israel. *Journal of Personality and Social Psychology*, 64, 817–26.

Mikulincer, M., Gillath, O., & Shaver, P.R. (2002). Activation of the attachment system in adulthood: Threat-related primes increase the accessibility of mental representations of attachment figures. *Journal of Personality and Social Psychology*, 83, 881–95.

Middleton, M.J., & Midgley, C. (1997). Avoiding the demonstration of lack of ability: An underexplored aspect of goal theory. *Journal of Educational Psychology*, 89, 710–18.

Moore, L.L., Lombardi, D.A., White, M.J., Campbell, J.L., Oliveira, S.A., & Ellison, R.C. (1991). Influence of parents' physical activity levels on activity levels of young children. *Journal of Pediatrics*, 118, 215–19.

Mormede, P. (1997). Genetic influences on the responses to psychosocial challenges in rats. *Acta Physiologica Scandinavica*, Suppl., 640, 65–8.

Morris, R.L., & Kavussanu, M. (2008). Antecedents of approach-avoidance goals in sport. *Journal of Sports Sciences*, 26, 465–76.

Moss, E., & St Laurent, D. (2001). Attachment at school age and academic performance. *Developmental Psychology*, 37, 863–74.

Mudrack, P.E. (1989). Defining group cohesiveness: A legacy of confusion. *Small Group Behavior*, 20, 37–49.

Mullan, E., & Markland, D. (1997). Variation in self-determination across the stages of change for exercise in adults. *Motivation and Emotion*, 21, 349–61.

Naylor, K., & Brawley, L.R. (1992). Social loafing: Perceptions and implications. Paper presented at the joint meeting of the Canadian Association of Sport Sciences and the Canadian Psychomotor Learning and Sport Psychology Association, Saskatoon, Saskatchewan, Canada, October.

Newcomb, A.F., & Bagwell, C.L. (1995). Children's friendship relations: A meta-analytic review. *Psychological Bulletin*, 117, 306–47.

Newcomb, T.M. (1953). An approach to the study of communicative acts. *Psychological Review*, 60, 393–404.

Nicholls, A.R., & Polman, R.C.J. (2007). Coping in sport: A systematic review. *Journal of Sports Sciences*, 25, 11–31.

Nicholls, J.G. (1984). Achievement motivation: Conceptions of ability, subjective, experience, task choice, and performance. *Psychological Review*, 91, 328–46.

——(1989). *The competitive ethos and democratic education*. Cambridge, MA: Harvard University Press.

Ntoumanis, N., & Biddle, S.J.H. (1999). A review of motivational climate in physical activity. *Journal of Sports Sciences*, 17, 643–65.

Ntoumanis, N., Biddle, S.J.H., & Haddock, G. (1999). The mediating role of coping strategies on the relationship between achievement motivation and affect in sport. *Anxiety, Stress and Coping*, 12, 299–327.

Ommundsen, Y., Roberts, G., Lemyre, P., & Miller, B.W. (2005). Peer relationships in adolescent competitive soccer: Associations to perceived motivational climate, achievement goals, and perfectionism. *Journal of Sports Sciences*, 23, 977–89.

Orth-Gomer, K., Rosengren, A., & Wilhelmson, L. (1993). Lack of social support and incidence of coronary heart disease in middle-aged Swedish men. *Psychosomatic Medicine*, 55, 37–53.

Padilla, S.G. (1935). Further studies on the delayed pecking of chicks. *Journal of Comparative Psychology*, 20, 413–43.

Paley, B., Cox, M., Burchinal, M., & Payne, C. (1999). Attachment and marital functioning: Comparison of spouses with continuous-secure, earned-secure, dismissing, and preoccupied stances. *Journal of Family Psychology*, 13, 580–97.

Papaioannou, A.G., Ampatzoglou, G., Kalogiannis, P., & Sagovits, A. (2008). Social agents, achievement goals, satisfaction and academic achievement in youth sport. *Psychology of Sport and Exercise*, 9, 122–41.

Parish, M. (2000). The nature of the patient's tie to the therapist (Doctoral dissertation, Adelphi University, 1999). *Dissertation Abstracts International*, 60, 6378-B.

Parish, M., & Eagle, M. (2003). Attachment to the therapist. *Psychoanalytic Psychology*, 20, 271–86.

Parker, J.G., & Asher, S.R. (1993). Friendship and friendship quality in middle childhood: Links with peer group acceptance and feelings of loneliness and social dissatisfaction. *Developmental Psychology*, 29, 611–21.

Parker, J.G., & Gottman, J.M. (1989). Social and emotional development in a relational context: Friendship interaction from early childhood to adolescence. In T.J. Bemdt & G.W. Ladd (Eds.), *Peer relationships in child development* (pp. 95–131). New York: Wiley.

Parsons, J., Adler, T, & Kaczala, C. (1982) Socialisation of achievement attitudes and beliefs: Parental influences. *Child Development*, 53, 310–21.

Pearce, C. (2009). *A short introduction to attachment and attachment disorder*. London: Jessica Kingsley.

Pearson, L., & Jones, G. (1992). Emotional effects of sports injuries: Implications for the physiotherapists. *Physiotherapy*, 78, 762–70.

Pelletier, L., Fortier, M., Vallerand, R., Tuson, K., & Blais, M. (1995). Toward a new measure of intrinsic motivation, extrinsic motivation, and amotivation in sports: The Sport Motivation Scale (SMS). *Journal of Sport & Exercise Psychology*, 17, 35–53.

Petitpas, A. Cornelius, A., & Van Raalte, J. (2008) Youth development through sport. In N. Holt (Ed.) *Positive youth development and sport* (pp. 61–70). London: Routledge.

Pincus, D., Freeman, W., & Modell, A. (2007). A neurobiological model of perception: Considerations for transference. *Psychoanalytic Psychology*, 24, 623–40.

Pintrich, P.R. (2000). An achievement goal theory perspective on issues in motivation terminology, theory, and research. *Contemporary Educational Psychology*, 25, 92–104.

Poczwardowski, A., Barott, J.E., & Henschen, K.P. (2002). The athlete and coach: Their relationship and its meaning. Results of an interpretive study. *International Journal of Sport Psychology*, 33, 116–40.

Poczwardowski, A., Barott, J.E., & Jowett, S. (2006). Diversifying approaches to research on athlete–coach relationships. *Psychology of Sport and Exercise*, 7, 125–42.

Prapavessis, H., & Carron, A.V. (1997). The role of sacrifice in the dynamics of sport teams. *Group Dynamics*, 1, 231–40.

Reinboth, M., & Duda, J.L. (2006). Perceived motivational climate, need satisfaction and indices of well-being in team sports: A longitudinal perspective. *Psychology of Sport and Exercise*, 7, 269–86.

Reinboth, M., Duda, J.L., & Ntoumanis, N. (2004). Dimensions of coaching behavior, need satisfaction, and the psychological and physical welfare of young athletes. *Motivation and Emotion*, 28, 297–313.

Repetti, R.L., Taylor, S.E., & Seeman, T.E. (2002). Risky families: Family social environments and the mental and physical health of offspring. *Psychological Bulletin*, 128, 330–66.

Reti, I.M., Samuels, J.F., Eaton, W.W., Bienvu, O.J., Costa, P.T., & Nestadt, G. (2002). Adult antisocial personality traits are associated with experience of low parental care and maternal overprotection. *Acta Psychoactica Scandinavica*, 106, 126–33.

Risser, W.L., & Preston, D. (1989). Incidence and causes of musculoskeletal injuries in adolescents training with weights. *Pediatric Exercise Science*, 1, 84.

Roberts, G.C. (2001). *Advances in motivation in sport and exercise*. Champaign, IL: Human Kinetics.

Roisman, G.I. (2009). Adult attachment: Toward a rapprochement of methodological cultures. *Current Directions in Psychological Science*, 18, 122–26.

Roisman, G.I., Holland, A., Fortuna, K., Fraley, R.C., Clausell, E., & Clarke, A. (2007). The Adult Attachment Interview and self-reports of attachment style: An empirical rapprochement. *Journal of Personality and Social Psychology*, 92, 678–97.

Rom, E., & Mikulincer, M. (2003). Attachment theory and group processes: The association between attachment style and group-related representations, goals, memories, and functioning. *Journal of Personality and Social Psychology*, 84, 1220–35.

Rose, E.A., Parfitt, G., & Williams, S. (2005). Exercise causality orientations, behavioural regulation for exercise and stage of change for exercise: Exploring their relationships. *Psychology of Sport and Exercise*, 6, 399–414.

Rothbaum, F., & Weisz, J.R. (1994). Parental caregiving and child externalizing behavior in nonclinical samples: A meta-analysis. *Psychological Bulletin*, 116, 55–74.

Rovio, S., Kareholt, I., Helkala, E., Viitanen, M., Winblad, B., Tuomilehto, J. *et al.* (2005). Leisure-time physical activity at midlife and the risk of dementia and Alzheimer's disease. *Lancet*, 4, 705–11.

Rowe, A., & Carnelley, K. (2003). Attachment-style differences in the processing of attachment-relevant information: Primed-style effects on recall, interpersonal expectations, and affect. *Personal Relationships*, 10, 59–75.

Ryan, R.M., & Deci, E.L. (2000). Self-determination theory and the facilitation of intrinsic motivation, social development, and well-being. *American Psychologist*, 55, 68–78.

——(2004). Overview of self-determination theory: An organismic dialectical perspective. In E.L. Deci & R.M. Ryan (Eds.), *Handbook of self-determination research* (ch. 1). Rochester, NY: University of Rochester Press.

——(2007). Self-determination theory and the promotion and maintenance of sport, exercise, and health. In M. Hagger & S. Chatzisarantis (Eds.), *Intrinsic motivation and self-determination in exercise and sport* (ch. 1). Champaign, IL: Human Kinetics.

Salo, J.A., Qouta, S., & Punamaki, R. (2005). Adult attachment, posttraumatic growth, and negative emotions among former political prisoners. *Anxiety, Stress, and Coping*, 18, 361–78.

Sarrazin, P., Vallerand, R.J., Guillet, E., Pelletier, L., & Cury, F. (2002). Motivation and dropout in female handballers: A 21-month prospective study. *European Journal of Social Psychology*, 32, 395–418.

Schaffer, H.R., & Emerson, P.E. (1964). The development of social attachments in infancy. *Monographs of the Society for Research in Child Development*, 29 (3).

Scharfe, E., & Eldredge, D. (2001). Associations between attachment representations and health behaviours in late adolescence. *Journal of Health Psychology*, 6, 295–307.

Schmitz, N., Kruse, J., & Kugler, J. (2004). The association between physical exercises and health-related quality of life in subjects with mental disorders: Results from a cross-sectional survey. *Preventive Medicine*, 39, 1200–7.

Schwarz, J.P., Lindley, L.D., & Buboltz Jr, W.C. (2007). Adult attachment orientations: Relation to affiliation motivation. *Counselling Psychology Quarterly*, 20, 253–65.

Segal R., Evans W., Johnson D., Smith J., Colletta S., Gayton J. et al. (2001) Structured exercise improves physical functioning in women with stages I and II breast cancer: Results of a randomized controlled trial. *Journal of Clinical Oncology*, 19, 657–65.

Shankar, P.R., Fields, S.K., Collins, C.L., Dick, R., & Comstock, R.D. (2007). Epidemiology of high school and collegiate football injuries in the United States, 2005–6. *American Journal of Sports Medicine*, 35, 1295–303.

Shaver, P.R., & Clark, C.L. (1994). The psychodynamics of adult romantic attachment. In J.M. Masling & R.F. Bornstein (Eds.), *Empirical perspectives on object relations theories* (pp. 105–56). Washington, DC: American Psychological Association.

Shaver, P.R., & Hazan, C. (1988). A biased overview of the study of love. *Journal of Social and Personal Relationships*, 5, 473–501.

——(1993). Adult romantic attachment: Theory and evidence. In D. Perlman & W. Jones (Eds.), *Advances in personal relationships* (vol. 4, pp. 29–70). London: Jessica Kingsley.

Shaver, P.R., & Mikulincer, M. (2002). Attachment-related psychodynamics. *Attachment and Human Development*, 4, 133–61.

——(2005). Attachment theory and research: Resurrection of the psychodynamic approach to personality. *Journal of Research in Personality*, 39, 22–45.

Shaver, P.R., Belsky, J., & Brennan, K.A. (2000). The Adult Attachment Interview and self-reports of romantic attachment: Associations across domains and methods. *Personal Relationships*, 7, 25–43.

Shaver, P.R., Collins, N.L., & Clark, C.L. (1996). Attachment styles and internal working models of self and relationship partners. In G.J.O. Fletcher & J. Fitness (Eds.), *Knowledge structures in close relationships: A social psychological approach* (pp. 25–61). Mahwah, NJ: Erlbaum.

Shaver, P.R., Hazan, C., & Bradshaw, D. (1988). Love as attachment: The integration of three behavioral systems. In R.J. Sternberg and M.L. Bames (Eds.), *The psychology of love* (pp. 68–99). New Haven, CT: Yale University Press.

Shouldice, A., & Stevenson-Hinde, J. (1992). Coping with security distress: The Separation Anxiety Test and attachment classification at 4.5 years. *Journal of Child Psychology and Psychiatry*, 33, 331–48.

Shulman, S. (1993). Close relationships and coping behavior in adolescence. *Journal of Adolescence*, 16, 267–83.

Sibley, C.G., & Overall, N.C. (2007). The boundaries between attachment and personality: Associations across three levels of the attachment network. *Journal of Research in Personality*, 41, 960–7.

——(2008). Modelling the hierarchical structure of attachment representations: A test of domain differentiation. *Personality and Individual Differences*, 44, 238–49.

Siebold, G.L. (1999). The evolution of the measurement of cohesion. *Military Psychology*, 11, 5–26.

Simpson, J.A. (1990). Influence of attachment styles on romantic relationships. *Journal of Personality and Social Psychology*, 59, 971–80.

Simpson, J.A., & Rholes, W.S. (1994). Stress and secure base relationships in adulthood. *Advances in Personal Relationships*, 5, 181–204.

Simpson, J.A., Ickes, W., & Grich, J. (1999). When accuracy hurts: Reactions of anxious-ambivalent dating partners to a relationship-threatening situation. *Journal of Personality and Social Psychology*, 76, 754–69.

Simpson, J.A., Rholes, W.S., & Nelligan, J.S. (1992). Support seeking and support giving within couples in an anxiety-provoking situation: The role of attachment styles. *Journal of Personality and Social Psychology*, 62, 434–46.

Skodak, M., & Skeels, H. (1949). A final follow-up study of 100 adopted children. *Journal of Genetic Psychology*, 75, 85–125.

Slade, A. (1999). Attachment theory and research: Implications for the theory and practice of individual psychotherapy for adults. In J. Cassidy & P. Shaver (Eds.), *Handbook of attachment: Theory, research, and clinical applications* (pp. 575–94). New York: Guilford Press.

Slater, M.R., & Sewell, D.F. (1994). An examination of the cohesion–performance relationship in university hockey teams. *Journal of Sports Sciences*, 12, 423–31.

Slough, N.M., & Greenberg, M.T. (1990). Five-year olds' representations of separation from parents: Responses from the perspective of self and other. In I. Bretherton & M.W. Watson (Eds.), *Children's perspectives on the family*. New Directions for Child Development (vol. 48). San Francisco: Jossey-Bass.

Smith, E.R., Murphy, J., & Coats, S. (1999). Attachment to groups: Theory and measurement. *Journal of Personality and Social Psychology*, 77, 94–110.

Smith, R.E. (1986). Toward a cognitive-affective model of athletic burnout. *Journal of Sport Psychology*, 8, 36–50.

Smith, S. (2003). Peer relationships in physical activity contexts: A road less travelled in youth sport and exercise psychology research. *Psychology of Sport and Exercise*, 4, 25–39.

Snook, G.A. (1982). Injuries in intercollegiate wrestling: A five-year study. *American Journal of Sports Medicine*, 10, 42–4.

Sonkin, D. (2005). Attachment theory and psychotherapy. *California Therapist*, 17, 68–77.

Sperling, M.B., Foelsch, P., & Grace, C. (1996). Measuring adult attachment: Are self-report instruments congruent? *Journal of Personality Assessment*, 67, 37–51.

Spink, K.S., & Carron, A.V. (1993). The effects of team building on the adherence patterns of female exercise participants. *Journal of Sport Exercise Psychology*, 15, 39–49.

Spitz, R.A. (1946). Anaclitic depression. *Psychoanalytic Study of the Child*, 2, 313–42.

Spitz, R.A., & Wolf, K.M. (1946). The smiling response: A contribution to the ontogenesis of social relations. *Genetic Psychology Monographs*, 34, 57–125.

Sroufe, L.A. (1990). An organizational perspective on the self. In D. Cicchetti & M. Beeghly (Eds.), *The self in transition: Infancy to childhood* (pp. 281–307). Chicago: University of Chicago Press.

Sroufe, L.A., & Fleeson, J. (1986). Attachment and the construction of relationships. In W. Hartup & Z. Rubin (Eds.), *Relationships in development*. Hillsdale, NJ: Erlbaum.

Sroufe, L.A., & Waters, E. (1977). Attachment as an organizational construct. *Child Development*, 48, 1184–99.

Stathopolou, G., Powers, M., Berry, A., & Smits, J. (2006). Exercise interventions for mental health: A quantitative and qualitative review. *Clinical Psychology: Science and Practice*, 13, 179–93.

Steiger, H., Van der Feen, J., Goldstein, C., & Leichner, P. (1989). Defense styles and parental bonding in eating-disordered women. *International Journal of Eating Disorders*, 8, 131–40.

Stein, H., Jacobs, N.J., Ferguson, K.S., Allen, J.G., Fonagy, P. (1998). What do adult attachment scales measure? *Bulletin of the Menninger Clinic*, 62, 33–82.

Stipek, D., & Hoffman, J. (1980) Development of children's performance-related judgements, *Child Development*, 51, 912–14.

Sullivan, H. (1940). *Conceptions of modern psychiatry*. New York: Norton.

Sullivan, M.J.L., Tripp, D.A., Rogers, W.M., & Stanish, W. (2000). Catastrophizing and pain perception in sport participants. *Journal of Applied Sport Psychology*, 12, 151–67.

Suomi, S.J. (1991). Up-tight and laid-back monkeys: Individual differences in the response to social challenges. In S. Brauth, W. Hall, & R. Dooling (Eds.), *Plasticity of development* (pp. 27–56). Cambridge, MA: MIT Press.

——(1997). Early determinants of behaviour: Evidence from primate studies. *British Medical Bulletin*, 53, 170–84.

——(1999). Attachment in rhesus monkeys. In J. Cassidy & P. Shaver (Eds.), *Handbook of attachment: Theory, research, and clinical applications* (pp. 181–97). New York: Guilford Press.

Taylor, I., Ntoumanis, N., & Standage, M. (2008). A self-determination theory approach to understanding antecedents of teachers' motivational strategies in physical education. *Journal of Sport and Exercise Psychology*, 30, 75–94.

Teti, D.M., Sakin, W.J., Kucera, E., Corns, K.M., & Das Eiden, R. (1996). And baby makes four: Predictors of attachment security among preschool-age firstborns during the transition to siblinghood. *Child Development*, 67, 579–96.

Theodoulides, A., & Armour, K.M. (2001) Personal, social and moral development through team games: Some critical questions. *European Physical Education Review*, 7, 5–23.

Thompson, R.A. (2000). The legacy of early attachments. *Child Development*, 71, 145–52.

Thompson, R.A., & Limber, S. (1990). 'Social anxiety' in infancy: Stranger wariness and separation distress. In H. Leitenberg (Ed.), *Handbook of social and evaluation anxiety*. New York: Plenum.

Thorpe, W.H. (1956). *Learning and instinct in animals*. London: Methuen.

Thune, I., & Furberg, A. (2001). Physical activity and cancer risk: Dose-response and cancer, all sites and site specific. Proceedings for the American College of Sports Medicine symposium on exercise and cancer, October, 2000, Ontario. *Medicine and Science in Sport and Exercise*, S530–S550.

Tinbergen, N. (1951). *The study of instinct*. London: Clarendon Press.

Tonge, B. (1994). Separation anxiety disorder. In T.O. Ollendick, N.J. King, & W. Yule (Eds.), *International handbook of phobic and anxiety disorders in children and adolescents*. New York: Plenum.

Torquati, J.C., & Vazsonyi, A.T. (1999). Attachment as an organisational construct for affect, appraisals, and coping of late adolescent females. *Journal of Youth and Adolescence*, 5, 545–62.

Treasure, D. (2001) Enhancing young people's motivation in youth sport: An achievement goal approach. In G. Roberts (Ed.), *Advances in motivation in sport and exercise*. Champaign, IL: Human Kinetics.

Treasure, D.C., Duda, J.L., Hall, H.K., Roberts, G.C., Ames, C., & Maehr, M.L. (2001). Clarifying misconceptions and misrepresentations in achievement goal research in sport: A response to Harwood, Hardy, and Swain. *Journal of Sport and Exercise Psychology*, 23, 317–29.

Trinke, S. (1995). Hierarchies of attachment relationships in adulthood. MA thesis, Department of Psychology, Simon Fraser University, Canada.

Trinke, S.J., & Bartholomew, K. (1997). Hierarchies of attachment relationships in young adulthood. *Journal of Social and Personal Relationships*, 14, 603–25.

Tripp, D.A., Stanish, W., Reardon, G., Coady, C., & Sullivan, M.J.L. (2003). Comparing postoperative pain experiences of the adolescent and adult athlete after anterior cruciate ligament surgery. *Journal of Athletic Training*, 38, 154–7.

Truchon, M. (2001). Determinants of chronic disability related to low back pain: Towards an integrative biopsychosocial model. *Disability and Rehabilitation*, 23, 758–69.

Turman, P.D. (2003). Coaches and cohesion: The impact of coaching techniques on cohesion in the small group sport setting. *Journal of Sport Behavior*, 26, 86–104.

Ullrich-French, S., & Smith, A.L. (2006). Perceptions of relationships with parents and peers in youth sport: Independent and combined prediction of motivational outcomes. *Psychology of Sport and Exercise*, 7, 193–214.

——(2009). Social and motivational predictors of continued youth sport participation. *Psychology of Sport and Exercise*, 10, 87–95.

Urdan, T.C. (1997). Achievement goal theory: Past results, future directions. In M.L. Maehr & P.R. Pintrich (Eds.), *Advances in motivation and achievement* (vol. 10, pp. 99–141). Greenwich, CT: JAI Press.

Urdan, T., & Turner, J. (2005) Competence motivation in the classroom. In A. Elliot & C. Dweck (Eds.), *Handbook of competence and motivation*. New York: Guilford Press.

Valenza, E., Simion, F., Cassia, V., & Umilta, C. (1996). Face preference at birth. *Journal of Experimental Psychology: Human Perception and Performance*, 22, 892–903.

Vallerand, R.J. (2001). A hierarchical model of intrinsic motivation in sport and exercise. In G.C. Roberts (Ed.), *Advances in motivation in sport and exercise* (pp. 263–320). Champaign, IL: Human Kinetics.

——(2007). A hierarchical model of intrinsic and extrinsic motivation for sport and physical activity. In M. Hagger & N. Chatzisarantis (Eds.), *Intrinsic motivation and self-determination in exercise and sport* (ch. 17). Champaign, IL: Human Kinetics.

Vallerand, R.J., & Reid, G. (1984). On the causal effects of perceived competence on intrinsic motivation: A test of cognitive evaluation theory. *Journal of Sport Psychology*, 6, 94–102.

Vallerand, R.J., Deci, E.L., & Ryan, R.M. (1987). Intrinsic motivation in sport. In K.B. Pandolf (Ed.), *Exercise and Sports Sciences Reviews* (vol. 15, pp. 389–425). New York: Macmillan.

van den Boom, D.C. (1994). The influence of temperament and mothering on attachment and exploration: An experimental manipulation of sensitive responsiveness among lower-class mothers with irritable infants. *Child Development*, 65, 1457–77.

van der Horst, F.C.P. (2009). John Bowlby and ethology: A study of cross-fertilization. Doctoral thesis, Centre for Child and Family Studies, Leiden University.

van Ijzendoorn, M. (1995). Adult attachment representations, parental responsiveness, and infant attachment: A meta-analysis on the predictive validity of the Adult Attachment Interview. *Psychological Bulletin*, 117, 387–403.

van Ijzendoorn, M., Schuengel, C., & Bakermans-Kranenburg, M. (1999). Disorganized attachment in early childhood: Meta-analysis of precursors, concomitants, and sequelae. *Development and Psychopathology*, 11, 225–49.

Vasta, R., Haith, M.M., & Miller, S.A. (1999). *Child Psychology: The Modern Science* (3rd Ed.). New York: John Wiley & Sons.

Vaughn, B.E., Egeland, B., Sroufe, L.A., & Waters, E. (1979). Individual differences in infant–mother attachment at twelve and eighteen months: Stability and change in families under stress. *Child Development*, 50, 971–5.

Vazou, S., Ntoumanis, N., & Duda, J.L. (2006). Predicting young athletes' motivational indices as a function of their perceptions of the coach- and peer-created climate. *Psychology of Sport and Exercise*, 7, 215–33.

Vilhjalmsson, R., & Thorlindsson, T. (1998). Factors related to physical activity: A study of adolescents. *Social Science & Medicine*, 47, 665–75.

Walker, N., Thatcher, J., & Lavallee, D. (2007). Psychological responses to injury in competitive sport: A critical review. *Journal of the Royal Society for the Promotion of Health*, 127, 174–80.

Walsh, T.M., Symons, D.K., & McGrath, P.J. (2004). Relations between young children's responses to the depiction of separation and pain experiences. *Attachment & Human Development*, 6, 53–71.

Wang, C.K.J., & Biddle, S.J.H. (2007). Understanding young people's motivation toward exercise: An integration of sport ability beliefs, achievement goal theory, and self-determination theory. In M. Hagger & N. Chatzisarantis (Eds.), *Intrinsic motivation and self-determination in exercise and sport* (ch. 13). Champaign, IL: Human Kinetics.

Wang, C.K.J., Chatzisarantis, N.L., Spray, C.M., & Biddle, S.J.H. (2002). Achievement goal profiles in school physical education: Differences in self-determination, sport ability beliefs, and physical activity. *British Journal of Educational Psychology*, 72, 433–45.

Wartner, U.G., Grossmann, K., Fremmer-Bombik, E., & Suess, G. (1994). Attachment patterns at age 6 in South Germany: Predictability from infancy and implications for preschool behaviour. *Child Development*, 65, 1014–27.

Waters, E. (2000). Notes on attachment as grand theory. Unpublished manuscript.

Waters, E., & Cummings, E.M. (2000). A secure base from which to explore close relationships. *Child Development*, 71, 164–72.

Weidmann, U. (1956). Some experiments on the following and the flocking reaction of mallard ducklings. *Animal Behaviour*, 4, 78–9.

Weimer, B.L., Kerns, K.A., & Oldenburg, C.M. (2004). Adolescents' interactions with a best friend: Associations with attachment style. *Journal of Experimental Child Psychology*, 88, 102–20.

Weiss, M.R., & Smith, A.L. (1999). Quality of youth sport friendships: Measurement development and validation. *Journal of Sport & Exercise Psychology*, 21, 145–66.

——(2002). Friendship quality in youth sport: Relationship to age, gender, and motivation variables. *Journal of Sport & Exercise Psychology*, 24, 420–37.

Weiss, M.R., Smith, A.L., & Theeboom, M. (1996). 'That's what friends are for': Children's and teenagers' perceptions of peer relationships in the sport domain. *Journal of Sport & Exercise Psychology*, 18, 347–79.

West, M., Sheldon, A., & Reiffer, L. (1987). An approach to the delineation of adult attachment: Scale development and reliability. *Journal of Nervous and Mental Disease*, 175, 738–41.

West, W., Rose, S.M., Spreng, S., Sheldon-Keller, A., & Adam, K. (1998). Adolescent Attachment Questionnaire: A brief assessment of attachment in adolescence. *Journal of Youth and Adolescence*, 27, 661–73.

Westre, K., & Weiss, M. (1991). The relationship between perceived coaching behaviors and group cohesion in high school football teams. *The Sport Psychologist*, 5, 41–54.

White, R.W. (1959). Motivation reconsidered: The concept of competence. *Psychological Review*, 66, 297–333.

White, S.A., Kavussanu, M., & Guest, S. (1998). Goal orientations and perceptions of the motivational climate created by significant others. *European Journal of Physical Education*, 3, 212–28.

Widmeyer, W.N., & Williams, J.M. (1991). Predicting cohesion in a coacting sport. *Small Group Research*, 22, 548–70.

Widmeyer, W.N., Brawley, L.R., & Carron. A.V. (1985). *The measurement of cohesion in sport teams: The Group Environment Questionnaire*. London, Canada: Sports Dynamics.

Widmeyer, W.N., Carron, A.V., & Brawley, L.R. (1993). Group cohesion in sport and exercise. In R.N. Singer, M. Murphey, & L.K. Tennant (Eds.), *Handbook of research on sport psychology* (pp. 672–92). New York: Macmillan.

Wiese-Bjornstal, D.M, Smith, A.M., & LaMott, E.E. (1995). A model of psychologic response to athletic injury and rehabilitation. *Athletic Training: Sports Health Care Perspectives*, 1, 17–30.

Wiese-Bjornstal, D.M., Smith, A.M., Shaffer, S.M., & Morrey, M.A. (1998). An integrated model of response to sport injury: Psychological and sociological dimensions. *Journal of Applied Sport Psychology*, 10, 46–69.

Wilson, P.M., & Rodgers, W.M. (2004). The relationship between perceived autonomy support, exercise regulations and behavioural intentions in women. *Psychology of Sport and Exercise*, 5, 229–42.

Woodall, K.L., & Matthews, K.A. (1989). Familial environment associated with Type A behaviors and psychophysiological responses to stress in children. *Health Psychology*, 8, 403–26.

Wylleman, P. (2000). Interpersonal relationships in sport: Uncharted territory in sport psychology research. *International Journal of Sport Psychology*, 31, 555–72.

Youngblade, L.M., & Belsky, J. (1992). Parent–child antecedents of 5-year-olds' close friendships: A longitudinal analysis. *Developmental Psychology*, 28, 700–13.

Zasler, N.D., Martelli, M.F., & Nicholson, K. (2005). Chronic pain. In J.M. Silver, T.W. McAllister, W. Thomas, & S.C. Yudofsky (Eds.), *Textbook of traumatic brain injury* (pp. 419–36). Washington, DC: American Psychiatric Publishing.

Zeijlmans Van Emmichoven, I.A., van Ijzendoorn, M.H., de Ruiter, C., & Brosschot, J.F. (2003). Selective processing of threatening information: Effects of attachment representation and anxiety disorder on attention and memory. *Development & Psychopathology*, 15, 219–37.

Index

Lightning Source UK Ltd.
Milton Keynes UK
UKOW06f1715071215

264286UK00004B/531/P